advance praise for

Please Forward

Cynthia Joyce exhumes the colloquial, hyper-literate voice of a population that is never so open as when its citizens are talking amongst themselves. In the process, she has brought to light the one thing outsiders could never comprehend, at least until now: the deep emotional scar Hurricane Katrina's levee breaches left on those who survived the disaster.

> Brett Anderson
> Restaurants critic and features writer
> NOLA.com | *The Times-Picayune*

These are postcards from a city that was on the very edge. They are selfies shot against a backdrop of unprecedented catastrophe. For survivors of Katrina, the collected blog posts will kick up raw memories, some cherished, some still harrowing. Readers lucky enough to have only wondered what disaster is like will find an answer. It's all here: the terror, the confusion, the compassion, the self-absorption, the posturing, the misinformation masquerading as insight—above all the ties that held us together and made recovery possible.

> Jed Horne,
> Author of *Breach of Faith, Hurricane Katrina and the Near Death of a Great American City*

Most of us never got the real story of Hurricane Katrina. The real story lies in these heartbreaking pages: stories of good people who built happy lives for themselves, watching those lives get ripped apart by 15 feet of toxic flood water. *Please Forward* offers a riveting montage of devastated voices waiting to hear from lost family members, waiting to be treated with respect by the outsiders who invaded their city, and waiting to see if there was anything left to rebuild once the waters finally receded.

> Heather Havrilesky,
> *New York Magazine* columnist
> author of *Disaster Prep*

T0116564

please forward

how blogging reconnected new orleans after katrina

UNO Press
Manufactured in the United States of America
All rights reserved
ISBN: 9781608011087

Book and cover design: Alex Dimeff

Library of Congress Cataloging-in-Publication Data

Please forward : how blogging reconnected New Orleans after Katrina
/ edited by Cynthia Joyce.
    pages cm
 ISBN 978-1-60801-108-7
1. Hurricane Katrina, 2005--Blogs. 2. Citizen journalism--Louisiana-
-New Orleans. 3. Social media--Louisiana--New Orleans. 4. Disaster
relief--Louisiana--New Orleans--Blogs. 5. Community development-
-Louisiana--New Orleans--Blogs. 6. New Orleans (La.)--Social
conditions--21st century--Blogs. I. Joyce, Cynthia.
 HV636 2005 .N4 P54 2015
 302.23'140976335--dc23
                                        2015011412

UNO PRESS
unopress.org

please forward

how blogging reconnected new orleans after katrina

edited by cynthia joyce

UNO PRESS

Dedicated to the memory of Marcia Beard,
who heard it all

TABLE OF CONTENTS

Introduction...17

2005

Kelly Landrieu: Lost..25

Mike Keller: Watch Out....................................25

Greg Henderson: The Horror...............................26

Kelly Landrieu: I Don't Know What to Say.............29

Richard Read: What It's Like.............................30

Email from FEMA director Michael D. Brown:
Re: U OK?..32

Ann Glaviano: Yes, It Could Be Worse.................33

Scott Delacroix, Jr. MD:
Thankfully, an Overcast Morning.......................36

Pls. Fwd: Condition of New Orleans....................39

Jordan Flaherty: Notes from Inside New Orleans.......40

A technical request:
Email from Margaret M. Grant,
Special Assistant to the President......................42

Josh Marshall: A DMV Nightmare on Steroids.........43

Rob Walker: Regarding New Orleans....................47

Kelly Landrieu: It's Official..............................51

Andy Carvin: CNN, Katrina and the Rhetoric of
the War Zone...51

Joshua Cousin: Bookman Lives!!.........................52

Email from FEMA director Michael D. Brown:
Subject: Pets..55

Joshua Cousin: The Thing with My Dog.........................56

David Olivier: Evacuation Oddities...............................56

Troy Gilbert:
Tetanus Shots and a Regimen of Augmentin...................58

Joshua Cousin: The Traditions of New Orleans................62

Jeanne Nathan: Training for the Catastrophe..................64

Allen Boudreaux: Destin Dentist....................................66

Clifton Harris: Where Do I Begin?................................68

Brooks Hamaker: Waves..70

Scott Broom: Pls. Fwd-from Maryland Reporter..............74

Jon Smith: My New Orleans...80

Josh Marshall: Power Lines..82

Michael "T Mayheart" Dardar:
You're in Good Hands...85

Abram Himelstein: New Orleans in Exile.......................87

Clayton Cubitt: Sour Times...90

Richard Read: Home, Briefly...92

Troy Gilbert: There's the Spirit......................................96

youbetshiraz: Pet Recovery Question.............................98

Josh Norman: Dolphins and Dogs.................................98

Kelly Landrieu: Dilemma..101

Mike Keller: Out of Place Smiles...................................102

David Olivier: Eastward Ho!...106

Josh Norman: Lessons Learned from Time Away.............107

Joshua Cousin: The Dogs................................110

Michael Homan: Allstate, Please Call....................111

MarilynSue: Katrina Pets for Sale.......................112

Kiersta Kurtz-Burke: Please Hold Down the Fort..........112

Ariana French: Elsewhere—Not New Orleans...............115

Suli: Rogue Rescuers...................................116

Kiersta Kurtz-Burke: Extended Curfew...................117

Wayne Leonard, Entergy CEO:
Snapshots from the Front...............................120

Human Rights Watch:
Ross Angle Prisoner Testimony..........................124

Clifton Harris: Don't Look for Closure.................125

Sara Ford: Blogging from Katrina Ground Zero:
Waveland, MS Day 1.....................................128

Kelly Landrieu: So, This Guy...........................132

David Olivier: No Pets Found Inside....................132

Kiersta Kurtz-Burke: It's Raining Men..................133

David Olivier: My Favorite Grumpy Quote................135

Josh Neufeld: ERV......................................135

Ann Glaviano: Gutting Houses...........................137

Craig Giesecke: I'm 51! I'm 22!........................143

Michael Tisserand: Ground Zero.........................144

Joshua Cousin: Cheddar Discrimination..................152

Blake Bailey: A Trip to the Devastated
Lower Ninth Ward.......................................153

David Olivier: A Topography of Normal........................158

Catherine Jones: No Losing Us..................................160

Wade Rathke: Close to Home....................................163

Joshua Cousin: Cheddar is Back Home!........................167

Catherine Jones: The Love, and the Recipes..................167

Bart Everson: Random Electronic Squawking..................170

Justin Lundgren: "Didn't He Ramble"...........................173

Ariana French: Grrr. 179

Michael Homan: Refugee or Concentration Camp
on I-10 and Causeway?..180

Clifton Harris: Homesick for the Holidays.....................182

Dar Wolnik: Look and Leave.....................................183

Clifton Harris: Cliff's X-Mas Wishlist #11....................185

Greg Peters: Neanderthal Assholery............................186

Dedra Johnson: Men in Trucks..................................189

Clifton Harris: New Year, New Life, New Energy............190

2006

Tara Jill Ciccarone: Servility with a Smile......................195

Deborah Cotton: Meltdown Town..................................198

Dedra Johnson: Chocolate City...................................202

Nikki Page: Deadwood-Salami Fest...............................204

William Joyce: Katrinarita Gras..................................206

William Joyce: Dick Cheney Shot His Friend, But He
Killed Our Cover..211

Joshua Cousin:
The Day I Realized I Was A Part of New Orleans
Public Schools' Greatest Organization..........................212

Greg Peters: These Were American Citizens..................214

Peter King: Katrina Fatigue..217

Sean Nelson: An Icon Came Forward...........................220

Dedra Johnson: Nagan's Businessman Solution.............224

Jack Ware: Confess, Ya Bastard!................................225

Cree McCree: Bipolar and Proud of It (I Think)..............227

Dedra Johnson: Who's Right to Return?.......................230

Francie Rich: Ann O'Brien Obituary.............................232

Luckydog: All the Stories Were Hard...........................235

Mark Folse: A Terminal Condition................................240

Jason Brad Berry: Obligatory Reckoning......................243

Allen Boudreaux: New Orleans is Rising......................245

John Boutte—The Musician...246

Josh Neufeld: Ringing the Closing Bell on Katrina..........248

Maitri Erwin:
Day 368: Why Don't You Quietly Rebuild
and Get On With Your Lives?.....................................248

Ann Glaviano: Broken City..253

Eve Troeh: Katrina Kitsch...254

Bill Loehfelm: A Katrina Memoir in Numbers.................257

Kalamu ya Salaam: They Want the Music,
But...They Don't Want the People................................261

Clifton Harris:
Things I Thought About While Driving............................264

Mark Moseley:
Why the Superdome is a Sacredome,
Not a Thunderdome...264

Da Po'Boy: Jesus in Cleats...273

Clifton Harris: Not Feeling the Hype...........................276

Maitri Erwin:
Day 393: The Cradle of Musical Culture......................277

polimom: The Best Football Game Ever..........................278

Clifton Harris: Who's Your Daddy, Vick?.......................279

Ashley Morris: Who Dat, Indeed..................................279

Andrea Boll: The Marriott in Four Acts.........................281

Bart Everson: Warren Easton Marches Again................287

Swampish Thoughts:
Where I Got Them Shoes, Desire Area Edition..............288

Matt McBride:
Why Don't We Know What Will Happen?....................291

Harry Shearer: The Blues Come Home..........................293

Mominem: The Very First Saints Game.........................296

Mominem: Darkness Continues...................................298

Letter from the People of New Orleans
to Our Friends and Allies..299

2007

Adrienne Lamb: Blue Notes.......................................309

Bart Everson: March for Survival Speech......................312

Ashley Morris: Real Leadership................................315

Greg Peters: Define Tragedy................................318

Clifton Harris: Why Come?................................319

Chef Chris DeBarr: Crawfish Boil Salad.......................321

Michael Homan: Congressional Testimony.....................323

Dan Baum: The Pie Men................................329

Chef Chris DeBarr: The Balm of Sawdust.....................332

Elizabeth McCracken: Ever-After-Katrina.....................334

Chef Chris DeBarr:
God Willing and the MF-ing Levees Don't Break.............339

Jason Brad Berry: Two Mythical Creatures
Appear On The Same Day................................344

Nola Fugees: Declaration of Secession.......................345

Chef Chris DeBarr:
The Long and Winding Road Where?.......................350

Karen Gadbois: Demolition................................353

Karen Gadbois: Show Us the Lists..........................353

Phil Dyess-Nugent: Helen Hill and Me.......................356

Robert X. Fogarty: Two Years Later... 368

Laureen Lentz: Imminent Danger List........................369

Francis Lam: Banh Mi and East Biloxi.......................373

Steve Allen: Willie Tee Is Dying................................376

Acknowledgments................................381

Contributors................................385

INTRODUCTION

Barely ten years later and it's already impossible to recall with any precision the depths of uncertainty that was life post-Katrina. For about six months after the storm, my hands shook too hard for me to write down much of anything. I was incredibly grateful to all those who did, to all those who, either professionally or quasi-publicly, struggled to make sense of that dramatically distorted reality. Explaining what it was like in the disaster zone post-Katrina was not only difficult—it was constantly required of everyone who lived through it.

Which is why, even though a print collection of online writing might seem to be beside the point, it's worth resurfacing the digital remnants, words that have otherwise since been forgotten or lost in a shuffle between servers, relegated forever to Page Not Found status. The internet, it turns out, is not forever.

This anthology is a cross-section of online-only entries that were written between August 2005-August 2007, one that reveals a layer of post-Katrina life that wasn't typically picked up by traditional news outlets or preserved in any official record. It's as much a testament to lost memories as it is to memories about what we lost.

There were no search-optimized metrics for determining what to include here: these posts weren't necessarily the most-viewed, most-emailed, or the most commented-upon. Some were stumbled upon serendipitously. Many were suggested not by the writers themselves, but by other bloggers in their blogroll. The writing stands now as a remarkable achievement that deserves to be read in context, side by side, preserved in a format that isn't immediately subject to crashes—a reminder of how this epic event was one of the first to be collectively documented on such a large scale, and how the process of doing so helped to empower an entire region during its long recovery.

Brewster Kahle, the founder of the Internet Archive and its Wayback Machine, says the average lifespan of a webpage is about 100 days before it changes or disappears. In other words, we are increasingly incapable of reconstructing our own past. Much of the collective digital diary of Hurricane Katrina has already been lost. At least a quarter of the leads I received for this project were dead-ends, pieces you wouldn't even know were missing unless you specifically went looking for them.

Reading these posts now, it's possible to feel the immediacy of a collectively documented moment. Blown apart but finding one another online, evacuees all asked the same questions: When can we go back? Where are my people? Where is the government? Where is the mayor? What about Mardi Gras? Together, professional and do-it-yourself writers created an online text that was immediate, responsive, and specific to the needs of a traumatized and dispersed community. Joshua Cousin, while writing his *Note from the Book* blog from a public computer set up at the Houston Astrodome, became a point person for the New Orleans marching band community; likewise, Creative Alliance of New Orleans director Jeanne Nathan, sending out email newsletters from a temporary home in Baton Rouge, started organizing her community of cultural ambassadors.

"There is plenty of garbage on the roads for strays to eat and therefore I find myself not caring all that deeply about how the animals were affected," wrote the former *Biloxi Sun-Herald* reporter Josh Norman on the blog he coauthored with his colleague Mike Keller in "Dancing with Katrina." Both Norman and Keller shared in the Sun-Herald's Pulitzer Prize, but sentiments like this one would never make it into the "official" news story: "Maybe in a few months I'll be worried how Flipper and Lassie fared, but now, I'm more worried about what my neighbor on a Section 8 housing allowance and welfare is going to do..."

Meanwhile national bloggers like Josh Marshall of *Talking Points Memo* and Andy Carvin constantly challenged the media coverage: "The rhetoric of Katrina is that of a war zone, not a natural disaster," wrote Carvin. "We may not want to frame it using the language of war, but we lack the language to frame a disaster of this magnitude otherwise."

While many of the missives included here were written without any assumption of ever finding a large audience, anonymous writers with handles like "Dambala" at *American Zombie* (since revealed to be muckraker extraordinaire Jason Brad Berry) were helping to steer the news agenda. Unofficial community ambassadors who had access to reliable information and large mailing lists—people like ACORN founder Wade Rathke and Houma Tribe Historian Michael Dardar—stepped into editorial roles, becoming cheerleaders and civic leaders in the early efforts to organize and plan for rebuilding. Emails and official correspondence were forwarded many times over, contributing to a critical online information ecosystem.

For those fortunate enough to have regular access to a computer, blogs functioned as a public forum for mourning. They also became a vehicle to express outrage, a means of finding solidarity, and a galvanizing force for "citizen journalists" (whether or not they'd ever aspired to that title). What made the New Orleans blogosphere so robust post-Katrina was its newfound mission of enforcing a kind of crowd-sourced accountability. That kind of constant, unrelenting scrutiny had never before been applied with such force, or such precise focus.

There are plenty of great pieces I didn't include here, including possibly the most notorious blog post of that era—"Fuck You, You Fucking Fucks" by Ashley Morris, the late patron saint of New Orleans bloggers and cofounder of the ongoing Rising Tide conferences. Like Morris, many of New Orleans' most dogged and devoted political bloggers were providing commentary and counterpoints to press reports, which they linked to and quoted at length. Because those posts don't lend themselves to a narrative laid out in print, they're underrepresented here. Several were included in *A Howling in the Wires*, published in 2010, which highlighted a dozen or so of the most prominent voices to emerge when the survival of the city was still not a foregone conclusion.

Each of these entries is an important reminder of a time, and of an online community, that we've assumed, wrongly, would be impossible to forget. It was not a small favor to ask people who've only recently recovered from what was most likely the worst trauma of their lives to go back and consider their personal recordings for the sake of this project. While most contributors here weren't professionals writing "for publication," so many of them really ought to make their entire blog available in book form. My hope is that this collection might inspire people to go searching for more of their words.

2005

LOST

KELLY LANDRIEU, *MINERVAE*

Destruction and destruction and Monroe, La.

Anxiety. Most of my people are accounted for, except for two—one who was staying in the Lower 9th and one Uptown.

Apparently Lakeview is extensively flooded. I fear I may have nothing left to go home to. I am sick with worry over people and, I hate to admit it, things.

However, I did bring my $400 worth of schoolbooks with me. And one pair of flip-flops.

My phone is out, guys. I hope everyone is safe. This is like a nightmare that I can't shake.

AUGUST 29, 2005. 2:52 P.M.

WATCH OUT

MIKE KELLER, *EYE OF THE STORM*

The dispatch is telling everyone to watch out. Mississippi Power is not generating power right now, but high levels of electricity are resident in the line in something called "backfeed."

There are also reports of gas leaks near downed power lines. Someone just reported in, yelling about needing to sift through the debris and there have been several calls of "signal 25," meaning dead bodies. Someone just called asking if a rescue team was needed.

It sounds pretty bad out there.

If you are reading this outside of the coastal counties of Mississippi and are considering coming back, just hold on. They probably won't let you through.

Mark, the Reuters photog who camped out last night, just came back from a scouting mission.

He said there is no city of Gulfport anymore.

AUGUST 30, 2005

THE HORROR

GREG HENDERSON

Thanks to all of you who have sent your notes of concern and your prayers. I am writing this note on Tuesday at 2PM. I wanted to update all of you as to the situation here. I don't know how much information you are getting but I am certain it is more that we are getting. Be advised that almost everything I am telling you is from direct observation or from reliable sources. They are allowing limited Internet access, so I hope to send this dispatch today.

Personally, my family and I are fine.

My wife and two young girls are now safe in Jackson, Mississippi, and I am now a temporary resident of the Ritz Carlton Hotel in New Orleans.

In addition, this hotel is in a very old building on Canal Street, which sustained little damage.

Many of the other hotels sustained a significant loss of windows and we expect that many of the guests may be evacuated here.

Overnight on Monday the water arrived. Now Canal Street, true to its origins, is indeed a canal.

The first floors of all downtown buildings are underwater.

I have heard that Charity Hospital and Tulane Hospital are limited in their ability to care for patients because of flooding.

Ochsner is the only hospital that remains fully functional. However, I spoke with them and they too are on generators and losing food and water fast.

The city has no clean water, no sewage system, no electricity, and no real communications.

Bodies are still being recovered, found floating in the floods.

We are worried about a cholera epidemic. Even the police are without effective communications.

A group of armed police are here at the hotel trying to exert some local law enforcement.

This is tough because looting is rampant. Most of it is not malicious looting. These are poor and desperate people with no housing, no medical care, no food and no water trying to take care of themselves and their families.

Unfortunately, some people are armed and dangerous. We hear gunshots frequently.

Most of Canal Street is occupied by armed looters who have a low threshold for discharging their weapons.

We are still waiting for a significant National Guard presence.

The health care situation here has dramatically worsened overnight. Many people in the hotel are elderly or small children.

Many others have unusual diseases.

We have set up a makeshift hospital in the French Quarter Bar in the hotel.

There is a team of about seven doctors and pharmacists. We anticipate that this will be the major medical facility in the central business district and French Quarter.

Our biggest adventure today was raiding the Walgreens on Canal Street under police escort.

The pharmacy was dark and full of water. We basically scooped entire drug sets into garbage bags and removed them.

We are anticipating dealing with multiple medical problems and acute injuries.

Infection and perhaps even cholera are anticipated major problems.

The biggest question to all of us is: Where is the National Guard?

We hear jet fighters and helicopters overhead, but there is no real armed presence, and hence the rampant looting.

There is no Red Cross and no Salvation Army.

We are under martial law [Ed. This was a commonly repeated but infamously false rumor], so a return to our homes is impossible.

I don't know how long it will be and this is my greatest fear.

The greatest pain is to think about the loss, and how long the rebuilding will take.

That, and the horror of so many dead people.

I DON'T KNOW WHAT TO SAY

KELLY LANDRIEU, *MINERVAE*

I don't know what to say.

I am sick with worry about two friends I can't find. If anyone heard from Emily Manger, please let me know. The last I heard, she and her boyfriend were going to ride it out in his house literally on the Industrial Canal in the Lower Ninth.

I can't wrap my mind around the fact that we have all possibly lost virtually everything. They are saying one week before we can go back, and chances are we will have to leave again for perhaps a month. I'm not sure where I am going to head to, but I cannot stay in Monroe. I may try to join up with everyone in Memphis. Since there is little chance of school starting up again, and since I probably have nothing left (my house is in the Lakeview area) I may just try to start over somewhere else. I don't know.

I am lost.

WHAT IT'S LIKE

RICHARD READ, *STURTLE*

I can't tell you what it's like to be in New Orleans right now. I can only tell you what it's like to not be there.

Obviously, I want to know that my house is okay. I'm not too worried about the things in it—we managed to secure most stuff before we left—I just want to know that it's still standing. It's a stupid psychological thing, but to me, if the house is still standing, there's a possibility that things will return to normal at some point down the line.

I want to stop thinking about the minutiae of my daily life. I want to stop thinking about work, and the multiple jobs I had running at the print shop in Metairie—a print shop that is most likely underwater now—and how that's going to affect my marketing plans for the year. I want to stop thinking about our theatre company and how our schedule is going to be thrown off, and how we're going to have to postpone the project that we've been giggling about for years. I want to stop thinking about other things, other plans, other projects that will have to be cancelled, put off, or drastically re-envisioned. I want to stop thinking about paychecks and bills and all the practical things that I usually think about—things that, thanks to direct deposit and online bill payments and other modern miracles, would normally manage themselves.

I want to stop watching the news. It's deadening, and the broadcasters are prone to get things wrong. Yesterday, reporters kept talking about a levee break in the Upper 9th Ward (my neighborhood), when, in fact, the break was in the Lower 9th Ward, which is further away and is separated from us by another system of levees. I guess the confusion is to be expected when you've got non-New Orleanians trying to make sense of our byzantine neighborhood naming systems—but that doesn't make it any less unsettling.

Not least of all, I want to express my gratitude to our hosts. The mayor is saying that we won't be able to get back to town for another week, and that utilities won't be up and running for several more. I love spending time with Drew and Don, but I feel very, uncomfortable imposing on them for that long. Hell, I wouldn't feel right camping with my own family for that long. But Drew and Don have been nothing but accommodating.

And to CNN: would it kill you to do a flyby of the Faubourg Marigny? I mean, really, just one good pass up Royal Street....

EMAIL FROM FEMA DIRECTOR MICHAEL D. BROWN: RE: U OK?

```
-----Original Message------
From: Brown, Michael D ███████████████
To: James, Tillie ██████████████████
Sent: Tue Aug 30 22:52:18 2005
Subject: Re: U ok?

I'm not answering that question, but do have a question. Do you know of anyone who dog-
sits? Bethany has backed out and Tamara is looking. If you know of any responsible kids,
let me know. They can have the house to themselves Th-Su.
```

On Tuesday, August 30, one day after the levee breach in New Orleans, FEMA director Mike Brown took the time to find a dog-sitter for himself back home in Washington. It would be another nine days before he ordered FEMA to "start planning for dealing with pets" of evacuees. State and federal law now mandate that provisions be made for pets during an evacuation.

YES, IT COULD BE WORSE

ANN GLAVIANO, *WHAT THE HELL IS WATER? THIS IS WATER*

YES, IT COULD BE WORSE. And that doesn't make this any better. Yesterday I finally got in touch with my Aunt Pattie. They're staying at a hotel off Siegen. She came to visit me at the restaurant, along with Aunt Ellen, Uncle Tim, Cullen, Aunt Shannon, Lee, Kurt, Mimi, and Grandpa—and I kept watching the door for them—and kept waiting for my mom to walk in. I wanted her to. I wanted her to but she never did. Then my family was at the door and I ran across the restaurant and tackled my uncle. Aunt Shannon cried when she saw me.

They'd let me use the office phone to call the hotel. When I got my Aunt Pattie on the phone—this was at about 6 p.m. Tuesday night; the last relative I'd spoken to was my brother at around 10 p.m. Sunday—she signed off our phone conversation saying, "Okay, I'll see you, I'm so glad you called— Mimi and Grandpa are coming—I'll call the restaurant if something changes but I'll see you in a little bit—" Then she paused and said, "You know everything's gone, right?"

I didn't see the news till Monday night. I knew St. Bernard (where my family lives) would be underwater. I was sitting with Abby, Barrett, Jacob, and his cousin and brother—we're from Metairie, the West Bank, Destrehan. We're watching CNN at Barrett's house (Barrett said, "Why is this crap still on?" and Jacob's cousin said, "She hasn't seen it yet"—my house didn't have power, still doesn't) and we're identifying neighborhoods, or trying to, from the helicopter shots—but it all looks like houses and water, houses and water, and that same pan across the Clearview Mall parking lot, Target and Zea's with the roof torn off.

I'm learning the geography of the city from this aerial view. I didn't realize the 17th Street Canal was the one right by my house, at the end of Vets, separating Jefferson and Orleans Parish. All I knew about the 17th Street Canal was that it was between "eight-by-yo-mama's" and "six-pack-a-Dixie" in the "12 Yats of Christmas" song. We're watching CNN and they're talking about the breach in the 17th Street Canal and I sang, "17th Street Canal," and after a beat, Abby sang, "Dix pack of sixie," and I was glad to be with a bunch of motherfucking New Orleans refugees right then.

All day yesterday I was so glib because none of it is real. I had a hair appointment on Magazine Street at 1 p.m. today. It wasn't until I was reading the WWL TV forum and watching the live feed online— it wasn't until I saw Blanco crying and Landrieu saying, with great force, "You should get down on your knees"—that's when I lost it. I was alone at Rikki's house doubled over.

Then I went to work.

I cried over cheese and onion enchiladas (the lady said she didn't want the onions) and people were tipping like crazy. Like crazy. You could tell the New Orleans tables, they were the families with little kids and the parents slamming back beer and margaritas. The husband at fifty-three said he wanted chicken quesadillas, eighty-six peppers and onions, and I asked the wife if she wanted the peppers and onions on her quesadillas.

She looked at me blurrily and said, "You know, at this point I really don't care," and I said, "What part of New Orleans are you from?" They were from Kenner. I told her I was from Metairie and hadn't been able to get in touch with my mom, dad, or brother since Sunday; she looked at me like a horrified, sympathetic mother.

The table behind them was from Covington and then the Shackletons sat down at eighty-one when my aunts and uncles left. I wouldn't have known it was them, except the dad was wearing a white polo with *St. Catherine of Siena Men's Club* embroidered on it. I touched his shirt and said "I graduated from there," and as it turns out, Sydney and Adam are sitting right there, unrecognizable now to me, but I was on Quiz Bowl with Adam when I was an eighth-grade girl and he was a seventh-grade boy, and Sydney was in Michael's class. This is what happens when New Orleans comes to Baton Rouge.

I walked out of work with 120 dollars on a Tuesday night and went to Chelsea's, where Shuchin bought me a lemon drop, and PJ's friend serendipitously brought out a bourbon and Coke that he didn't want, and then he bought me a tequila shot because I'd never done one and he's from New Orleans and so is PJ and everyone at Chelsea's was a refugee and we toasted to that. I was too drunk to drive home, so Anson brought me to Barrett's, where I showered and slept.

Today I got voicemail messages for the first time since Sunday. My phone hasn't rung in three days. From Dallas, my dad says: "I am safe, please get in touch." From his dorm in Natchitoches, my brother says: "Have you been able to get in touch with Mom, because the first extended is this weekend and, uh, I don't know what I'm doing."

The first extended weekend. I'd completely forgotten. All the LSMSA (Louisiana School for Math, Science, and the Arts) kids are required to leave campus. Michael is supposed to come home for a visit.

I told Barrett, "I've got to figure out a way to get Michael home."

He said, "What home?"

SEPT. 1, 2005

SCOTT DELACROIX, JR., MD

Thankfully, an overcast morning.

People had now been there for 36 hours. I was getting tired of lying to people and telling them to hold on a little longer for a ride. Ambulances and buses were more frequently arriving to transport patients, but again, getting the elderly and large families aboard was problematic considering the pushing and shoving when a bus arrived. One of the volunteers approached me and said that there was a medical convoy that had arrived to help and wanted to know where to set up. I walked about 2 blocks and met Gordon Bergh and the Austin City EMS. Gordon asked how he could help and where I wanted them to set up. They had a command and control station, 4 ambulances, and 8–10 EMTs. We discussed a plan to set up a triage station on the opposite site of the current one. Now our "hospital" had swelled to encompass both the East and Westbound lanes of Interstate 10. Helicopters still landing.

About 3,000–5,000 people still in our location. I received word that the FEMA official said that they were pulling out. Until this point, FEMA was providing no medical assistance, but they were helping to obtain transportation for these people. The transportation was inadequate to say the least, and now they were pulling out? I approached the official and asked him whether it was true that they were pulling out and if so why. I was told that yes they were leaving, and he was unsure why. His comment was that the decision had been made by "people above my pay grade" as he shrugged his shoulders. Rumor was that shootings in New Orleans had spurred someone higher up in FEMA to pull back. This was ridiculous. We were 1.5 miles outside of New Orleans proper. At that time, we had no security problem. We did not have a security problem until later that day when transportation slowed almost to a standstill. No more FEMA, very little transportation. No coordination. It is Thursday—3 days post storm! There was no gunfire at our location. Only people in dire need of medical assistance and transportation. The lack of transportation for the people caused more of them to become medical patients. Dehydration and exhaustion. The FEMA official walked away leaving our crew, the local EMS crew from Austin City, and a mass of people—patients lying on the Interstate in their own urine and feces.

Supplies were still minimal—oxygen, albuterol, IV fluids. I was rationing 2 bottles of nitroglycerin. No aspirin for ACS [acute cardiac syndrome]. Found the largest bottle of 2 mg of alprazolam (Xanax) I had ever seen—500 count. Immediately rolled one up in some cheese from an MRE (Military-issued meal ready-to-eat) and fed a big pit bull that had been scaring patients and myself for the past couple of hours. He went to bed until Friday morning (he was OK). State police were there to keep the general population off the Interstate lanes: about 3000–5000. Every time a bus would pull up to take the general population, the elderly and young would get shoved out of the way, and there was nothing that we or the state police could do without causing a riot. We attempted to put mothers with small children into some of the ambulances, but there were just too many hospital patients.

Triage continued through the day. Helicopters continued landing. We did accomplish clearing out the initial side of patients. With Austin EMS's help, they took over the triage while some of us tried to clean the area. There was trash everywhere. People had urinated and defecated where they lay waiting for transportation. We had cut holes into some of the cloth cots and placed boxes under the holes for sick patients to relieve themselves. It was a mess. This area is something out of a UNICEF commercial.

I ran into one of my Charity Hospital patients under the I-10. He had been evacuated from an apartment building in Mid-City with 150 seniors without water. He said they were in dire need of help. We spoke with the air traffic controller (military) and talked with Gordon from Austin City EMS. Coordination between the state police and the communications trailer from Austin was our best asset. *Still no FEMA. No transportation and no coordination* other than among ourselves on the ground. We were allotted a BLACK HAWK helicopter to fly water into the building. I hate flying. Two EMS technicians from Austin City, 4 state police officers from Houma, Louisiana, armed with AR-15 semiautomatic rifles, myself, Nick the EMT from New Orleans, and the ER doctor from Baton Rouge. Also accompanying us was a news crew from Austin KXAN 36 (an NBC affiliate) with reporter Rich Parsons. Austin City EMS would be pulling out of this area as soon as we returned. Bulletproof vests on, we loaded the chopper with water and MREs and took off. This was the first (and I hope only time) I would be seeing patients with a bulletproof vest, a .38 revolver in my scrub pants, and a white coat with .38-caliber cartridges jingling in my pocket. We flew into the city around 6:00 pm. Amazing site of destruction and flooding. The city where I grew up was underwater.

While many citizens banded together in the aftermath of the storm, some communities took on a siege mentality as reports of gunfire and looting ricocheted across social media and cable. Incidents like the walling off of Gretna and the shootings at the Danziger Bridge laid bare divisions that the region could no longer hide.

-----Original Message-----
> From: XXXX
> To: Bayou Fern
> Sent: Fri, 02 Sep 2005 20:55:07 -0400
> Subject: Condition of New Orleans

Hi everyone,

I've been in Gretna since Tuesday morning. Since I probably have more first-hand info than anyone you'll meet, I thought I'd take the time to write something out. I'm currently living in Gretna. I'm part of Entergy's restoration effort on the Westbank. I help coordinate the teams that scout the damage. Further, since I have an Entergy truck, I can go pretty much anywhere my truck can take me (except the Northshore, that's Cleco territory)...Gretna is the safest place on the Westbank right now. The Gretna cops have made it into an armed camp, and are working hand in hand with us. We've received no help from JPPD. The city was sending its refugees over the CCC, they were gathering under the Expressway in Gretna, and looting Algiers. Gretna has put a stop to that. They have a firing line blocking the bridge. Anyone coming over is sent directly onto buses—I'm not sure where they send them. I have more info on the Westbank, if there are specific questions, email me, and I'll get you some info (maybe even check on your house)...

SEPTEMBER 2, 2005

NOTES FROM INSIDE NEW ORLEANS

JORDAN FLAHERTY

I just left New Orleans a couple hours ago. I traveled from the apartment I was staying in by boat to a helicopter to a refugee camp. If anyone wants to examine the attitude of federal and state officials towards the victims of Hurricane Katrina, I advise you to visit one of the refugee camps.

In the camp I just left, on the I-10 freeway near Causeway, thousands of people (at least 90 percent black and poor) stood and squatted in mud and trash behind metal barricades, under an unforgiving sun, with heavily armed soldiers standing guard over them. When a bus would come through, it would stop at a random spot, state police would open a gap in one of the barricades, and people would rush for the bus, with no information given about where the bus was going. Once inside (according to the heavily armed police and soldiers standing guard) evacuees would be told where the bus was taking them—Baton Rouge, Houston, Arkansas, Dallas, or other locations. I was told that if you boarded a bus bound for Arkansas (for example), even people with family and a place to stay in Baton Rouge would not be allowed to get out of the bus as it passed through Baton Rouge. You had no choice but to go to the shelter in Arkansas. If you had people willing to come to New Orleans to pick you up, they could not come within 17 miles of the camp.

I traveled throughout the camp and spoke to Red Cross workers, Salvation Army workers, National Guard, and state police, and although they were friendly, no one could give me any details on when buses would arrive, how many, where they would go to, or any other information. I spoke to the several teams of journalists nearby, and asked if any of them had been able to get any information from any federal or state officials on any of these questions, and all of them, from Australian TV to local Fox affiliates, complained of an unorganized, noncommunicative mess. One cameraman told me, "as someone who's been here in this camp for two days, the only information I can give you is this: get out by nightfall. You don't want to be here at night."

A TECHNICAL REQUEST: EMAIL FROM MARGARET M. GRANT, SPECIAL ASSISTANT TO THE PRESIDENT

-----Original Message-----
From: Grant, Margaret M. <Margaret_M._Grant@who.eop.gov>
To: Paine Gowen <gowenp@GOV.STATE.LA.US>
Sent: Wed Sep 07 16:06:54 2005
Subject: Am in need of a copy of the Gov's 9/2 letter to the President

Could you send a copy of the Governor's 9/2 letter to the President to 202-456-7015. We received two other letters the Governor sent, one to the President and one to AG Gonzales. We found it on the Gov's website but need "an original" for our Staff Secretary to formally process the requests she is making. We are on the job but appreciate your help with a technical request. Thx!

Subject: Am in need of a copy of the Gov's 9/2 letter to the President

As soon as I can get back to my folders....I will send to you.

Paine Gowen
Executive Assistant to the Governor
Office of the Governor
Sent from my BlackBerry Wireless Handheld (www.BlackBerry.net)

JOSH MARSHALL, *TALKING POINTS MEMO*

11:19 AM

It's almost awe-inspiring to see the level of energy and coordination the Bush White House can bring to bear in a genuine crisis.

Not Hurricane Katrina, of course, but the political crisis they now find rising around them.

As we noted yesterday, the storyline and the outlines of the attack are now clear: pin the blame for the debacle on state and local authorities.

So, let's get all the facts out on the table now. And let's not be afraid to let them all fall where they may. There's no need to make saints of Gov. Blanco or Mayor Nagin. In such a storm of error as this, it would not surprise me if they made a number of them too. But the reason you have a federal government and particularly a FEMA in cases like this is that it is in the nature of local and state authorities to be at least partly overwhelmed in disasters of this magnitude. Read what Ed Kilgore wrote a couple days ago at TPMCafe...

> Anyone who's been involved in a disaster response episode will tell you the first few days are characterized by absolute chaos. Basic logistics are fouled up; communications systems are paralyzed; a thousand urgent needs must be triaged; a vast welter of well-meaning but tunnel-visioned federal, state and local agencies, plus private charitable organizations and volunteers, rush in; local elected officials are forced in front of cameras to inform and reassure the affected population.

> Somebody has to be in charge of the chaos, and that's FEMA's job.

This is just one of the many reasons why the White House's main excuse—that the locals didn't tell us what to do—is such a grim joke.

But let me, just for starters, focus in on one specific case. Administration officials gave a series of blind quotes for an article that appeared in today's *Washington Post*.

One passage reads as follows...

> Louisiana did not reach out to a multi-state mutual aid compact for assistance until Wednesday, three state and federal officials said. As of Saturday, Blanco still had not declared a state of emergency, the senior Bush official said.

I don't have the details yet on the first point about the multi-state mutual aid compact. The state authorities seem to be saying that there was little point in making the request since the nearby states were also hit by Katrina. Indeed, this article says that Blanco accepted an offer of National Guard troops from New Mexico on Sunday, but that the paperwork didn't arrive from Washington until Thursday.

But let's focus in on the second point. Had Blanco still not declared a state of emergency as late as yesterday?

On the state of Louisiana website you can find this letter Gov. Blanco sent to President Bush on August 28th; that was last Sunday, just on the eve of the hurricane's landfall. Basically the letter is a laundry list of requests for aid and assistance from the federal government, invoking various laws, and so forth.

Some of the key passages include...

> Under the provisions of [the relevant
> federal law], I request that you declare an
> emergency for the State of Louisiana due
> to Hurricane Katrina for the time period
> beginning August 26, 2005, and continuing
> ... In response to the situation I have taken
> appropriate action under State law and
> directed the execution of the State Emergency
> Plan on August 26, 2005 in accordance with
> Section 501 (a) of the Stafford Act. A State
> of Emergency has been issued for the State
> in order to support the evacuations of the
> coastal areas in accordance with our State
> Evacuation Plan....Pursuant to 44 CFR §
> 206.35, I have determined that this incident
> is of such severity and magnitude that
> effective response is beyond the capabilities
> of the State and affected local governments,
> and that supplementary Federal assistance
> is necessary to save lives, protect property,
> public health, and safety, or to lessen or
> avert the threat of a disaster...

The referenced state declaration of emergency
was apparently declared on August 26th—that is, the
Friday before landfall.

There's also this Statement on Federal Emergency
Assistance for Louisiana, which appears on the White
House website dated August 27th, which begins:
"The President today declared an emergency exists
in the State of Louisiana and ordered Federal aid to
supplement state and local response efforts in the
parishes located in the path of Hurricane Katrina
beginning on August 26, 2005, and continuing."

Key excerpts include...

> ...Specifically, FEMA is authorized to identify,
> mobilize, and provide at its discretion, equip-
> ment, and resources necessary to alleviate the
> impacts of the emergency.

Now, it seems to me there are three points that make sense to raise with all this data.

The first is the importance of keeping an eye on the big picture and that is the fact that this whole conversation we're having now is *not about substance, but procedural niceties*, excuses which it is beyond shameful for an American president to invoke in such a circumstance. We don't live in the 19th century. All you really needed was a subscription to basic cable to know almost all of the relevant details (at least relevant to know what sort of assistance was needed) about what was happening late last week. The president and his advisors want to duck responsibility by claiming, in so many words, that the Louisiana authorities didn't fill out the right forms. So what they're trying to pull is something like a DMV nightmare on steroids.

Second, as long as the White House wants to play this game, there are various invocations of federal statutes in this proclamation. And we'd need a lawyer with relevant experience to pick apart whether the right sections and powers were invoked.

Third—and this is key—even on its own terms, the White House's claims seem false on their face. The plain English of this documents shows that states of emergency had been declared on both the state and federal level before the hurricane hit and that at the state's request the president had given FEMA plenary powers to "identify, mobilize, and provide at its discretion, equipment and resources necessary to alleviate the impacts of the emergency."

REGARDING NEW ORLEANS

ROB WALKER

As soon as it became clear that Hurricane Katrina was going to hit New Orleans, and for many days after it did hit, I was asked by various people to write about or comment on the event and, for lack of a better word, its "meaning."

I was asked because we lived in the city for about three and a half years, and I published a small book about that time. The specific nature of the request varied. Somebody wanted me to talk about "the arts and culture of New Orleans." Somebody else wanted me to write something on the "psyche" of the place, in a way that would "draw a picture of the world that lives, fatalistically but also optimistically, with the proximity of natural disaster." Mostly they wanted an explanation of what it is that makes New Orleans different. Again: they wanted meaning.

When Katrina's eye passed just east of the city Monday morning, I was on an airplane from Newark to Las Vegas. I was headed to a trade show for the apparel and fashion industry. I was worried and distracted, but when I landed, the early word on the hurricane was that, for New Orleans at least, things looked better than expected.

And I spent the next several hours hustling around the city's enormous convention center, a strange bubble where the only news that circulated was about the authenticity of this hipster streetwear line or gossip about the hottest "urban" brands. Meanwhile, the news in the real world was changing.

In a hotel room, I watched events unfold on television. People were stranded. There was looting. By Tuesday morning a levee had failed, water was now rising through the city, and it was clear to me, at this point, that a nightmare was unfolding. The looting was getting worse, the number of people who were stranded was clearly larger than originally thought. It was at about this time that the requests for an explanation of New Orleans, its specialness, and its meaning, began to arrive in greater numbers.

It looked to me that what was happening in the city was that there were quite likely hundreds or maybe thousands of people who were going to die in their attics in poor, mostly black neighborhoods; the rule of law was collapsing; a majority of the city was now said to be flooded; there was no word on when power might be restored; even the hundreds of thousands who did get out of the city were now in an open-ended homeless and jobless limbo. And I did not feel like explaining New Orleans. I felt like crying.

Many times it has been pointed out that New Orleans is different from most places partly because it is surrounded by water, and has lived for hundreds of years with the possibility of this kind of disaster. Perhaps, it is often speculated, there is a connection between this and the city's almost un-American joie de vivre; at the very least, there is something of the fatalistic in the juxtaposition of the goodtime life and the constant threat of destruction.

That may all be correct. It may also be correct that the perfect metaphor for this carnivalesque place is the mask: the constructed façade that hides another identity, quite possibly a much less attractive one. So many people think of New Orleans as a picturesque vacation town, a zone in which to act wild and crazy for a time in an atmosphere appropriately soaked in the carefree, the possibly dangerous—and the authentic.

The aftermath of Katrina will, I suspect, have the effect on many people of feeling that they have seen a mask fall away. Certainly anyone who has lived in or really knows New Orleans already knew that behind the beauty of the French Quarter and the Garden District lay a sprawling and sometimes desperate underclass. Generally this is mentioned only in the "arts and culture" context, as a backdrop to, say, the creation of jazz, or more recently, the rise of several major rap stars. But obviously it is just as true in a socioeconomic context: The city has long been full of people living in brutal poverty; the city has long been full of cheap violence.

I was back at home in Jersey City by late Tuesday night, watching with anyone else who cared just how badly things can fall apart, and reading reports of the systematic theft of guns, of a forklift commandeered to rip through the metal gate protecting a drugstore, of shootouts, of breakdowns in basic social behavior. It is likely that as the stories of life in the Superdome and Who's Right in the city for those days eventually reach us, they will be ugly and grim. It is hard to believe the idea of the city that care forgot disintegrating into chaos and misery. It makes me angry and it breaks my heart.

I have written many words in the past about what it is that I think makes New Orleans special, different, unique. I have written them in tones of love, and I have meant them. At the moment, however, I feel that thinking about what sets New Orleans apart is, while understandable, not the right thing to do. The reason is that if a mask is falling away, then the attempt to localize what we see is also an attempt to be distant from it. That is a comfortable approach to take, but it is also the wrong approach. It is comfortable to acknowledge brutal poverty and cheap violence in New Orleans, rather than to acknowledge brutal poverty and cheap violence in the United States. And it is comfortable to think that there must be something different about the people of New Orleans because they were so willing to live right on the edge of mortality; they must have some strange penchant for denial.

We all live on the edge of mortality. A penchant for denial is the most unstrange thing in the world. Masks are a routine function of daily life—and they were of course precisely the thing being sold at that fashion and apparel convention that I was so anxious to escape. A penchant for denial is what allows most of us to gossip about fashion or search for meaning or otherwise go about our business in one city, while the social contract dissolves and trapped people die of thirst in another. Disasters, large and small, natural or otherwise, are always proximate. Learning to live with that is not what sets the people of New Orleans apart, it is what binds them to us.

This—more than any of the many things about the city that are special, unique, irreplaceable—is the reason you should care about New Orleans, and its people, and their future.

KELLY LANDRIEU, *MINERVAE*

It's official. Everything I own, besides my briefcase and my backpack with my least favorite clothes, is gone. Family in town tried to get to my house. Impossible. Every book. Every notebook, journal, shoe, piece of antique furniture...soaking in sewerage right now.

I don't even know how I am going to look for work in Memphis. I seriously look like a refugee. If you saw the things I "evacuated" with, you would laugh. (I was planning on riding out the storm at my parents and then heading back to my place. I was one of the cocky it's-going-to-turn people.) I'm alive. That counts for something. But I really do not feel like being an adult about it right now.

CNN, KATRINA AND THE RHETORIC OF THE WAR ZONE

ANDY CARVIN, *KATRINA AFTERMATH*

Has anyone else noticed how CNN has mobilized its best war correspondents—Christiane Amanpour, Nic Robertson and Jeff Koinange, most notably—to cover Katrina?

I've watched reports from Amanpour and Robertson, and heard some of Koinange's reportage; for all intents and purposes, they're covering it as if they're embedded in a war zone. Robertson patrols a neighborhood, describing harrowing accounts of Hurricane victims fighting for survival; Amanpour wears a khaki vest that feels as if it's one fashion step away from a flak jacket.

News anchors like Paula Zahn have described reporters trailing national guard troops as "embedded"—a term that previously was reserved for reporters caught in the thick of it in Afghanistan and Iraq. Meanwhile, we hear of police going out "on patrol," with lead members "on point." First responders go out on "recon" missions, not just search and rescue. Citizens and law enforcement have been killed by "friendly fire." And perhaps most ubiquitous, survivors of the storm now exist as "refugees."

The rhetoric of Katrina is that of a war zone, not a natural disaster. We may not want to frame it using the language of war, but we lack the language to frame a disaster of this magnitude otherwise.

SEPT. 6, 2005

BOOKMAN LIVES!!

JOSHUA COUSIN, *NOTE FROM THE BOOK*

What's up y'all. I have made it though the Winds and Waters of Katrina and now my home is ASTRODOME!!

I'll be back in a few weeks...or months... AAAAAAAH!!! BLOGGERS I'll be here someday!!

KATRINA WAS A KILLER!!

One loss but we made it through!

A quick run-through: My Name is Joshua Cousin. I am a Survivor of Katrina. Not only the storm, but the Flood after.

Riding out the hurricane was fine. Strong winds for 3 days knocked down houses & trees and EVERYTHING ELSE. Well, while my building stood strong, we just looked at the wind currents from my hallway. The waters were still low. We had fun sticking our heads out in the rain…it was some fun.

Unfortunately that fun became tragedy. One of my older cousins who rode out the storm in my house, he was the only loss in our family (so far).

Gregory Estes….He was cool people. The whole time he was at my house, he read the Bible. And quoted it also. He was studying to be a church deacon. He talked about how he loved his family as a whole. He even said it himself. "If the lord wants me to die, he'd take me out in this hurricane."

He also said that "This is me and my kids' first real hurricane and I know they'll remember this for the rest of their lives." He was jolly the whole day…until he realized that one of his kids was at my cousin's. He walked his way through 3 or 4 feet of water. He got to a lower-lying area where waters were about 8 to 12 feet. He died while trying to save a boy's life. He was on his way to save his daughter & drowned.

YEAH IT'S SAD!!! He left behind 8 kids. When we made it here (in Houston) we told his mom and everything, they were devastated.

All we could do at first was hope that he was alive and stop worrying and crying. So we rode out the storm four more days at home. Those were some long nights. The water kept rising….Coast Guards and residents who found boats came to get residents to the interstate. From the time the rescue mission started from the time we made it to the Interstate…

Wild stuff. Sleeping on the interstate is rough. That military food was great, though.

We all shacked up our group to get on the buses. We also left our dog behind, which broke our heart... we took that ride though the city. There were dead bodies and overflowed homes throughout the whole thing. Everything was flooded until you got to the French Quarter. Yet Canal Street, Tulane areas looked like ...well, canals. We passed up by Charity Hospital only to find all windows blown out. Later we found out that they will be closing it down. We all cried because Charity Hospital is THE BEST HOSPITAL IN THE WORLD

... My WHOLE family was born there.

YYYEEEEEEEEEEAAAAAAAAAAHHH

The bus stopped in Lafayette. I wanted to go to Opelousas by My Future Wife Bethany. She also thought I was dead until I called her. Same as other family, like my brother who attends Texas Southern University. He came to the dome. I've seen so many childhood friends here, it's wild.

I don't know man, it's so much. I've talked to many people about the storm, and God, and why this happened... it's crazy ... I'll have more next time.

I talked to FEMA, they're having connection problems. I'll go back later though. OHH!! Shout out to SWACFANS.com members for wanting to help me out. Same to the member of the other Forums I'm on. Wow. It's wild y'all.

EMAIL FROM FEMA DIRECTOR MICHAEL D. BROWN:
SUBJECT: PETS

From: Brown, Michael D
Sent: Thursday, September 08, 2005 10:38 AM
To: Lokey, William; Altshuler, Brooks; Picciano, Joe; Carwile, William; Sherman, Ron
Cc: 'john.jordan2@us.army.mil'
Subject: Pets

I want us to start planning for dealing with pets. If evacuees are refusing to leave because they can't take their pets with them, I understand that. So, we need to facilitate the evacuation of those people by figuring out a way to allow them to take their pets. Bill and Ron, this may not be an issue for you in AL and MS, but it is a huge issue in LA. Please get some sort of plan together to start handling the pets. Thanks. MB

THE THING WITH MY DOG

JOSHUA COUSIN, *NOTE FROM THE BOOK*

I only had 1 dog, His name was Cheddar but we called him "Chat" for short. He tried to sneak on the bus with us, but we left him on the interstate. He was a 1-year-old beagle with a red/brown nose. We had a Makeshift Tag, with my sister's phone number on it. There is a pic of him biting me in this blog somewhere. He had ink from the marker we used on one of his legs. He was limping last time we saw him because of a cut on his toe. But he did manage to jump across those concrete separators. (They are about 3 feet high...) He did that on 3 feet—it made me happy, until we left him all alone.

EVACUATION ODDITIES

DAVID OLIVIER, *SLIMBOLALA*

The choices that one makes of what to take when evacuating for a hurricane can be illuminating. Some are just straightforward: clothes, toiletries, essential documents, etc. But there are other choices, the idiosyncratic, non-essential ones that can reveal a lot about a person.

Here is a sampling of some of the things the folks here have evacuated with::

Sarah and I:
- Rum.
- Limes.
- A juicer.
- Simple syrup (we thought this was just a three day evacuation—we figured a mean old hurricane is was no reason not to have good daiquiris).

Ana:
- The fancy, purple purse that her mother gave her, by far the fanciest purse she has ever owned. It's very nice.

Phillip:
- A guitar.
- A mini-Marshall portable amp.
- His brother's "Davioke" book (his brother, Dave's, song book for karaoke with live accompaniment—oodles of hits from recent decades—it's a remarkable treasure).
- A crystal paperweight with a laser-etched illustration of a light house.

Zack:
- A jar of Creole mustard (the local New Orleans variety) because, as he rightly points out, you can't get it anywhere else.

Miranda (she takes the cake on evacuation oddities):
- Her darling stuffed bunny, "Bun-bun."
- 3 really good down pillows.
- All of her Netflix movies.
- Her grandmother's dentures.
- And last but not least, the really weird, mutant double-goat-paw-thingy that normally hangs on the wall of her living room. Talk about odd.

TETANUS SHOTS AND A REGIMEN OF AUGMENTIN

TROY GILBERT, *GULFSAILS*

Another bizarre and surreal day on top of so many bizarre and surreal days.

At 8:00am this morning our "team" of pet rescuers headed out to the boat launch at the intersection of Veterans Highway and Fleur De Lis...that's on the overpass that crosses the 17th St. Canal where you drive from fair normality to extreme devastation and uninhabitability.

Our team is made up of one veterinarian, one Iberia Humane Society member, one St. Mary Humane Society member, a New Orleans lawyer whose home in Lakeview had four feet of water in it, and myself... one of the amazing things you'll understand after you keep reading is that our "team" definitely grew larger... regular old New Orleanians who simply wanted to do something were coming up and volunteering on the spot. Even if it was just to sit there and talk to the cats, they all wanted to do something to help.

Armed with two flatboats, around 30 cages of varying sizes, and three pairs of chest-high waders, we set out to work launching the boats, which is fairly difficult because this ain't a boat launch...it's a road and the slope is not that sharp. The trucks were at the point of stalling and taking on water as we backed down the street.

We struck out on our first missions for a few specific cats and birds. We were definitely NOT well organized; we learned a lot of lessons today...

I feel that before I continue I need to explain something about why most of these pets are in this predicament. No one, at least that we know of yet, knew that there was going to be a levee breach. Many people stayed and rode the storm out, and ended up being rescued. They were not allowed to take pets out with them on helicopters or boats. Many people evacuated figuring that their pets would be ok. Some were out of town. Whatever.

On our first run, we rescued five cats. This took almost three hours. As we pulled back up to the "boat launch" a Coast Guard patrol was right next to us, having saved an old man in his seventies. He was covered in rashes... He had been living in his house filled with that water for 13 days. They got someone's dad, or grandfather, or brother. We got five cats.

It was at this point a guy named Mike joined our crew. Early thirties, an auto mechanic, his house and his mother-in-law's house are both underwater. He had been coming out there for the last three days hoping to get someone to take him to rescue his mother-in-law's pug. It turns out that she is Ronnie Virgets' girlfriend. Virgets is a New Orleans character, writer, and all around true New Orleanian, who had been missing for several days and was feared dead. Anyway, he was rescued... but the pug was left behind.

Mike joined Kelsey and I as we made another run. He ended up working with us all day.

We tried to make a run to get the pug, but quickly discovered a major obstacle. The railroad and her low bridges. A lot of Lakeview roads go under the trestle, and with the water as high as it is, it's impassable. We actually considered hauling the boat up and over the railroad at one point.

We had to move on though, there were other pets. He never complained, but I know that Kelsey and I both understood that no matter what, we were going to get into that house to get the pug—dead or alive. If there was anything we were going to do that day, we were going to get Puck.

By the time of the end of our third run, we were exhausted, covered in that water, hot, and were considering calling it a day. We were totally beat. But what started happening is that random people would start come up to us and plead for us to rescue their pets. How can you say no to that?

By this time, one of the things we had learned is how to read a house for survivability. One story equals death. Raised one stories, a chance. Not much of one, but it was possible. As it turned out, we only rescued animals that either had a second story or the owners had left the attics open. I apologize if this is disheartening to some, but it's the way things are. We have a lot of loss down here.

Sometimes, even after this had been explained, people would still plead and we would end up taking some of them out, even when we already knew what the answer was going to be.

A great exception to that was this one family—I don't even know their names—but the parents had stayed and were rescued themselves on Tuesday after Katrina, and were forced to leave behind their Boxer and a cat. We took the daughter with us...dogs are a serious issue. You can control cats somewhat...but dogs guard.

We motored up to their house and the daughter started calling the dog's name and lo and behold he stuck his head out an open window. Almost all the pets we got were incredibly malnourished and on the verge of total dehydration—they had mucus coming out of their noses, a sure sign. Bailey was like this. Mike and I helped the girl up through the second story window as he didn't want to have anything to do with either of us climbing up. This smallish girl took the cage that we handed to her, got the dog in, and then lifted it up to the windowsill for the two of us to grab hold of. Remember, a standing and shifting 75-lbs dog that you're holding in a large cage over your head while you're standing in a non-secured, drifting boat is not an easy task. But we got him down and the cat.

Back at our HQ at the launch, the area was crawling with 82nd Airborne, LAPD Cops, paramedics from Chicago, doctors from Minnesota, Cajuns wearing white shrimp boots and talking French, reporters, SWAT... everyone you can imagine.

We literally would have these 82nd Airborne guys and Search & Rescue guys coming over thanking US. These guys told us over and over again that it was killing them to see and hear these stranded pets without being able to do anything about it. They were coming up to us and asking, "Are you sure that cat over there has water?" It was incredible....

...From 8:00am to 6:15pm we rescued a total of 9 cats, 3 dogs, and a rabbit.

Unfortunately, a lot of times these pets hide, and they do this in a house that we've never, of course, been in and you simply after your best efforts can't find them. So, we leave them food and water and hope for the best.

Also, unfortunately, we'll never be able to get to all of them.

But the real victories are when you cage up those cats or dogs and then watch Kelsey call the owners. She stands there telling these displaced New Orleanians, who are all over the country, that their pets are alive. They start balling, crying. Kelsey starts crying. Amazing.

If you'd care to make a donation to the Iberia Humane Society—they'd surely appreciate it to help cover some of their expenses.

We will no longer be taking family members out on the rescues with us—it's too dangerous. Unless you want to volunteer, and you have a boat.

SEPT. 10, 2005

THE TRADITIONS OF NEW ORLEANS

JOSHUA COUSIN, *NOTE FROM THE BOOK*

On my way here, there was a guy on our bus with a Zulu Social Aid & Pleasure Club shirt on. It reminded me of all the traditional things we cherish in N.O.

Street Musicians and Performers
Locally Famous Musicians, Singers, Rap Artists
Second lines (Jazz & Brass bands)
The Social Clubs & Organizations
High School Marching Bands & Units
THE BRIDGE!!
Battle of the Bands
The Bayou Classic
Mardi Gras
The Mardi Gras Indians
THE FAMOUS RESTAURANTS AND FOOD!
The Whole Thing with Projects, Wards, Sets & Streets.
Block Parties
Our Slang

Tulane, UNO, Loyola, SUNO, Dillard, Xavier, Delgado... ALL GONE
Charity Hospital
The Superdome
Tad Gormley Stadium—Alerion Field, New Orleans' Own Olympic Track
Dooky Chase Restaurant, across from the Lafitte
St. Charles Avenue
Napolean Avenue
Blaine Kern studios—where the floats come from (Where My HS Band Did Conventions Daily)
The grave sites
Bayou St. John
Jazz Fest
Flambeaux
New Orleans All Star Band
The New Orleans Saints
The Superdome
The crawfish
The nightlife

There's a whole lot more to it, but that's all I can think of at this time :)

Man...everyone's big question...WHAT ARE WE GONNA DO FOR MARDI GRAS?

We know that they celebrate it in other cities like Mobile, Alabama and Galveston, Texas, but they can't do it like N.O does it. I guess all the pics I took were worth it.

TRAINING FOR THE CATASTROPHE

JEANNE NATHAN

Forwarded message ----------
From: <xxx@aol.com>
Date: September 10, 2005 at 5:44 PM
Subject: Fwd: On a hopeful note...

Hey all, we have been so out of touch because of terrible communications. Tannen and I are ok, with Catahoula Pola, and border collie Eric, ensconced in a "Walmart Contemporary"-decorated apartment in the Garden District of Baton Rouge...camp furniture in primary colors collected in one night, with kitchen accessories from Target. We are both working on recovery and redevelopment in various ways.

All our family in New Orleans got out. We have yet to hear from artist friend James Lalande, who told us "good night Irene, good night...I'll see you in my dreams" as he refused to leave his Bywater home...I hope he got out. Our house in New Orleans, re: a report from Lolis Elie yesterday, is ok. The musician's union parking lot three houses away is a staging ground and heliport for the National Guard. Mississippi House, which was in the direct path of the east quadrant of the eyewall, is still standing in fallen fields of pine trees.

It is very hard to get your arms around this catastrophe, despite the training we have had during the long-term catastrophe we have been experiencing in New Orleans over the past years. This was not a surprise, as many have been saying. Working on the America's Wetland campaign, we have been sending out emails warning we are in a state of emergency, with a tsunami on the way. We hung a 20′ ruler off a balcony in the French Quarter on the first day of the hurricane season to call national attention to our plight. We have been hearing warnings about the "bowl" of water we would become, and the 100,000 without cars for more than 20 years.

Tannen, prescient as he always is, and not wanting to tie his shotguns down in the garden yet again, just delivered them to a studio last week in preparation for smashing them to become a "painting" called "Category Five." And I got us out early, discerning the difference between "cone of uncertainty" and "convergence of models."

We stayed with Ray Mabus last week, enjoying the serenity of his home built on an old gravel pit...gave me hope that the gravel pit near us in Mississippi, which has been providing land fill for the Port of Gulfport... might not turn out so bad after all. Now we are trying to work with no phone or internet access for possibly two more weeks.

But the other thing about this Atlantis–like disaster...is that it is impossible to feel too badly for yourself when so many others are hurting so much more. At first we mourned. But Tannen's inevitable optimism launched us into an aggressive strategy to help shape recovery in a way that will mean "building better" rather than just "building back." Wouldn't it be something if we put parks on the MS Gulf Coast, and pushed development further back? I have been driving along the beach counting the few green spaces left for years. I was down to two.

And in New Orleans, maybe now we can get the financial help we need to revive our once beautiful neighborhoods...and revive the social and cultural fabric of our city. Here's to the future.

At first I thought we might lose a lot of people...and we will lose some. But the more I listen to these talk radio shows up here, and run into refugees at Walmart, the more I hope we will come back together in the city... the world we love. Stay in touch...and send money to the Louisiana Disaster Recovery Foundation... our state's official fund set up by Gov. Blanco, with a blue ribbon board of national foundation folks to help. 877.435.7521, or louisianahelp.org. If you're from New Orleans or the Gulf Coast...please let us know how and where you are!

Jeanne Nathan
President
Creative Industry

SATURDAY, SEPTEMBER 10, 2005

DESTIN DENTIST

ALLEN BOUDREAUX, *UNAPOLOGETIC*

This terrible situation has its bright side in that it has brought out the good in so many people. I realize that sounds silly and trite but the sympathy and kindness of strangers that I have personally experienced has been incredible, to say nothing of the aid my friends have offered. I don't want to be pitied, but it makes life a little easier to be treated like a welcome guest— and at least here in Destin, that has been the case.

Yesterday I had a root canal, again. I had one earlier in the summer, which went well; this one had been started by my dentist at home about a week before the storm, and I was scheduled to have it completed this week. For obvious reasons, that didn't happen, and I've been on a constant flow of over-the-counter pain meds since I got to Florida, so I decided that enough was enough and made an appointment with the only endodontist in town.

I got there, filled out the paperwork, and explained the situation first to an assistant, then to the dentist. Then the chair went back, they took X-rays, and got to work. It was worse than I had expected—when the dentist keeps saying "wow" and "oh my" and "this is really bad," it's not a good sign. Apparently it had become pretty infected since the process had been started in New Orleans—which explains the pain I had been in. She kept going, explaining that because of the infection, this would be painful—anesthetic or not. And it was. But I soldiered through it—it helps if you just try to think of the pain as "warmth."

By the end, the dental assistant whispered to me that she had never seen anyone take that much pain that well... but hey, she probably says that to everybody. Anyway. So I go to the front to pay for the procedure, and the dentist tells me that since my first dentist in New Orleans had probably filed the insurance claim on that tooth, and because of the situation with the storm, she knew I had better things to spend my money on—there wouldn't be a charge for this.

Maybe it was the pain, maybe it was being in the position of accepting rather than giving charity—more likely it was just the sheer generosity—I broke down crying right there, told them how much I appreciated it through my tears, hugged the dentist, thanked her again...all the dental assistants in the office were crying by the time I left.

CLIFTON HARRIS, *CLIFF'S CRIB*

Where do I begin?

Two weeks ago the only thing on my mind was my tailgate party for the Saints first game. Today I am at square one in life, having lost every possession I own in Hurricane Katrina. It's quite a shocking turn of events when you wake up one day and realize that 31 years of life, memories, and work are swept away in an instant. My entire family and most of my friends lost everything. I never thought we would all be starting over together at the same time. Who do you lean on? Everyone is in the same situation. If I had to describe what I feel at this moment it would have to be shock, depression, and a loss of will. I just wish I knew where my grandmother was right now.

The pain I feel inside is compounded by the realization that the government and the rest of the world looks at the people from my hometown as second-class citizens not worthy of dignity. The treatment we have received in other cities since this happened has been helpful but also degrading. Don't let the images on TV fool you. On April 28th, I had a job, a house, a dog that I loved dearly, and a wonderful circle of friends and family support. I didn't depend on a handout and I really don't want any now, but since my life has been washed away in toxic floodwater I have no choice. Where do I go from here? Only time will tell.

I don't know if I can ever feel truly secure in my own city again. I don't know if the circumstances of how I left will ever allow me to feel like I truly belong anywhere else either. I guess I am in emotional limbo when it comes to my place in this country. I would be lying if I said that New Orleans was the cleanest, most honest, and most rewarding place to live. Some of the things that go on there can take a lot out of you mentally. I won't mention the draining humidity and heat and the unwritten racism in the area that almost assures the entire area won't prosper. Even with all that, I have an almost obsessive love for the place that won't die until I do. Call me foolish, but I have always waited for the day when things would turn around. I guess that day is near because it can't get much worse than it is now.

I don't know what the future holds for me or the Big Easy. I do know that there are some friends and people that I may never see or hear from again because of this storm. Some are deceased and others will be too shaken emotionally to ever come back. The hardcore people like myself will be back one day. I just don't know how you get over something like this. I want one night of sleep without dreaming of something back home and one day where I don't start crying out of the blue.

I don't know if that will ever happen again.

I hope I find my grandma.

WAVES

BROOKS HAMAKER, *MAYHAWMAN*

It's not very pretty, no matter the brush used to paint it.

Tonight, I watched one more endless video stream "live from the mean streets of New Orleans." It occurred to me that, unless you happen to be from New Orleans or have spent a whole lot of time there, there is no way that you can understand what it's like for natives to watch these scenes unfold.

We're scattered across the country, but we scan the same images, looking not for dead bodies or the occasional looter, but trying to identify where in the hell the cameras are pointed. New Orleans has many, many identifiable neighborhoods. In a flash, a native can figure out what part of town is being shown. St. Stephen's Church? That's Napoleon and Magazine. Wagner's Meats (You can't beat our meat!)? That's Claiborne Avenue. Those cars all up and down the middle of the street? People moved them there to keep them out of the water. It usually works. This time, sadly, there may not be anyone to go back and reclaim the car from the neutral ground.

I've spent a great deal of my life (not to mention money) hanging around New Orleans in the thick of the food-and-music scene. So when I see shots of neighborhoods, I think of clubs, restaurants, and bars. Maybe it sounds cold, but the first thing that I thought of when I heard that the water was rising fast in the industrial canal and flooding the Ninth Ward was what would happen to the Saturn Bar, St. Roch Cemetery, and the Captain's Houses.

When the 17th Street Canal broke, I heard about it on local radio station WWL. Loyal and attentive listeners were told that the canal had broken "right behind Deanie's on the City Park side," and that "Sid Mar's had washed through the hole." A foreigner listening to the radio might not make much sense of that, but if you were from New Orleans, you knew exactly where they were talking about.

Another long shot of Rampart Street: The cameras cross over Treme, going for one more long, too-often repeated shot of the Vieux Carre. Look down and see the Municipal Auditorium, WWOZ, Peristyle, Mama Rosa's, and the Funky Butt. All of these places have gotten my time and money over the years. I saw Van Morrison, The New Orleans Brass, and Harrah's Temporary Casino in the Auditorium. I remember when OZ was on top of Tipitina's at Tchoupitoulas and Napoleon, and when it moved to Armstrong Park. I listened to late-night shows with back-to-back appearances by J Monque'd and Ernie K. Doe (One of the wildest nights in regularly scheduled radio history. The tapes are still traded among those in the know.) I remember (though not very clearly) stumbling down St. Louis Street from the Funky Butt after a long night of real jazz with Astral Project, or the Dozen, or any of dozens of the unsung and underpaid heroes of the New Orleans music scene.

As the water rose, many of us mentally checked off the streets that held our favorite restaurants and clubs. Not only would we be very unlikely to be eating there or listening to music there any time soon, but we wondered what was going on with the people who had worked there.

With the exception of a lucky few, most people in New Orleans have been born and raised living hand-to-mouth—including the owners of many of the funky little dives that tourists often fall in love with. And if the owners aren't getting rich, think about your waitress, or the guy who washes the dishes, or parks your car, or carries your bag. These folks didn't live where tourists often travel, but they had homes just like you and me, and the areas that they lived in have been among the most severely affected. Many of these people have left New Orleans for good—but the ones that return? Man, will they have some stories to tell. Epic tales of long trips, hardship, strange customs in stranger lands, and finally of their triumphant return to the City that Care Forgot (no moniker could be more accurate at the moment). That's what I am waiting on. Those stories.

I'm waiting to drive in on Friday afternoon, weary from a long day at work but not so tired that I am willing to pay the parking thieves for one of their little spots. I will circle around on Esplanade, make the turn onto Chartres, and head back to Frenchman Street, looking for a free spot in the block behind Doerr Furniture, just past Santa Fe Restaurant. I'll grab my stuff, double-check to make sure I didn't leave anything in the car that I might ever want again, and stroll off down Frenchman: past Snug Harbor, Café Brasil, Mona's, the Praline Connection, a cool tattoo parlor that tempts me every time I go by it, and finally out of the Faubourg past Checkpoint Charlie's. I'll cross Esplanade and make a right. On down to Royal Street and into the Quarter, past the block of residential property, past the Golden Lantern (Home of the Mr. Leather Contest, where I was once the celebrity "straight" judge), Bennachin African Restaurant, Mona Lisa's, and into the Verti Marte. I'll get a newspaper, a quart of milk, a couple of bottles of club soda, a couple of Hubig's pies (lemon, thanks) and a pint of whatever Ben and Jerry's looks right. I'll go outside, walk across the street, unlock the door, and walk into the courtyard, marveling as I always do at the fact that it's been there so long and looked so much the same all these many years.

Once I put my things up, I'll head back, tripping down Gov. Nicholls to Decatur and through the French Market. Over to the Moonwalk, all the way down the river, past the Aquarium. There, I'll walk over and ask where my son's brick is (I never can remember where that damn thing is). Once I satisfy myself that it's still there, I'll walk a few blocks down Canal and make the right back into the Quarter onto Royal. I'll probably check in at the Monteleone, just to make sure that the Carousel is still going 'round, and then I'll go past the Supreme Court Building (formerly known as the Wildlife and Fisheries building, formerly known as the old Supreme Court Building—this is a very complicated structure), past the folks lining up for dinner at Brennan's that evening, past the antique stores, the cool old gun shop, the Rib Room in the bottom of the Royal Orleans (maybe they will enlarge the rooms, finally, as they redo it), and then, just before I get home, I'll stop in at P.J.s and get a large iced coffee to go. A real iced coffee, made that way that apparently no one else in the Deep South knows how to make it— big go cup, ice, dark-roast coffee (no chicory, no cow, thanks). And then I'll go back home and put my feet up and watch WWL as they report on the latest Saints disaster.

Many of the places I have mentioned might be unfamiliar to you, but if you have ever been to New Orleans—even once—others were not. I know you pictured those landmarks, along with what were once unremarkable places, and you remembered that trip. You might have a photo on your wall of you and some loved one standing in front of General Jackson with

St. Louis Cathedral in the background. Or maybe, on some shelf, you have a hurricane glass from Pat O's of hard-earned Mardi Gras beads hanging from a rearview, or a couple of Carnival doubloons tucked into a dresser drawer. A ticket from the Superbowl or the Final Four pinned behind a Superdome magnet on your fridge. No matter the souvenir you chose to keep from your visit, one thing is sure, you left part of your heart in New Orleans. We can't wait until you can come back and try to find it.

Author's note: When written in 2005, the below email was merely an impassioned note between friends. It was not a blog post, news account, or any other form of professional journalism. Ten years later, in a new era of social media that is always "on the record," that is an important distinction. The accounts and opinions are my own and not of any news organization.
—Scott Broom

---------- Forwarded message ----------
From: Madison
Date: September 14, 2005
Subject: RE: New Orleans

Thought you'd be interested in this note from Scott Broom, an old fraternity brother who is a reporter and was on the scene.

—Madison

I did 5 days down there covering the activities of Maryland's National Guard, a group of medical volunteers, some Baltimore public works guys, and a 75-member urban search and rescue task force based here.

The whole thing is mind-numbing. I've been to a lot of disasters—but the scale of this is so out of proportion it sets you off balance. Things you haven't seen much of on TV: The interstate disappears into the water at will—people drive wildly against traffic in the available lanes and dodge Chinook helicopters landing on the overpasses. There is little order as we know it. Rail cars and barges are found hundreds of meters from train tracks and waterways. Fleets of 18-wheel Hazmat carriers are tossed around and busted up. The breach of any one of them on a normal day would be grounds for evacuating a small town—I saw dozens. There are dead dogs everywhere. The thirsty, starving canine survivors congregate at National Guard checkpoints and sleep under the Humvees to get out of the abusive tropical sun. Some locals have taken to shooting them since there is no hope of a humane rescue. Everyone is armed (including us). There are now so many cops they are guarding other cops—who are being guarded by the military. The looters left with the busses from the Superdome. Meanwhile, the town is crawling with out-of-town, late-coming geeks in clean BDU's who have Motorola radios and three-ring binders full of their bullshit "emergency protocols." These contemptible twits should all be shot. Here's why: The search and rescue team I followed found rotting bodies in trees and in attics. Almost all of them were elderly. A lot of them might be alive today if anyone had their act together.

The urban rescue outfit we followed was a "dream team" complete with its own police protection, boats, communications system, Hazmat decon, food, water, logistics. Problem is, they sat unused for three precious days. Up to 10 days after the storm, there was still literally no one in charge to report to or take an assignment from. The Maryland guys found their own assignment the old-fashioned way—they went on recon.

We ended up in St. Bernard parish where outside non-military rescuers were only just getting in 10 days post-hurricane. When we got there, the entire parish was being run by a manic, homeless fire chief in a tee-shirt and sneakers. He had no trucks or usable communications system. FEMA was nowhere to be seen. The National Guard was there trying hard—but they had no equipment to handle rescues or Hazmats (which were everywhere). The soldiers were doing real well on security and medevac—but not much else. The parish's homeless DA had been living in the courthouse since the storm. He was dazed and looked like Robinson Crusoe. The building was surrounded by wrecked boats. The coroner was a local doctor, now homeless and wearing scrubs because he had no clothes. I found him alone in the tropical steam at the nursing home where 30 old people died. He said he'd found them a week before, but word didn't get to the outside world 'til the day we got there. He was waiting for someone to come with a refrigerated truck. No one ever came. The fire chief and all the surviving volunteers were wearing guns and driving wrecked pickups spray-painted for ID. All this was 10 days after the storm. There was still the prospect of saving PEOPLE yet the federal focus seemed to be on securing a refinery and a wharf. It was a cluster-fuck.

The Maryland team set up communications and logistics for the locals so they could take control. When FEMA finally did show up (one guy) there was nothing for him to do and he had nothing of value (like command and control communications) to offer. The rescuers gave him a pat on his little pointy head and sent him away to fill out forms while they got on with finding rotting corpses and the very occasional survivor hold out. To their credit, FEMA did have a medical team that was doing some good at the refinery office.

St. Bernard had 67,000 residents. I don't think I saw 5 percent of the homes that looked salvageable. Spilled oil and chemicals from the refineries contaminated vast areas. Some guardsmen got coughs and rashes because they had no Hazmat gear. The Marylanders set up decon for the whole parish.

Elsewhere, downtown NO was filled with TeeVees, like us—tons of cops, soldiers, firefighters, and dreaded managers. Everyone was from somewhere else. The place was still flooded. Shit was catching on fire all the time. The military handled it by air dropping water a-la forest fires. We toured the garden district on St. Charles. It was mostly dry—very salvageable!! The rest of the town looked just like on CNN. We smuggled in booze and did some drinking with three Buffet-like locals who were living in a restaurant near the D-Day museum. They told us the cops made them hold the flashlights while colleagues in uniform cleaned out electronics stores before the wind even stopped blowing. The looting started at the top—they swore.

We were staying in the town park over in Gretna. The West Bank and most of West Jefferson Parish was badly wind-damaged and powerless—but dry because the levees there held. The only open biz was a bar. We traded gas, food and money for beer. The girls were driving to Lafayette everyday to restock the coolers and generators. Good arrangement for us. No plumbing or electric meant pissing in the bushes, baby-wipe baths, and MREs. Real food was hard to come by. We did pull a "Yogi" one day when I whiffed a grill with meat on it at the downtown command post. We dressed up like cops in our Kevlar vests and radios—which got us a heaping helping intended for real rescuers. (Does that make us looters or thieves??).

I interviewed the mayor of Gretna, who was more than eager to tell me how "proud" he was that he sealed off the town from looters in the days after the storm. He was the guy who sent cops to the bridge to turn back old ladies and kids fleeing death and chaos at the Superdome. He was unashamed that he was sending them back to the gates of hell when his town was high, dry and a lot safer—with a good road (rt. 90) for evacuation. Every local official I talked to in the parishes said they would have done the same (or did). They let me know with all the code words that the low-income blacks of New Orleans are to be regarded as animals who got what they deserved. Nice town. Good luck, y'all.

Among the saddest moments were after we left town. There are refugees everywhere on the roads. They're drifting like Okies in the dust bowl. You don't see them on TV because they aren't in a dome somewhere. It looks like some don't have family or friends in other places. Some are hanging around for the prospects of salvaging homes in one of the dryer zones. Many will have nothing left at home, but don't know it yet. There are A LOT of them out there. They appear to be largely ignored by the Red Cross and others simply because they are not concentrated anywhere and they are hard to communicate with as a diaspora.

Here are a few observations:

1) You can stock up the Superdome with enough food, beer, soda and security for 70-thousand every time the NFL comes to town—but I guess somebody forgot to call the caterers when Katrina showed up on radar 5 DAYS OUT. What an OUTRAGE— especially since the Superdome has been in the emergency plan for years.

2) Local firefighters and coastguardsmen are your heroes. When the shit hits the fan, they show up—and stay on the playing field until the last man is standing. Even when it's clear no one else is coming to help.

Next time put a local fire chief in charge.

3) A significant number of New Orleans cops are criminals in Kevlar and blue. (I guess that's not a revelation).

4) National Guardsmen are your next-best heroes. They're regular guys who are all about "can-do" even when they don't have the gear to work with. Problem is, someone has to send them.

5) Guys with clean pants, Motorola radios and three ring binders full of bullshit should be shot on sight—before they have a chance to send a rescue team to Baton Rouge for "training" and let your grandmother die of dehydration.

6) Get a generator, stock gasoline, and buy a shotgun. If it happens to you—you are on your own.

Sorry about going a little long here—I started writing and could not stop.

Look forward to hearing from you—

Best, Scott

I have pics if you want.

JON SMITH, *CORKNOLA*

I don't have a lick of psychological training, never even took a basic level college course. So far as I'm concerned the base tier of Maslow's Hierarchy is a good cup of coffee. I can't even begin to tell you the steps of grievance—loss, denial, sorrow, something else, I don't know. All I know is that by now I've felt everything I think I'm going to feel. I've felt the despair, the sorrow, the fear and the uncertainty. I'm tired of it and now all I feel is mad and homesick.

I'm starting to miss stuff. For the first two weeks of this web log all I received were questions, people wanting to know about their homes, their businesses, their neighborhoods. It felt good to get the questions, and it felt good to answer them. It gave me hope. Now that crazy people like me are getting back in, questions are getting answered, and although the news is slightly better for some, it is not really good for any of us. Although some of our individual homes might have been spared, our neighbor was not and this affects all of us equally. Although we were generally spared the horror of having our entire parish wiped out like St. Bernard, we did have our share of loss. Lakeview. Gentilly. The 9th Ward. A good chunk of Mid-City. Pockets of Faubourg St. John. Gone. Our culture took a body blow and I already miss it.

The one comment I keep hearing from you all is "I miss my New Orleans" and all I can say is I miss mine, too, and I wonder how it will look when it comes back. Does New Orleans exist despite us? I keep running into good friends at the strangest places in Baton Rouge, coffee shops, malls, gas stations. Everyone has a different story to tell, everyone has a different timeframe for when they want to get back. Yesterday I told my friend and fellow evacuee, George Brown, that the deck has been reshuffled and who knows how the cards are going to be dealt out. Who knows?

All I know is that I miss my stuff.

I miss my "Biggest Latte Ever" at Fair Grinds.

I miss my Thursday afternoon scene at the wine shop.

I miss my wine tasting group.

I miss running past the Pitot House along the Bayou.

I miss Rebirth at The Maple Leaf and doing shots of Bushmills next door at Jacques-Imo's.

I miss my old house and drinking my morning coffee looking out over the Bayou.

I miss Bud Rips and I still can't believe my wife went out on a second date with me even after I took her there for a few drinks on our first date.

I miss the Turtle Soup at Mandina's.

I miss getting my fresh La Spiga bread delivery.

I miss seeing my son's eyes light up when I brought him to "Mrs. Bar Bar's" house for daycare.

I miss The Chart Room and The Napoleon House.

I miss the accents and the attitudes. I miss the potholes.

I miss the fact that if you need to make a left turn on Airline Highway you're screwed.

I miss the Bud's Broiler #4 with sauce.

I miss Ronnie Virget's column in *The Gambit*.

I miss reading the Friday Lagniappe and lamenting at all the great live music I'm missing.

I miss the Radiators live at Tip's.

I miss the view of Place St. Charles looking down Royal Street, perhaps the best view of the Old and the New in our entire country.

I miss the long-ass red light at the corner of Esplanade and Wisner and the fact that if you need to make a left turn onto either street you're doubly screwed.

I miss the nasty Mardi Gras beads still hanging on the trees Uptown in November.

I miss The Joint on Poland Avenue: The finest Bar-B-Que in the city of New Orleans.

I miss Crescent City Steakhouse and listening to Anthony bitch about the Saints.

I miss the tranquility of the mossy oaks along City Park Avenue.

I miss my home.

I miss my New Orleans.

SEPTEMBER 14, 2005

JOSH MARSHALL, *TALKING POINTS MEMO*

Before getting to the meat of this post, let me stipulate that there are some cases where restoring critical infrastructure after a natural disaster is more important than restoring power to civilian neighborhoods, hospitals or even possibly saving lives.

That said, this seems awfully odd.

Today in the *Post* Dan Froomkin linked to an article in the Hattiesburg (Mississippi) *American*.

The article begins...

> Shortly after Hurricane Katrina roared through South Mississippi knocking out electricity and communication systems, the White House ordered power restored to a pipeline that sends fuel to the Northeast.

That order—to restart two power substations in Collins that serve Colonial Pipeline Co.—delayed efforts by at least 24 hours to restore power to two rural hospitals and a number of water systems in the Pine Belt…

"I considered it a presidential directive to get those pipelines operating," said Jim Compton, general manager of the South Mississippi Electric Power Association—which distributes power that rural electric cooperatives sell to consumers and businesses.

Later Compton is quoted as saying: "We were led to believe a national emergency was created when the pipelines were shut down."

Then it gets a bit more interesting as we hear how Compton got the word…

Dan Jordan, manager of Southern Pines Electric Power Association, said Vice President Dick Cheney's office called and left voice mails twice shortly after the storm struck, saying the Collins substations needed power restored immediately.

Jordan dated the first call the night of Aug. 30 and the second call the morning of Aug. 31. Southern Pines supplies electricity to the substation that powers the Colonial pipeline.

Mississippi Public Service Commissioner Mike Callahan said the U.S. Department of Energy called him on Aug. 31. Callahan said department officials said opening the fuel line was a national priority…

But just what was going on here? Cheney's office wouldn't talk. They referred the reporter to DHS. And they wouldn't talk either.

Is this how the national disaster response system works? Calls go out from the Vice President's office to local electric power utility operators giving national security directives on which power lines to get running first? Aren't things a bit more systematized than that?

This is also pretty early in the crisis, August 30th, the day after the storm hit. The Veep's office seemed really proactive about getting that pipeline flowing again. I trust it won't seem too persnickety to note a certain contrast between the urgency of this response and that to the rest of the crisis in the region?

The article says that, "substations were crucial to Atlanta-based Colonial Pipeline, which moves gasoline and diesel fuel from Texas, through Louisiana and Mississippi and up to the Northeast." Here's the map of the Colonial pipeline on the company's website. (It basically goes from Texas to New Jersey.) And the Colonial website says the company runs the "world's largest-volume refined petroleum products pipeline system." So with that and just a quick bit of research I've done this evening, the pipeline does seem like a fairly big deal.

But why haven't we heard more about this? At a minimum this seems like an important part of the story of what happened two weeks ago. But to the best of my knowledge it's gone wholly unremarked in the major national dailies.

YOU'RE IN GOOD HANDS

MICHAEL "T MAYHEART" DARDAR

Michael "T. Mayheart" Dardar served for 16 years on the United Houma Nation Tribal Council and was part of the tribe's hurricane relief and recovery efforts after Katrina and Rita. His family lost their home in Boothville, LA during Katrina and moved to Raceland, LA while he worked with the relief effort. One of his duties was to write commentaries and articles for the tribe's website, where this was originally published.

Houma families began to settle in the Venice area in the early decades of the twentieth century. We lived in extended family settlements along the passes that radiated off the Mississippi River.

"Striker's Woods," "Grand Pass," "the Half-Way House," "Spanish Pass" and "the Village" were some of the Houma Indian settlements that sprang up around Venice in an area that became known as "the Jump."

I was born in LaFourche Parish, in the Houma settlement below Golden Meadow, where my father's family originated. By the time I was three years old we were living on Spanish Pass. My dad had joined other family members there to trawl in the seafood-rich waters and to trap in the surrounding marshland.

The settlement on Spanish Pass consisted mostly of an extended Dardar and Billiot family. I remember my Aunt Rita had a big house that was jokingly called "the Ponderosa" while our smaller place was "the Green Acres."

My father was Raymond Mayheart Dardar, or just "Mayheart" in the memory of most Houmas. He was a trawler and a trapper. My early years were spent on a skiff trawling for shrimp in the summer and running trap lines through the marsh in the winter.

I don't remember a lot about Hurricane Betsy in 1965 other than evacuating to a relative upriver and the roof of the house we were staying in being blown off.

I was a little older when Hurricane Camille came in 1969, and the details of that time are much clearer in my memory. I remember leaving home on that September evening with my parents. We each took one change of clothes. My dad said he didn't think it was going to be that bad. It was the only time I can remember my dad being wrong about anything.

We returned weeks later to a devastated town and Parish. It was over a year before we could move back.

Through it all I remember my dad working hard and providing for us. Even though we lost everything, he made sure we never did without. I don't ever remember being hungry or feeling neglected.

My dad had strong hands, I can still see them "picking" shrimp and skinning nutria and muskrats. He used to like the Allstate ad slogan "you're in good hands," and he'd jokingly assure us we were in good hands with him. In reality it was no joke, I always felt safe and protected by those strong hands.

The wind and the water had taken all we had but I knew the strength in daddy's hands was enough to get us through.

As I sat in a conference room a few days ago reviewing photos of Hurricane Katrina's effects on Venice, I couldn't help but stare at my hands. I was thinking about my dad, who passed away some years back, and of my grandchildren (two of whom live with my wife and I), and I couldn't help but wonder about my hands.

I know I don't have all of the strength he possessed, but I do have the example he set. The Houma are a strong, resilient people who have faced many hardships over the years. I grew up hearing the stories about the Caminada hurricane, and the hurricanes of 1915 and 1926, and hurricanes of my lifetime. I heard stories of struggle and survival and I saw them replayed and brought to life with the strength of daddy's hands.

I look at my own hands and I have determination, I have hope!

SEPT. 16, 2005

NEW ORLEANS IN EXILE

ABRAM HIMELSTEIN

I am inside New Orleans, only it is not New Orleans. Ugly, silent and looking fairly ruined. And there's the smell: death, with rot and sewage. It's not the smell of death that is so upsetting. It's the lack of any living smells. No food cooking, no jasmine, no body sweat, not even fresh garbage.

Instead there is the smell of the muck, and the occasional very lost dog. And there is the National Guard, everywhere, riding around taking pictures of the destruction with their cell phones.

But mostly there is the silence. Think moonscape. Think the Claiborne underpass, with no one barbecuing or hanging out playing dominoes; the ball courts, with no one playing. The occasional Humvee rolls by, or a convoy of open-bed trucks, and we wave, and the National Guard soldiers wave back.

The day began in Houston, rolling out of bed at 6 a.m., electric with one idea: I am going home. Soon I will see my town, look in on the places I love. Find my friends who I hope are hiding out safely, explaining why my e-mails are going unanswered. I am going with my friend Davy, a reporter for "This American Life," and we make the deeply familiar drive through Beaumont, Lake Charles, Lafayette and Baton Rouge. We take the old highway, Airline Drive, from Sorrento, planning what we will say at the checkpoint, but we are waved through without getting to show our papers, and suddenly, before my brain can adjust, we are in New Orleans.

We are Uptown, and I struggle to get my bearings, but I find my way to my parents' house, armed with the e-mailed checklist, wondering about lootings and flood levels and smells, and wondering, because we were given no instructions at the checkpoints, should we be worried about the police or National Guard?

We open the car door and stagger through the smell, waving with relief to the neighbors who are home to show the contractors what is to be done. When we get into the house, I am not sure what to make of it. The good news is that no one has touched the house. The bad news is that the muck has been there and smells like it is still downstairs. We begin to look for the things on my mother's list: birth certificates, house deeds.

No. 9 on that list: "Please DO NOT open the refrigerator door, as it will smell much worse if the suction is broken."

No. 10: to see if our boat is by the house. We are relieved to find it gone, so we can imagine that it was of use to someone during the flood.

After my parents' house, Davy and I drive to my wife's and my house, in the Fifth Ward, near Bayou St. John, taking the side streets. There is no traffic for blocks, for miles. There are no traffic lights working, and many of the roads are not clear to drive. Occasionally we see National Guard vehicles. Not knowing our status, we wave, and they wave.

When I see an RTA bus driving the streets, I'm overjoyed to see a sign that the city is functioning. But as we get close, it is being driven by the National Guard and reads, "Barracks." It isn't a reference to Barracks Street.

Our house is exactly as we left it, no damage that I can see, no evidence that water came inside. I call my wife, Shana, and tell her the news and ask her if there is anything she wants. We are both too shocked, after thinking about our home being destroyed as we watched CNN, to remember a single thing that we want. So I close the door and avoid the dog on the street, wishing that I had food for him. The local Humvee passes by, and I duck back into my house, trying not to take chances.

After our house, there is the checking on friends, who are impossible to find, and the checking of our friends' houses, which are in varying degrees of standing, and then there is the reporting to be done. Davy hopes to interview some of the police officers who stayed the whole time, but we don't see any, and the one policewoman I call tells me that there are orders not to talk to reporters because an interview went poorly last week. I get choked up thanking her for staying when New Orleans needed her most.

But mostly there is no one for Davy to interview, so we drive the streets while he takes photos of the boats and helicopters in the streets. Occasionally we see other people cleaning up their houses, walking debris to the curb. Mostly we see reporters taking pictures of the same sights.

We hear the curfew is 6 p.m., so at 5 we make our way to Molly's, in the French Quarter, and after the day of emptiness it is a relief to see people. I see friends of mine, finally, and we argue over who gets to buy the round of drinks. But mostly Molly's is swarmed with media people, and the vibe is of a fraternity of war reporters.

The feeling that our town is hosting a crew of people with misguided ideas about our city isn't new. It's just that there aren't the living people, the living smells, to put the crazy out-of-towners into the proper context. For the record: New Orleans isn't a dangerous place. It is a smelly, inconvenient place where the citizens aren't allowed on the streets after 6 p.m. and where the out-of-towners are in charge.

New Orleans is my favorite town to show out-of-towners around. I can't wait until we are all back, getting to show the out-of-towners again, rather than asking permission.

SEPTEMBER 18, 2005

SOUR TIMES

CLAYTON CUBITT, *OPERATION EDEN*

I want so desperately to have good news for you. Trust me, this is not for your benefit, but for mine, for my family, for my mom, for the hundreds of pitiful and proud people I've talked to here. Some good news, some hope, even just a little thimble full, would save some lives. But there is none. Not even a thimble full. No, I take that back, occasionally good news travels in from outside, like a birdsong though an open window. It's as if Katrina left in her wake a huge zone of Bad, where no new Good can gain a foothold.

All the Good we get has to be imported from exotic far away lands, like Missouri, or New York. Places where people have homes, and electricity, and phones, and running water, and a future. Those of you who've given, who've bought prints from me, or donated money, you've sent us some good news. That's what we're surviving on. Thank you.

But down here, the Bad just keeps lingering. While I was in what's left of my mom's Eden, photographing what happened to her few belongings, she tripped over a fallen tree in the backyard and fell on her face. Katrina did this to her.

We rushed her to the motor home medical clinic at the local distribution center, and a nice volunteer doctor from Florida checked her out, after he was done checking out the little fat kid who had accidentally split his foot wide open with an ax while trying to clear his dad's yard.

In 100-degree heat she sat there, and I watched as what was left of her dignity and pride slowly drained out of her. I could see it happen, right as she apologized to the doctor for having unshaven legs, *but we haven't had running water this whole time, so I feel bad you have to touch them.* The doctor was charming and said *nonsense, don't apologize,* but it was too late, and Katrina and the 100 degree heat evaporated my mom's reserve of dignity and all I could do was watch, because dignity drains much faster than you can fill it back up.

We listened to Johnny Cash's "Hurt" on the way back to our shelter, and my mom silently cried a little, and I put my hand on her shoulder and couldn't say anything, because Johnny already said all that needed saying.

HOME, BRIEFLY

RICHARD READ, *STURTLE*

When I turn the corner, the house looks mostly as we left it. There are a couple of strips of weatherboard missing from the second floor, but they came off weeks ago when we were just starting the tropical storm alphabet, during Cindy. Most of the homes around me are fine, too. An awning torn off, a few tree limbs down. Nothing too big.

I get closer and see that our dormer window is gone. On the far side of our house, the neighbor's 30-foot-tall loquat tree has fallen. It slid alongside our house on its way down, taking out the fence, a couple more sideboards, some windowpanes, and one complete window. The hand of Fatima is still hanging by the front door, though. So is the snooty French, "Attention: Chien Lunatique" sign. There's a mark spray-painted on the front of the house, presumably by the National Guard. I can't translate it entirely, but I think it means "No dead bodies inside."

The door is heavy and swollen. That's not surprising: midway through September, it's still sweltering and very, very humid in New Orleans. I give the door a kick and breathe a sigh of relief: nothing's changed. Glass on the floor from a shattered window, but otherwise, it's okay.

There's no smell of death in the air. I'm hopeful for Lola.

I get to the kitchen, and there are still two full bowls of cat food on the floor: the SPCA must've come early on and taken her away. I put my bag on the table and call around just to make sure. No answer. Great.

I open the door to the study and make my way to the back. It's high noon, so there's no light coming directly through the windows. It's dark and stifling. Jonno made me a list of clothes and supplies. I just want to get them and get out.

I look around and see that there's not much damage. Some more small trees and shrubs are down in my neighbor 's yard. A handful of my potted plants have died. I walk back to the kitchen to get my duffel bag and start packing.

Then I see her: a long, low lump stretched across a side table. I take a step toward her and call out "Lola?" but she doesn't respond.

The pieces quickly fall into place: during the storm, the door to the study slammed shut, trapping her in the back of the house for nearly three weeks, a few crucial feet away from bowls of food and a tap that's still dripping. Lola's eyes are slits, green and lifeless. I call her name again, stroke her back, but nothing.

Without thinking, I say, "I'm sorry." I keep repeating it: "I'm sorry, I'm sorry, I'm sorry, I'm sorry." I say it again and again as I walk back to the yard, and though the words stay the same, the inflection changes: now, I'm furious. I'm furious at the SPCA, the Humane Society, every organization I contacted one day after the storm and who've obviously been conducting rescues in the area. I'm furious with neighbors who could've checked on her. I'm furious with friends who could've gotten in. But of course, I'm most furious with myself. Lola is feisty and stubborn, and on the handful of occasions I've tried to put her in carriers, I've lost significant amounts of blood. In the rush of our evacuation, it was simpler to leave her behind in a well-stocked house. I never anticipated that something as simple as a tricky door latch, an inch-long piece of metal, would decide whether she lived or died.

I pick up a shovel and start to dig, but the ground is strangely hard. I'm sweating like a pig, maybe two or three of them. I grab a post-hole digger and try again. It's no easier. I'm still repeating, "I'm sorry, I'm sorry." It gives me a focus, something to keep my mind occupied, something to keep me from feeling too sad and guilty just yet. I'm making no progress with the digging. It's going to be a very shallow grave.

I hear a tiny clinking and a meager "meow." The neighbor's cats must've started using my water garden for drinking. I glance up, expecting to see the usual assortment of toms and black cats, and there's Lola, standing in the back door, looking at me.

It's one of those moments when I really, truly don't believe my eyes. It's like after someone's died, you think you see them from the corner of your eye, but you turn your head and realize there's no one there at all, or maybe it's just a coat rack, or perhaps a passerby happens to have a gait similar to that of your mother or grandfather or best friend from college.

A full five seconds later, I rush over to Lola, pick her up, and bring her to the kitchen. I put her next to the running tap, but she's not interested. Maybe the water smells contaminated to her, or maybe she's been drinking from the toilet for the last 20 days. I place her on the ground by the food, and her mood changes. For the first time, I notice that she's skeletal, and she's clearly starving.

I leave her to eat while I start packing. Five minutes later, I've put her in the cat carrier I brought from Lafayette, and we're out the door. I take her back to my office, where my coworkers and members of the National Guard (who have commandeered our offices, turning them into a temporary base of operations) peek in on her. I leave her in their hands and rush off to look in on other homes and pets. No luck with the outdoor cat at a friend-of-a-friend's house. I leave her as much water as I can in an upturned trashcan lid and move on. I pass by another friend's home and notice she's lost a bit of her roof—nothing too big, but she'll want to know. I take a picture and move on.

I arrive at my pal Jim's house, which looks to be in very good shape. I see that the National Guard has come by his place, too; they spray-painted their mark on his sidewalk, which is more considerate than what they've done at mine, I suppose. Beside his door, there's another mark—it says "SPCA" with a big "X" by it. Cool: they didn't get my cat, but at least they got to Jim's. I enter the house, just to make sure.

I call around, looking in all the hiding places I know she likes. Finally, I peek under the bed, and sure enough, there she is: curled up in a ball, hidden in the lining under the box spring. I prod her a bit, and she meows. After a bit, she slips to the floor, and I try to put her in a second carrier I've brought, but she's shy and runs away. Ten minutes later, she runs behind the bathtub, and I know she's not coming out. I open the three gallons of water sitting on the kitchen table and fill up every mixing bowl and saucepan I can find. I turn on the tap just a trickle (though his water isn't running yet), crack open every can of cat food in the pantry, look in on her once more, lock up and go. She's gotten by for several weeks on far less, and with power coming back on and people gradually returning, I'm hopeful she'll do okay 'till I can get back again.

THERE'S THE SPIRIT

TROY GILBERT, *GULFSAILS*

Crazy night.

I've sat here for the last three weeks, my Katrina solitude interrupted only by two people over a total of 22 days, not counting the random survivalist neighbors. And then suddenly: three lawyers, two scientists, a librarian, an Emeril's chef and me. New Orleans came roaring back last night, and if I had any doubts about her survival—they were quashed.

That defiant, self-deprecating, shoot-the-bird-at-the-devil-while-drinking-a-Huge-Ass-Beer New Orleans' humor and attitude IS alive and well.

These friends were all trickling in, making their way back into the city from places like Memphis, Big Bend National Park, Atlanta, Annapolis, Alabama, and other points. All seeking a first-hand view of their homes in either Orleans or St. Bernard Parish. Their discoveries were mixed—some shockingly good news, and of course, some bad.

The most startling news came from Curt and Alice, whose home in old Arabi, that's in St. Bernard Parish, turned out to only have moderate roof damage—no water. We laughed a bit, because Curt had only married his native New Orleans wife nine months ago—moving down here from Seattle at the same time and experienced Hurricane Cindy and then this. Welcome to New Orleans, bud.

Our resident chef hooked us up with what was my first home-cooked meal since the event—red beans, steamed broccoli, green beans, dirty rice, salad, collard greens and a pork loin...heaven.

For lunch yesterday they all had their first MRE, prefaced by an MRE training seminar. The little Tabasco bottles are a huge hit, but the general consensus is that Rumsfeld needs to work on his jambalaya and creole rice recipes.

With a lot of beer and drinking happening, the funniest moment of the night was the rehashing of George Bush's speech in front of Jackson Square. Not only was it bizarre for us to hear the President saying the words "second line," we couldn't imagine what the rest of the country thought of that. But we nearly died when someone said they expected Bush to break out an umbrella and a napkin at the end of the speech and start "second lining" with Cheney, the first wives, and whoever else in front of the Cathedral. It was really too damn funny...maybe you had to be there...I don't know.

There was an interesting dialectic happening also. All these exiles were fascinated by my stories—yet all I wanted to hear was their exile stories. It was killing me to hear about free admission to Graceland, comped meals, exile drinking gatherings in the middle of nowhere, boozy nights of hanging up "Viva Nagin" signs off overpasses in rural Alabama...it was killing me, even though I understood the incredible frustration they all had with simply not even being able to see their homes, neighborhoods and city. I know I'd be climbing the walls.

What was truly amazing, though, were the stories of families taking care of families. The media harps on the exiles housed in camps and the Astrodome or wherever...but the truth is that large amounts of New Orleanians have also been taken in by their extended family. Eight and nine people living under one roof. Family taking care of family.

It was a good night.

PET RECOVERY QUESTION

YOUBETSHIRAZ ON CORKNOLA.BLOGSPOT.COM

Like too many of us, I have a cat stranded in my apartment (at 41 Allard Blvd) while I commute from Baton Rouge to Ochsner for work (I am an RN in the Transplant Stepdown unit). I am ready to go get him anytime, but I am alone and have no pass to the area. Could I enlist your help in some way? Since we are currently reduced to a barter economy, I would gladly trade a few days of hard labor helping you clean up in exchange for a chance to rescue Sam (angry, lonely cat). I have contacted many working rescue groups already, but I have no idea if they have been able to get to my pet. If there is another way I can help you, please let me know. You have no doubt received many other requests for aid, so I do understand if there is nothing you do for me in this matter. I can be reached in BR at 225-XXX-XXXX (home of Catherine and Chris)

JOSH NORMAN, *EYE OF THE STORM*

I was asked to put the following story and informational tidbit on the blog from a friend (Hi-dy-ho, northern bureau Bears!) because of all the animal questions we've been getting and because of the international attention those dolphins from the marina are getting.

1) There were also some smaller, younger dolphins who were transferred to swimming pools at a Best Western and a Holiday Inn up Hwy 49. There's actually a photo on this blog (of not the best quality) of one of the swimming pools with said dolphins and their trainer the night before the storm. Anyways, not all the smaller dolphins made it. Why has their plight not made the news?

2) A friend from work, let's call him Lil' Mookie because I like that name, told me the following story early last week (all quotes are rough remembrances of what my friend told me): Lil' Mookie's house was destroyed, so he was staying with his parents. One day, they discover a pit bull—of the large variety—in their backyard in an otherwise ruined-by-Katrina neighborhood. The dog was obviously not in a good mood so they start shouting and throwing things in its general direction to get it out of their yard so they could feel safe to go outside. Surely, this dog had survived the storm on its own and was rather freaked out, because the dog did not move a muscle, despite the noise and threats.

Eventually, Lil' Mookie's father goes to get his gun. Lil' Mookie says, "No dad, don't shoot it," and takes the gun from him.

Lil' Mookie decides to fire off a few rounds into the ground in front of the pit bull to scare it away.

"Bang! Bang! Bang!" goes the gun and the dog looks up at Lil' Mookie as if to say, "What the f**k do you want?"

So Lil' Mookie's dad decides to call the cops. Cops come in about an hour and, by that point, the pit bull had wedged itself under the family's deck and was shaking and growling.

The cops start to coax the dog out from under the deck and when it pokes its head out a little, "Bang!", they shoot it between the eyes. The dog took a step like it did not know what had happened and drops dead.

"What the hell did you do that for?" yells Lil' Mookie. "We didn't want you to kill it!"

"C'mon, kid," said the cop. "You know how many calls we get for this? Do you know how many of these animals there are out there? Even if we had enough space for it, which we don't, all the dogs we throw in together are so freaked out, they're tearing each other apart. That thing could have had rabies too, for all we know. Not that we had the time or resources to test for it. Besides, we also don't really have the time to deal with that sort of thing in general now, there is still that whole natural disaster, medical emergencies and looting thing to deal with."

And off they took the dog's corpse.

Things have, of course, gotten better since then. I've seen animal activists and control specialists from all over the country in their vans driving around recently.

What I want to say is, at least one third of all South Mississippians lost their homes. Thousands lost their jobs. Hundreds lost their lives.

There is plenty of garbage on the roads for strays to eat and therefore I find myself not caring all that deeply about how the animals were affected. Maybe in a few months I'll be worried how Flipper and Lassie fared, but now, I'm more worried about what my neighbor on a Section 8 housing allowance and welfare is going to do with her 8-year-old daughter and herself now that we've been asked to leave our apartment complex and there are no available apartments.

DILEMMA

KELLY LANDRIEU, *MINERVAE*

My buddy T., a Clintonian Democrat and a city attorney of New Orleans, sent the following to me today:

This test only has one question, but it's a very important one.

By giving an honest answer, you will discover where you stand morally.

The test features an unlikely, completely fictional situation in which you will have to make a decision.

Remember that your answer needs to be honest, yet spontaneous.

Please scroll down slowly and give due consideration to each line.

You are in Florida, Miami to be specific. There is chaos all around you caused by a hurricane with severe flooding. This is a flood of biblical proportions. You are a photojournalist working for a major newspaper, and you're caught in the middle of this epic disaster.

The situation is nearly hopeless. You're trying to shoot career-making photos. There are houses and people swirling around you, some disappearing under the water. Nature is unleashing all of its destructive fury.

Suddenly you see a man floundering in the water. He is fighting for his life, trying not to be taken down with the debris. You move closer. Somehow the man looks familiar. You suddenly realize who it is.

It's George W. Bush!

At the same time you notice that the raging waters are about to take him under...forever.

You have two options—you can save the life of G.W. Bush or you can shoot a dramatic Pulitzer Prize winning photo, documenting the death of one of the world's most powerful men.

So here's the question, and please give an honest answer: Would you select high-contrast color film, or would you go with the classic simplicity of black and white?

SEPTEMBER 24, 2005

MIKE KELLER, *EYE OF THE STORM*

I was told to talk about things and not keep them pent up inside. I always thought that was silly because I'm hard. But I got sick last night and now I feel pretty close to crap. Maybe things are getting to me. Maybe I'm not as hard as I think. Or maybe I haven't been eating enough Spam.

So maybe I'll talk to the blog compose screen and maybe I won't send this out. God, even to this point I feel like I've written more "I's" than any journalist worth his salt should write in his entire professional career.

For a while I've been going under the assumption that the disaster part is over and people are on to rebuilding—either in South Mississippi or somewhere else. But today I went out to a little, forgotten town on the border of Louisiana called Pearl-ington. I went to see how they were holding up against Rita's winds. The article should be in the paper tomorrow. I talked to survivors and disaster relief people. I got some good quotes.

A photog and I rolled up to the Salvation Army distribution center. They are also sheltering about 40 people. Rita's rains made the Katrina-beaten ground soupy and everything was covered in a layer of grime. The Salvation Army people kept calling it a camp, which freaked me out for some reason.

A woman pushing a bike with a cart attached to it navigated the muddy road. The photog wanted a pic of her so I started chatting with her. She was really a lovely woman. The right lens of her glasses was scratched enough to almost obscure her eye. Her name was Carolyn.

It turns out that she, along with almost everyone in the community, had to swim out of her home as it was swallowed by rising water from the Pearl River and the surging seawater of the Gulf. She said there was noise above her for hours that was probably tornadoes spawning off of Katrina. She said they sounded like helicopters right overhead.

"The wind was screaming," Carolyn said. "I never heard anything like it."

In those conditions, when land turns to water, everything living is only concerned with surviving. All offense is shut down. Everything just swims and tries to find something to hold onto to keep from being sucked out to sea.

"I had snakes and lizards crawling on me," she said.

When she went into the water and gave up her home, she brought her "10-pound puppy," which clung to her as she found a pine tree and clung to it. She held onto that tree for two or three hours, she wasn't sure which, and her puppy held onto her.

She smiled when she talked about hanging on and saving her dog—a small victory in a forest of so much defeat.

And she didn't stop smiling when she talked about living in a tent mauled by Rita's winds in front of the remnants of her house or about her other losses.

"I lost all 14 of my kitties," she said.

Or there was the dude named Jon-e from Rochester. I didn't ask him why his parents named him that or whether he was joking, because that's what his Salvation Army badge said. Seemed like a nice guy, too, what with the coming down here to help people piece together their lives.

He was the first person to refer to the place as a camp. I told him that his camp smelled like human waste.

"I've been through this neighborhood since I got down here," he said. "I'm used to the smell of rotten flesh and black mold."

He smiled. I smiled. I thanked him for taking the time to talk. He went back to directing supply trucks into the parking lot of the camp. With photog in tow, I went on my merry way.

Then we went to go see a woman down the street who was making $724 in government disability a month. Her name was Dallas. She had four friendly mutts who really liked my crotch.

She was sitting there in a tent in front of her house, one of those brightly colored dome ones. Dallas was real nice, too. She was a construction foreman, -woman, -person before falling 13 feet off of a scaffolding.

I lied. The tent wasn't actually in front of her house. Her house was first filled with water, then picked up off its foundation, then turned about 45 degrees counterclockwise, then moved about thirty feet to the front of what used to be her yard. The house, which was overrun with gnats inside, had been redone two weeks prior.

Dallas also lost her two cars, a small boat and its trailer, her shed with a weed whacker and a new chainsaw inside and two travel trailers. That was pretty much everything except her life and her four dogs.

She swam out of her house, too. She made it to an oak tree several yards up the road and climbed out of the water onto a branch fifteen feet off the ground. She was joined by her three neighbors and eight dogs.

"I got eighteen pigs and piglets, too," she said. "They all made it. I don't know how. I guess they climbed on a roof."

She apologized for not cleaning the house before having visitors. I apologized for not knocking off the rancid mud onto her rancid muddy floors. I let her go but told her I expected fresh cornbread the next time I came calling.

People are not on to rebuilding, many are still just trying to survive. When it rains they get wet. Old men sitting on the side of the road scrape cold gruel out of an MRE packet.

Civic leaders are saying that it is time to get used to a "new" normal. As soon as we talk about death and despair without vacant eyes and out-of-place smiles, then maybe it will be time to get on. Now we have to confront something that seems, feels, a lot like shell shock.

Thanks for listening, blog compose screen.

EASTWARD HO!

DAVID OLIVIER, *SLIMBOLALA*

Goggles? Check. Respirator? Check. Extra gas? Crap. No extra gas. Once again, gasoline is in short supply, and those precious red, plastic cans are sold out. Oh, yeah. And I have to figure out the best way to drive around 2 million de-evacuating (devacuating?) Houston-ites.

Rita has blown over, and the trip is back on. I'm heading east tomorrow (I hope) to Nicholson, Mississippi, an hour outside of New Orleans where I'll meet up with John and Zack, and we'll form a sort of neo-apocalyptic Three Musketeers of reconstruction, wielding our hammers with fury and might. Or something like that.

At various moments, this thing has felt like it must be a different century. Mass population migrations? Packing provisions? Leaving the womenfolk and children behind?* This stuff doesn't happen anymore, right? When Katrina blew through, it rolled back the clock and created a new frontier in the middle of the Gulf South with New Orleans at its epicenter, a no-man's-land, surrounded by concentric rings of progressively increasing normalcy. In the passing weeks, the normalcy has gradually flowed back in (although Rita briefly put that on hold). Now some things are really back up and running. Others are still in the stone age.

I'm looking forward to going back, and taking the first little step towards rebuilding our New Orleans lives, even though I know it won't be easy seeing my home like that.

And I have no idea when my next post will be. Check back in. If I don't manage to update in the interim, I'll definitely have plenty to say when I get back in a few days.

* This is not a comment on my gender politics. It's just how things have worked out.

SEPTEMBER 28, 2005

JOSH NORMAN, *EYE OF THE STORM*

Lessons learned from my time away:

1) It is hard for many people outside of this area to care about what is happening in Mississippi because it is even harder to understand. What happened in New Orleans was a palpable and photogenic tragedy. What happened here is simply mass destruction and devastation on an incomprehensible scale.

When I left the Peace Corps, I was warned about the relative indifference of the rest of the world, especially from my fellow Americans, in regards to what I did and what I went through. The following conversation was frequent.

"Wow, you were in Africa?" a curious individual would ask.

"Yep," I would reply.

"What was it like?" the curious individual would ask.

At this point, I wouldn't know what to say. Try summing up any two-year period of your life in which your ideas on humanity, happiness, metaphysics, social interactions, hygiene, language, right and wrong, up and down, and the way the world turns were completely turned on their head.

Sometimes, I would be curt.

"It was a learning experience," I would often say.

On other occasions, I would be thorough and give anecdotes about my cat getting eaten, my projects (and my house for that matter) being stolen from, my illnesses and the desperate squalor. I would also add the happy stories about smiles, sunsets and strong drinks.

Then, there would usually be a ridiculous question.

Example: "Were there any lions?"

At first, I was upset by this. Then, one day I realized how detached the questioner was from my experience and what had informed them about Africa to that point.

My point of relating those experiences is to put in perspective what happened last weekend when I was visiting with my Peace Corps friends, all of whom went through similar difficulties after their time abroad.

"So you live in South Mississippi now, huh?" one would ask.

"Yep," I would reply.

"It's really messed up down there, huh?" the next question would be. Or, "What's it like?"

"It's a learning experience," would be my reply.

When I would get into details, try and expand upon the experience a bit, I got this question occasionally: "So it's kind of an adventure, huh?"

"No, it's actually really f****d up," I would reply.

I relate all this not out of bitterness. I wanted people to not care or talk that much about what was happening. I went to the Green Mountains to detach myself as much as possible from Mississippi.

But it was a little jarring to hear Peace Corps volunteers, who had dealt with the difficult questions themselves, turn around and lay them on me.

I suppose that you can't understand it until you see it, smell it, live it. I know that all the reporters who come here from elsewhere stay a while and then leave still don't get it. Shoot, even I don't really get it.

I see, smell, feel, taste and hear the devastation all the time. I saw Hurricane Katrina coming and I watched her go.

Yet I don't understand the situation fully.

I loved Mississippi the moment I got here. Great food. Great outdoors. Great people.

To see it ripped to shreds, though, has left me confused and wanting a better picture or frame of reference for the whole situation. But even those who have been here decades don't get it, which brings me to the second thing I learned while roaming Vermont's lovely mountains...

2) The mental health of people living and breathing the disaster is precarious at best. Because we can't grasp the entirety of what's happening, we have no chance of gaining a routine. There is nothing comfortable about being here, let alone working and living in it.

It is nearly impossible to "recharge" for large, daily tasks while here. All that being here seems to do is break you down.

One of the hardest parts about Africa was how different everything was. The hardest part about here is how different everything has become.

There is no getting back to normal. I even disagree with the saying "Getting back to the new normal." The base that was there is gone. Building from the ground up means any kind of normal is gone.

It is hard to understand that.

Almost two out of every three dwellings in South Mississippi are gone or unlivable. To comprehend that, go outside, look at your block and say there-gone-gone-there-gone-gone as you glance from building to building. That's saying nothing about the jobs, schools and lives lost.

When people begin to get that, and few do and even fewer seem to try, it is beyond jarring. It is worse than being slapped, beaten or knocked out.

There is an immeasurable degree of humiliation in the face of a force not only beyond control but miles past understanding.

On to my final learning point...

3) There is no horizon.

The endgame is unforeseeable. A conclusion is impossible.

Therefore it is now a question of picking oneself up and learning to work and live with that.

SEPTEMBER 30, 2005

THE DOGS

JOSHUA COUSIN, *NOTE FROM THE BOOK*

After watching various network news stations I've realized that (my dog) Cheddar could have been either Adopted, Shot, or Stolen and Sold. Me & my sister are going crazy right now trying to find our dog.

We even saw a few dogs that looked like him on a show on Animal Planet that was recorded during Katrina Animal Rescue. But after calling them, they claimed that all these animals were surrendered by their owners.

That's a lie. We were forced to leave the animals. I hope we get our dog.

I feel like goin' back to N.O y'all...

SEPTEMBER 30, 2005

ALLSTATE, PLEASE CALL

MICHAEL HOMAN

We are having a hell of a time contacting our insurance adjustor for Allstate. On September 8th we were told his name was Steven Blethan. When we called his phone number we were told by a recording that he was in the Gulf Coast area and would return calls September 2nd. We called every day and left a message asking that he contact us. Then on September 22nd we called the 1-800 Allstate number and were told that we had a new adjustor for both wind and flood, and his name was John Dye. They said that he had been to our house on the 20th of September to take pictures. We have called him every day since the 22nd and left messages, and still no word from him. We tried desperately to get in touch with him while I was in New Orleans from the 23rd-26th of September. The thing is that we don't want to clean out our house until he sees firsthand the damage that the floodwaters did to the interior. So because he hasn't contacted us, the mold is growing and ruining more of our house every day. We don't expect the claim to be settled at this point, but is it too much to ask for a freaking phone call? So John Dye, if you are reading this, please please please call us back.

KATRINA PETS FOR SALE

MARILYNSUE

Yorkies are for sale here *http://groups.yahoo.com/group/ stealthvolunteers/files/*

and I posted the address for Rottweillers in my blog: *http://volunteertexas.blogspot.com/2005/10/pet-res cue-or-pet-theft.html*

I suppose they have other pets as well.
Isn't this stolen property?

Kiersta Kurtz-Burke and her husband Justin Lundgren are both physicians in New Orleans. They both rode out the storm with her patients in Charity Hospital.

PLEASE HOLD DOWN THE FORT

KIERSTA KURTZ-BURKE

New Orleans has always had the funk...but you can't begin to picture how funky it is until you try this: take a pair of shoes, submerge in muddy water—add some fish, a sprinkle of sewage, a heaping helping of oil—and leave it there for, oh, let's say three weeks. Drain the water and voila! Now do the same, but use a city instead of a pair of shoes...

Sorry for the mass email again. I'd love to be in more individual contact, but it seems difficult. We are staying with friends, some other refugees (which 9 out of 10 New Orleanians prefer to "evacuees") in Algiers, and have started the long road to recovery. We visit our old house and neighborhood daily, but it's kind of silly...mainly just stand around, talk to anyone we see, pick up fuzzy items and put them back, get filled with nostalgia, cry a bit, then feel guilty for crying when we look at other people who have it so much worse, wait for the insurance adjusters to come so we can start the cleanup.

Life is strange in stranger ways then we thought... they tell us it's a toxic sludge dump (don't drink the water! worse than Love Canal!) but the prices are more like Soho than Love Canal...$3500-4500 a month for an apt in a "livable area" like the Quarter or Uptown. Yet, the city is so empty—everything except the Ninth Ward is open, but not very many people came back. Or they came back, got some stuff, and went back to Houston, Atlanta, Sioux City, or wherever they are making a home now.

But there are glimmers of a normal life...a cafe opens, everyone crowds in. The owner is there by herself...no employees have returned. She calls out: "no fridges, babies, no milk...just coffee black." No one seems to mind, we're too busy discussing soil surges, water lines, Clorox vs. vinegar, black vs. green mold, and where to pick up MREs (Meals Ready to Eat) from the National Guard.

"The chicken tetrazzini isn't half bad if you add hot sauce...." Hey, we still talk about food a lot...signs of promise. We still got it.The owner calls out again, "Can y'all just hold down the fort while I go pick up my FEMA check?" She shows a regular how to use the cash register. A tired NOPD officer walks in, high-fives

and handshakes all around. Someone puts on music...
Rosie Ledet...and we remember why we loved this
stinky place to begin with.

Justin is back at work, his hospital in Jeff Parish did
well. He likes it, the routine, being around coworkers
again. I have been re-assigned to the Baton Rouge VA,
since the one here is defunct. Charity hospital's future
is unknown...we hear different things every day. A
naval hospital ship is parked in the port...we hear it's
the temporary Charity! Everyone prepares to go back
to work, some people just show up...but we're told by
the Navy: We are staffed by Naval personnel, don't
need ya. Besides, we'll only be here a few weeks. There
are 3700 employees at Big Charity...people are trying
to decide: can they live without a paycheck for another
month? Hope the feds bail us out, fix the building, or
set us up somewhere else? Or is it time to move on...
put Charity behind you, and get a job elsewhere? We
get wacky ideas...let's take over the naval ship and just
start seeing patients there! Let's just move into the old
building, what can they do to us? We're not even quite
sure who "they" are...what about the Superdome? No
one else wants to go to that haunted place, let's just
move our equipment over there, buy some generators,
and get going. A tent in the Wal-Mart parking lot is
proposed, and it all seems possible....

Well, darlings, thanks for listening to my ramblings.
Please hold down the fort, cause I need to go pick up
my FEMA check.

Love, Kiersta

ELSEWHERE—NOT NEW ORLEANS

ARIANA FRENCH, *LEVEETATION*

I try to stay positive about the future of New Orleans, for the most part...mostly for friends and family, and because that's where my home and job is (for now, anyway). But the truth is—I don't know. I don't know if I can stay past, say, Mardi Gras. The environmental stuff worries me. My job situation worries me. The mold in our house and my horrible mold allergies worry me. It's all a wait-and-see game.

I hate not being in control of my job situation, and I feel like I'm not in control of much of anything right now. So I'm kind of "shopping" for other cities. In a half-assed (half-hearted) way. I like Austin. I like NYC. I like them both a lot. But I'm not sure I like them enough to live there. And my husband insists we live somewhere where we have friends, so that narrows down the list. I insist we live somewhere with a soul, with a unique personality. That narrows down the list. Both of us want to live close to our parents, who live here in south Louisiana, so that narrows down the list.

New Orleans: job in doubt, environmental hazards, friends gone, debris and infrastructure problems, below-average salaries, close to family, has a soul (this is in doubt if the city becomes the Vegas of the South—thanks Nagin), has the best food in the country.

Elsewhere: Not New Orleans.

Every time I go through this pro-and-con list in my head, I get nowhere. It was gently suggested to me that I write this stuff down (thank you Blogger) to get it out of my head and so I would shut the fuck up about it. Heh.

I wish—I really, really, really wish—I wanted to move somewhere else. But I really liked New Orleans—the New Orleans before the storm. It's not going to be the same now.

It might be similar, and I hope it is, but New Orleans won't ever be the same.

OCTOBER 10, 2005

ROGUE RESCUERS

SULI, XPOSTED FROM *NOLA.COM MARIGNY FORUM*, KEN FOSTER

From the SPCA: NEW ORLEANS (10/06/05)—The Louisiana SPCA is warning residents to beware of activists breaking and entering homes, under the auspicious of animal rescue.

Groups of animal activists have come into the city since Hurricane Katrina, and are breaking and entering homes to remove pets. These groups DO NOT have permission to do this, and are NOT affiliated with the Louisiana SPCA, the only licensed animal control agent in the city.

"These are activists who are choosing not to play by the rules," said LA/SPCA Executive Director Laura Maloney. "They are breaking into homes without permission, destroying property and taking people's pets. Just yesterday, a group broke in to a New Orleans home while the family was sitting down, eating dinner!?"

Organized animal rescue efforts since the storm have been spearheaded by the LA/SPCA, and the organization has given official credentials to trained humane officers who lead the search and rescue work.

Please report any suspicious activity to the New Orleans Police Department, as any animal rescuers without LA/SPCA credentials can be arrested.

OCT. 11, 2005

EXTENDED CURFEW

KIERSTA KURTZ-BURKE

In the New New Orleans, most people are looking for a new job, a new place to live, or both. Some have found it...our friend Bob, teacher/principal for 30 years at the school he founded, is working construction and cleaning out refrigerators. Jeanine, also a teacher, is working the FEMA phone lines.

Jenn, a newly laid-off hospital colleague, serves us pizza at one of the few open restaurants. "It's weird," she says, "because I worked in a pizzeria in college and hated it, which is what inspired me to get my PhD....I guess I've come full circle." She wants to get another job in her field, but it probably won't be around here, and she can't bear to leave New Orleans yet. Dory, a former UNO professor, is hoping to parlay her volunteer job with the Red Cross into a paying one.

We run into Cassandra and Shelley in the Quarter... they are all smiles. Their house was ruined, but they scored a good gig cleaning rooms at a downtown hotel in exchange for room and board. Plus, Cassandra is a massage therapist, and the guests pay her cash, mostly Army Corps of Engineers guys.

"Cute?" I ask.

"Fifty-something suburban dads," she sighs. "But they're really nice people."

"You should get in with the Guard," I say. (She's single, after all.)

"WAY too young," she laughs. "I'm looking for the 30-year-old crowd."

"Insurance adjusters?" I offer. "Or roofers..."

Speaking of roofers, FEMA will send some guys over to put a blue plastic tarp over your damaged roof so the rain won't come in. A mere $1900 for the job—billed to your insurance company, or, if you don't have it, then to the federal government. Your tax dollars at work, folks. It takes a half an hour, and they use a staple gun.

Mayor Nagin ("Ray-Ray" when we're feeling the love) proposes a large casino district, "Las Vegas of the South." Charity Hospital is smack in the middle of it, so the administration stands to make beaucoup dollars on selling the land once they tear down the building. We can only hope they build a Charity Hospital-themed casino on the site—martinis intravenously! An unlimited buffet whizzes by on a gurney!—so that the former employees can get their jobs back. I'll be one of the doctors dealing blackjack, and a real nurse in a fake nurse uniform will get your drinks. Not a bad place to choke or have a heart attack—at least you'll be in capable hands.

Still, the weather turns cooler, and our spirits are definitely up.

They extended our curfew and we can stay out to midnight....Saturday we see signs all over town with magic marker: 2nite Hot 8 Brass Band @ Le Bon Temps. And we go, and it is magical. Like the first time your hear live music in New Orleans. The crowd is frenzied, happy reunions with old friends...(by the way, a strange effect of the hurricane is that I have become a "double-hugger." You know, a slow, close hug, with an extra squeeze at the end. Usually the realm of drunk guys and/or hippies and/or elderly aunts, the double hug is now officially my m.o.).

The band sounds great and leads the crowd in chants like "Katrina, you gotta do better than that," and "New Orleans, bring it back, bring it back."

I see Ravi at the end of the bar, but it's too packed to get across, so we mouth words and do sign language.

"You okay?" he says.

I give the thumbs-up sign.

"House?" he makes a roof with his hands.

I wrinkle my nose and shake my head side to side.

He nods sadly, "Us, too."

"How's the baby?" I say while cradling the air. "She's great, so great," he grins.

We never did make it across the bar—the National Guard rides up at midnight and tells us all to go home. They look tired, but are quite gentle about it all.

But next time I see Ravi, I'm definitely gonna get close enough that I can give him a double hug.

SNAPSHOTS FROM THE FRONT

J. WAYNE LEONARD, ENTERGY CEO

From 1999 to 2013, Wayne Leonard was the CEO of Entergy, Louisiana's second-largest company and New Orleans' lone Fortune 500 firm. Hurricane Katrina caused massive damage to the company and raised doubts about whether they would be forced to move operations out of New Orleans for good, especially after President Bush's recovery proposal included no money for the utility.

Against the urging of elected leaders from outside Louisiana, Leonard declared in 2006 that it would remain in New Orleans.

People have been e-mailing me a lot lately. The messages are not questions or complaints but often times long, thoughtful essays on how the recent adversities have made them, not angry or bitter over their loss, but thankful for what they have. The people writing often cite my messages as a source of comfort that I know what they are going through. But the truth is I don't. I can only imagine.

Other than my immediate family, all my relatives live in the Midwest. I did not have to help evacuate them, worry for their safety or grieve their loss. My home in New Orleans was almost completely spared while others around me suffered considerable damage. On the West Bank where I live, we had plenty of wind but none of the ravages left behind by flooding. In some respects I feel almost guilty to have been so lucky. But as "luck would have it," it does allow me to focus (without as many personal issues to confront) on what we can do to help all of you, and to make sure Entergy gets through all of this as strong as ever.

But as for my messages, whatever comfort you might get comes not from me, but the inspiration of your fellow employees.

My messages are often just observations of what I have seen and heard the people out there, not just on the job, but on a mission...

...A man named Jeffery Hughes works for us in the Chalmette area. Jeffery rode out the storm in his house. Well, he started out in his house. As the water rose, Jeffery and some buddies moved to the attic. The water kept coming. Jeffery and the buddies soon found themselves debating how they would exit the attic.

With a piece of two-by-four, strong muscles and a hefty dose of adrenaline, the group forced open a hole in Jeffery's roof where they soon realized that "they needed a taller house."

Seeing a boat off in the distance, Jeffery swam to the boat and found its bilge pump still operable. Rescuing his buddies from the disappearing roof, Jeffery made his way to "higher ground" so to speak. Here, he remained for a few days before being rescued.

But the most impressive part of this story is that after being rescued, Jeffery went to work the next day. He joined his fellow linemen without hesitation, working very long days, in the heat surrounded by the stench of rotting food.

Our line people have a difficult task; they have to work in a devastated, putrid environment. In addition to the smell and the devastation around them, there are the bugs. People in the field everyday and night tell me that the flies are huge. I don't want to even think about what they have been eating to get that big.

The military is right when it says an army moves on its stomach. Food is imperative in an operation such as ours. Many people who spent most of their pre-Katrina days behind a desk, using the latest technology and in air conditioning now find themselves assembling lunches for hundreds of people. And they're happy to do it.

People are laughing and joking. They swap "how did you make out in the storm stories" and comment on how this was a whole lot more interesting than submitting invoices to PEARL. Every job is important. If it weren't, we wouldn't be doing it.

But when you're doing paperwork all day, sometimes you wonder if you're really making a difference, a contribution. You are, but when you're helping to feed people on the frontlines, you can see it. It doesn't matter if the "thank-you's" are there or not. You "feel" appreciated.

I know our people are grateful because food (i.e., sand-wiches) has become merely sustenance, fuel for a weary body. Any chance they get to eat something different, like a hot meal, they practically applaud. I'm not so sure I'd have the strength or the attitude to cheer about much of anything, if I had been putting in the long days and hard work these people have for so long now. But like our ad says, "All my heroes have always been cowboys!"

Then there are fascinating snapshots from the "cowboys" in the field. I heard of a man working on insulators on a 500 kv tower that were cracked and broken. He worked at the job with fierce determination and by the way, when the old insulators were brought down, the date that was written on the bundle was 1965. This was the year they were installed, the same year as Hurricane Betsy. Whoever put them up after Betsy should be proud. They survived everything Mother Nature dished out for 40 years.

Not all the work is high in the air. On a corner in New Orleans, I heard about gas workers that dug up a 21-inch gas line that last saw the light of day in 1910. That fact that we can find something buried in the ground from 1910 amazes me.

These guys are preparing to drain the water out of our natural gas system. They are over their heads in mud, struggling to dig around a water line and the old cypress timbers (scary thought) our forefathers used to build this line.

They tap the pipe and water shoots out about a foot. It smells horrible. (They tell me to imagine the worst thing you have ever seen on "Fear Factor," multiply it by 100 and you still won't know how vile this is.) And, it keeps on coming. They pump as fast as they can, but the water just keeps coming out of the line. They persevere and soon we will be able to restore gas service to the French Quarter and Central Business District.

Yes, I am proud to be part of this company. I am proud to say that I work for Entergy. Entergy people are exceptional in every way. They work hard, they are tireless. Everyday I am thankful for the people who are determined to get this done, the people of Entergy who are facing Rita and Katrina down with a smile even when sometimes their heart is breaking, not only for their personal losses, but having to witness the devastating loss of others everyday on the job.

It is my privilege, my joy, to be able to share the often inspirational stories of your lives. Thank you and please stay safe.

Wayne
J. Wayne Leonard
Entergy CEO

ROSS ANGLE (AS TOLD TO HUMAN RIGHTS WATCH)

Ross Angle finished serving ten days for a trespassing charge and was set for release on August 29th from Orleans Parish Prison.

"They shut off the phones on the 28th and told us that we couldn't call anyone. On the 29th they were supposed to let me out, but they told me they had to hold me because of the hurricane. At that point it wasn't even raining that hard. I said, 'You've gotta be kidding me.' My family was waiting for me. I've got a baby on the way, my lady is seven months pregnant. I had a job to get back to. I was stuck there. I couldn't even make a call to explain."

He didn't get to call his family until he was moved to St. Francis Parish Prison, a small rural jail, over a week later.

"I felt awful, my family was crying, no one knew what happened to me."

Angle did not have anything to eat or drink until the next Wednesday, when sandwiches were thrown over the fence onto the football field at Hunts Correctional Facility, where evacuated prisoners were taken before they were transferred to the facility that would hold them.

"I've never been in jail before in my life. I'm not a criminal. I wasn't even supposed to be there! By Tuesday at 6 a.m., the water was 3 feet high. We had no food, no lights, the toilets overflowed into the water that rose up to my stomach by the time they brought us outside. I'm still having nightmares thinking I'm surrounded by water in those walls."

He described his fear: "Picture waking up everyday in a prison somewhere—you don't even know where you are—knowing you were supposed to be free, not knowing how long they were going to keep you there. Not knowing if it would ever end. After they moved me, I kept asking for someone to look at my case and they just kept telling me 'we're waiting on the DOC guys, we don't know anything.' If my lady wasn't seven months pregnant calling them everyday and yelling then I would probably still be there. . . . It made me feel worthless. They treated me like I had no right to live. I'll never forget what I've been through."

"And you know what?" Angle said to the Human Rights Watch lawyer who interviewed him, "You're the first person who has told me they're sorry that I went through that."

OCTOBER 12, 2005

DON'T LOOK FOR CLOSURE

CLIFTON HARRIS, *CLIFF'S CRIB*

Well, I guess Mississippi isn't so bad. We have found an apartment right outside of Jackson and have finally told ourselves we will be here for at least six months. The apartment area is nice enough to be relaxed to the point that six months should fly on by. Lots of people I spoke with the first week after Katrina said there was no way they would ever return. I myself said out loud that I wasn't going back. Now, it's been a month and a half and I can sense the homesickness in a lot of their voices.

Now, this doesn't mean that I expect everybody to pack up their new lives and go back to the swamp.

That won't happen. What I am saying is that no one will ever get closure from this storm. I thought going home to see my house and the city would give me some closure in knowing everything was gone. It only made matters worse. I am going to give you a few reasons why we will never have closure.

How can you really just walk away and not even be concerned about what's going on? You will always feel the need to see what's going on with the rebuilding and recovery. We all really wanna know if rich people are going to come in and take over our neighborhoods. We all wanna know what it is going to look like and who's going to live where we played in the street. If they do take over the places we called home forever we will all be angry no matter if it's ten months or ten years from now.

We haven't gotten to the roughest part of the year for this even yet. The holiday period between Thanksgiving and Christmas in New Orleans was like a family and class reunion. No matter where we had moved to, that was the time of year to come home and spread love with all your family, classmates and childhood friends. The reason for this is because this is where our grandparents and parents always stayed. Now, they are gone too. This will be the first holiday season in my life that our family didn't spend at 2144 Benton St. That means there will be no chance of closure for anybody until January 2.

The rest of America has never caught on to the culinary wonder that is Patton's Hot Sausage. I feel like a fiend looking around every grocery store in Mississippi for Patton's or DD. There won't be any Patton's for a while, since it was under 10ft of water in the Lower Ninth Ward. These are truly dark days for me and my stomach. Even if you never move back, you know you got to go home for at least a hot sausage po' boy with cheese.

These other places are cool and normal, but New Orleans is different and odd. It's the kind of place you either have a feeling for or you can't live there. My dad always says New Orleans should have been its own country. If you were born, raised, and have been living in New Orleans more than 20 years, that will stick with you forever. There can be no closure, because the lifestyle and the attitude of the city is who you are. You can't get closure from yourself.

We are all products of Cool Can, Humpty Head, frozen cups, Tamborine and Fan, Wild Magnolias, Soul Rebels, Hot 8, Rebirth, gumbo, red beans on Monday, crawfish boils on Mother's Day, Super Sunday, Claiborne and Orleans on Mardi Gras, Shakespeare Park, Circle Food Store and, like my friend Neecha would say, "Sitting on the porch talking about nothing." That's who we are. The storm can't kill that. Even turning our shotgun doubles into townhouses can't kill it. It's in your heart and your personality.

Don't look for closure. Look for your own personal peace and spirit and adjust to your new life. Trying to get closure from something that is a part of you will only make you sad.

BLOGGING FROM KATRINA GROUND ZERO: WAVELAND, MS DAY 1

SARA FORD, *MICROSOFT DEVELOPER NETWORK BLOG*

My God, this is what an apocalypse looks like.

We left Seattle on 4pm on Saturday and arrived in Waveland Wednesday night at 11pm. We were delayed by the snowstorm in Denver, and we weren't able to get the truck pulling the U-Haul above 65. It was a long trip to say the least.

We found Waveland to be solid black in the night. Headlights miles away looked like odd glowing candles as they approached us on Hwy 607/90. If I were to take a snapshot of what my parents' street looks like, I wouldn't be able to identify it. Hell, I couldn't even identify it during the daylight.

On the "good" side of the tracks, houses are still standing, but are just ruined inside. There are just piles and piles of debris everywhere on the roads. And, I'm being constantly reminded that the piles were much higher weeks ago, as high as telephone poles.

This morning, Kyle, my dad, and I walked down Coleman Ave. Nothing is recognizable. It's amazing how you can drive down a street every day for the first 20 years of your life, then have all the landmarks removed, and next thing you know, you have no idea where you are at. People started spray-painting the names of streets onto the street itself so you knew where you were going.

Walking down the road, we were stopped by the Red Cross. They were driving around in a van handing out water and Poweraid to anyone who needed it. Of course, my first reaction is "oh no, I'm good. I'm from Seattle. I don't live here, so I don't need the water." Then 15 minutes later in the noon sun, as I'm baking, I wished I had taken them up on their offer. Now I'm starting to understand what life is really like down here.

We walked down Vacation Lane back towards the house, when we met a lady standing outside of what used to be her home. Again, it is so hard to hide emotions during such times. Normally, I'll ask someone "how are you" as a "hello, nice to meet you," but I have decided to stop asking that…

My family and I ate lunch at the Waveland Café, and I'm sure we'll be back tomorrow. It is hosted by www.christianlifeatthebeach.com. If you want to donate directly to Waveland, donate to this group. Microsoft: I'm working on setting up their 5013c with our giving campaign, so hopefully it'll appear on the giving campaign site soon. If it weren't for them, I would be a whole lot hungrier than I am right now. And so would many other people. Makes me teary-eyed thinking about it.

I have never been served food in such a fashion before. It was way too overwhelming when I was handed a plate of food by a high school girl from Florida. Seeing all the people waiting in line with their shopping carts to get donations, seeing people I grew up with in the same line waiting to get food. How do you take this all in after just a few hours?

I went to the "command ops" booth behind everything and said, "I'm a Microsoft employee, and I want to donate lots of money to keep this place up and running. Who can I talk with?" I doubt the volunteer had ever looked so happy since Katrina hit. I met the man in charge of the Waveland Café place. He's actually got a friend at MSFT that I have to look up when I get back. I got the direct number to the guy handling their funds, so not only will I be able to send them directly the fundraiser money (I was too scared to bring 1000 bucks in cash down there from the nearest working ATM/my bank), but I finally see a light at the end of the tunnel for getting Waveland Café hooked up with the Giving Campaign.

After we got back from the Café, I called my aunt to give us a tour of Waveland. We started off at my childhood home (aka, my babysitters when I was a kid). I practically lived there, and the lady who took care of me I consider to be my grandmother. The house is at least 50 yards from its foundation, maybe more. It went sailing across the neighbor's house and into the house next to it to stop it. There are parts of the shed and carport lying between. I made the mistake of looking inside. I don't know how to describe how a house can look "dead," but the childhood home where when I walked inside of it just last year called out to me, "Stay, be loved, be safe, take as long as you need" had died. There were no feelings of love emanating from the house, only death. No one was home—everyone in the family had evacuated (thank the lord), but the house itself had died, and a part of me died right there too. I learned the real meaning of "you can never go home again." I will never be able to go home again.

Since the house was tagged yellow, meaning it is safe to collect belongings, we're going to head back hopefully tomorrow to try to salvage some stuff. I just want something, anything to take back home, even if it is a light switch. Anything of interest will obviously be saved for my grandmother's family—bless their hearts. As I told her daughter on the phone, if you need to sell, you just make me an offer. I will rebuild.

We continued our "tour" of Waveland along the beach road. It's just more chaos, destruction, and disbelief. This is NOTHING like Camille. NOTHING. Camille was all about wind. This is all about water, and apparently water is stronger than wind.

After a while, you just shut down. It becomes just too much to take in, house after house after house just flattened like pancakes and then gutted by the water. We're talking 1000s of homes flattened like pancakes and gutted.

We stopped by OLA (my high school). The pictures said it all, but looking inside the school bus really got to me. Having played so many sports in high school, I spent a lot of time on the bus, just like all the other athletes. It was a sad sight.

One man at one of the stops on our tour said that he saw a wall of debris coming straight for him, not a wall of water, but a wall of debris. Can you imagine seeing something like that?

Anyways, our tour ended seeing Casino Magic Bay St. Louis washed ashore in Diamondhead. For those of you who don't know the area, the casino was on the wrong side of the lake/bay. It sailed completely across.

Tonight we went back to Waveland Café for dinner. I have always been on the "serving-side" of the soup kitchen line. Never had I been on the receiving line. I find it extremely hard to eat there; it's so emotional. And then when we get to the house, I'm starving again....

I'm off to bed now in my cousin's trailer (he was supervisor for the year at Casino Magic in Bay St. Louis, so he got a free trip to Disney World for this week). Right now, I feel terribly sad. There's some sort of cat howling competition going on right now outside. I feel their pain.

OCTOBER 17, 2005

KELLY LANDRIEU, *MINERVAE*

So this guy sent me the following message on Myspace:

> *I'm new to the New Orleans area and I'm lookin'
> for some people to hang out with, you know,
> show me the "cool" areas in town. I'm here doin'
> insurance work so I should be here for a while. I'm
> also lookin' for a sexual partner. If you're interested
> I have some pics I can send you. Hope to hear from
> you soon.*
>
> *Mike*

At least his method is straightforward. What a shame I'm not in New Orleans. I guess he'll have to keep "lookin'."

OCTOBER 18, 2005

DAVID OLIVIER, *SLIMBOLALA*

No Pets Found Inside

This is the front of our house. There are similar signs on thousands of other houses across New Orleans left by animal rescue groups: "1 cat rescued 9-31," "2 dogs rescued," "cat colony here ->," "3 cats rescued." It's a new feature in the city's already distinctive landscape.

I admire what these folks did. They saved the life of our tenant's cat. They saved the lives of thousands of other animals across the city. It was a truly decent thing to do.

I must add this though. Animal rescue folks—big hearts, small organizational skills.

The first group broke into our house and actually rescued the cat. That's good. The second group broke in, found no cat, and then spray-painted "no pets found inside." Understandable—it's a chaotic situation—lines of communication are jumbled. But while I was there, every day, weeks after the fact, multiple groups of animal rescue folks would come by and, despite the clear marker, try to re-rescue the cat. I would have to explain that it was long gone. They would then try to re-rescue the neighbors' cats and I would have to explain that those, too, were long gone. It was actually kind of painful to watch, all those good intentions with nowhere to go. I almost wanted to just bring in impostor cats for them to rescue just to validate their efforts.

Oh, well. Such, sometimes, is life.

OCTOBER 20, 2005

>>>From: Kiersta K-B:

It's raining men...in New Orleans.

You got your National Guard, FEMA, contractors, insurance adjusters, Army, plumbers, electricians, journalists, and an assortment of random dudes with guns and/or hammers, cranes, bulldozers, cameras ... not to mention the local barflies around town who never left. Estimation ratio is 20:1, men to women. Thoughts of reality TV possibilities run through my head: "The Bachelorette: New Orleans Edition!" Hmmm, gotta find a bachelorette who's not too picky about the whole "full set of teeth" thing...what about "Fear Factor: New Orleans Edition?" They can eat what's sitting in those duct-taped fridges on every curb. Bring those Real World kids back and give them some buckets and Clorox bleach, for Pete's sake. We need all the help we can get....

Justin and I, with Titus, are happily ensconced at our friend Mary's house uptown. I am working in Baton Rouge three days a week at the VA hospital, a brutal commute these days, so I am staying over some nights on a Finnish passenger ferry in Baton Rouge. Long story. It's more "Das Boot" than "Love Boat," but has the benefit of being very impressive to my three-year-old nephew, Benjy. "Tee-Tee is living on a boat!" he reports gleefully. Life is trickling back into New Orleans, we started the "demolition" phase on the house this week, forward march...still, the levees are not repaired, so we watch the newest hurricane carefully and keep a box full of photos and documents close enough to stick in the trunk at a moment's notice.

Jayme came down for a fabulous visit this weekend, hooray! First post-K visitor! She helped Justin peel apart water-logged letters, cards, etc., that my darling pack-rat-sentimental-fool-lover-of-paper-ephemera husband saved over the years. Some hilarious, some heartbreaking. We relaxed a lot, went out to hear Anders Osborne, had dinner, felt almost normal. Love carries us along.

Peace out,
Kier

DAVID OLIVIER, *SLIMBOLALA*

My Favorite Grumpy Quote From A Displaced New Orleanian: "Baton Rouge don't know what osso bucco is. Baton Rouge sucks."*

Apologies to the fine people of our state's capital. My city-mates sometimes become enraged when deprived of their specialty meat products.

OCT. 29, 2005

JOSH NEUFELD, *4-EYES*

Lee, my driver on Emergency Road Vehicle 1166, is a great team leader. He's about 55 and is from Seattle. He's sort of a Red Cross veteran, having worked with his wife on Hurricane Dennis in Florida. He loves being an ERV driver, and is also very conscious of the safety and comfort of the support people in back. He yells out every turn and bump before they happen, and always jumps in the back to help prep meals when we get slammed with people. (As I wrote about earlier, he also knows where all the blue water Port-a-Potties are scattered throughout the route. Bless him.) He's relentlessly positive and just has a great attitude.

At this point, after two weeks together, we've developed a real rapport. We have almost perfect division of labor, with him handling the driving and condition of the ERV and me running the back area. He lets me train new support people and basically follows my lead in that arena. The larger decisions about the route and ending the day's run are left to Bill. We work well together.

I like his style on the loudspeaker too. As we drive through the neighborhood, he calls out the menu, adding little flourishes to make it entertaining. The other night we had ham and sweet potatoes, so his riff went something like this: "American Red Cross with your free Dr. Seuss hot lunch today. We've got ham and yams served in a clam by hand by two guys named Sam in the back of a van. So come as quick as you can!" Corny, yes, but any bit of humor helps keep the day moving.

Bill flirts shamelessly with all our female clients over 40—he's the opposite of a dirty old man—and keeps up a constant patter with the neighborhood folks. One of his favorites is when someone asks him how he's doing. "I'm feeling so darn perfect, if I was feeling any better I'd have to be twins!" (One of our clients then replied, "Well, it's a good thing you ain't twins, then!" Good for her!)

Another favorite of his, when asked how he's feeling, is "Finer than frog's hairs on a Sunday morning." Recently, Tony gave him a new variation: "Finer than frog's hairs split four ways, sanded and greased. That's mighty fine."

He's also got one about using the Port-a-Potty. Something about how the "soap" in the "sink" in there "just doesn't lather up." You have to be as intimately familiar with the Port-a-Potties as we are to get it. And then there's the one he's told about his day off and how he got thrown off a public beach for wearing his thong bathing suit the wrong way. And of course he never passes up the chance to remark—whenever we have a woman as our third team member—that she has us out-numbered, "one to two." What a riot!

After the tenth time you hear Bill make the same joke, it starts to drive you crazy. After the 50th time, it becomes as soothing and familiar as a bedtime lullabye.

Bill and I are different in background, age, musical tastes, religion (he seems to be a pretty devout Christian, and I'm...nothing), and many other things, but we get along great. He's been a terrific partner on this disaster, and we have a good time on our runs. Most importantly, he seems as motivated towards our customers as I am, making sure everyone gets fed and not getting caught up in making it home exactly on time. (Surprisingly, there are many people here whose main motivation seems to be getting back to SeaBee base promptly every day. They seem to forget the whole reason we're here is to help the victims of the worst hurricane the U.S. has ever experienced.)

Anyway, I can truthfully say Bill has made every day here easier to get through, and I'm thankful we ended up together on the same ERV.

SUNDAY, OCTOBER 30, 2005

GUTTING HOUSES

ANN GLAVIANO, *WHAT THE HELL IS WATER? THIS IS WATER*

Today I drove with Michael to Mimi's house. Not the one in St. Bernard. The new one, off O'Neal Lane, way on the other side of Baton Rouge. I looked over at Michael: This is weird. We're going to Mimi's. This is how we get to Mimi's house now.

When we got there, Claire ran up to me and threw her arms around my waist and wrapped her legs around my leg and clung there, hanging, hello.

Kaylen, Kelsey, Kevin, Cullen: how is it? How are you?

Great! We're great!

I fixed myself a plate of beans and rice and sat down and asked them again. How's school?

We hate it. It's horrible.

They're all ready to go home. Except their parents bought houses in Baton Rouge, and they're enrolled in schools here, schools they hate, kids who don't want them. Kelsey explained: At St. Michael's, where the male/female ratio is like 1:3, the New Orleans boys are welcomed and the New Orleans girls are "intruders."

(Aunt Shannon and Uncle Tim went in together on a house and it's spacious, room enough for Uncle Tim, Aunt Elly, Aunt Shannon, Lee, Kurt, Cully, Erin. There's a pond in the backyard, a fake one with a plug-in fountain. I told Uncle Tim, "This is nice, weird but nice," and he said, "You know, yeah, it's nicer than my old house—but it's in Baton Rouge.")

The party was at Bethy's house, the whole extended family, Mimi and her two sisters and the kids and grandkids. Seeing everyone there was bizarre; it was my family but not our house. Still: Bethy lives five houses down from Uncle Tim and Aunt Shannon. Mimi lives two streets over, and Aunt Kay lives right behind Mimi. It's not St. Bernard but it's exactly like it was in St. Bernard.

I was so happy to see everyone. Mimi was so excited I thought she would bust. I hadn't even talked to her since the week after the hurricane. I miss them all, and I've been wanting to visit, but the traffic is so bad that I've stopped driving during the day unless it's within five minutes of my house and I can take a back way to get there.

Aunt Kay and I were talking while she snuck a cigarette, and Mimi came over, fussing. Aunt Kay was like, "Mama, not in front of Ann," and I thought Mimi was trying to take her cigarette away. But then she took a drag and told me, "Kay's teaching me how to smoke." It took me a minute to realize she was kidding. She smoked in college. I said, "Mim, what are you doing?" And she said, completely serious, "Well, Ann, you know, I didn't really want to take up drinking, so." She said the other day Grandpa confessed that when he saw Aunt Kay's Virginia Slims on the counter, it took everything he had in him not to sneak one.

That's when I realized how bad it is for them.

And still we are the lucky ones.

Aunt Kay has all the old pictures up in her new house: Mimi as a little girl, Granny and her sisters on the beach in '20s bathing suits. She'd put the old pictures on the second floor of her house in St. Bernard before they left. But all the pictures of her own kids were downstairs. They're ruined now. That's all I had cared about, before I knew about my house. The home movies and the baby pictures. I can't imagine them gone.

I played frisbee at Bethy's with a little redheaded girl, no relation, who looked like a ten-year-old Katie P. She had her hair all curled up on top of her head and she was good at throwing the frisbee. Uncle Mike's two-year-old, Ryan, was running around in a Batman costume. He looked at me and the little redhead and he put his hands on his hips and he said *OOOOOOOOOH YEAH*. Then he ran around in circles and shouted it, again, *OOOOOOH YEAH OOOH YEAH OOOH YEAHHHHH. Ooooooh yeah.*

Kelsey told me to come sit in her bedroom. She and Kaylen are sharing a room now; they bought new posters today: Led Zeppelin, Jimi Hendrix, Bob Marley, Pink Floyd. They bought them, I think, at Bed Bath & Beyond. Which is probably the same place they got their matching reversible purple/teal bedspreads. Kaylen asked me about waiting tables. She wants to get a job because she's got too much free time because her new school is easy and she has no homework. I asked the girls what they do in Baton Rouge for fun, and they exchanged glances and said: We walk. Sometimes, they said, we get chased by dogs. Claire came into the bedroom and Kelsey, irritated with the girl-talk interruption, told her to get out. Kelsey is Claire's surrogate mother and it was weird seeing her fuss.

—but Kelsey—
I played Barbies with you today.
—no you didn't—
Yes I did. On the internet, remember. (get out.)

Sibling bargaining. Michael was like that. He would chase me around the house wanting to play and I'd run into my room and slam the door, or try to, and if he caught it before it closed he'd stand on one side leaning and I on the other side leaning till the wood bowed or I could get it locked. And he would cry. And then if I would play with him, it was never enough. And he would cry. His adoration was thorough, endless, there was no satisfying him, and I felt horrible all the time. But he was almost six years younger than me. And it's not like we could play Barbies together. He dismembered my Barbies. And besides, I played Barbies better alone. If I sat on the sofa he had to sit next to me. And if I snuggled with him it only made him want to snuggle more. I told him, when we were both little, that he was a black hole of affection. My dad used to sit me on his knee and tell me how I was emotionally scarring Michael for life. That made me cry. Just like every time Michael got hurt, scraped knee busted lip, that time when he was three and nearly impaled his right eye on the coaster holder at Grandmotherdear's, I drew him a Band-Aid.

Hey, fix me a coke.
How many ice cubes?

This morning when I woke up, he was lying awake on the sofa in my apartment. It was 12:30 and we were supposed to be at Mimi's for 1. I told him get up. And do you want a shower. (Yes.) So get up. (He lay there.) Now. Get up. Hurry. (So he did.)

Later, after the party, we're driving down Siegen to the bus stop so he can go back to Natchitoches, and he's being quiet and I'm worrying about him, and I think: There's no one else in the world I can talk to like that. Who else can I tell to wake up now, and take a shower, and hurry up, and he'll actually do it. This is a weird point of sibling affection, but it's true.

In Kaylen and Kelsey's room, Aunt Kay and Aunt Ellen have joined us and they're sitting on the carpet. Beth comes in and says Uncle Mike's on the phone. She puts it on walkie-talkie mode so we can all hear him.

Aunt Kay says: Well, Mikney?

He says: Your house, the downstairs, is gutted.

To me this sounds scary, but evidently for her it's good news. And he took the kitchen cabinets down by himself. And next weekend, Saturday and Sunday, they're doing more work. He wants Kaylen and Kelsey to come help him pull nails.

I think: I want to go, I'll pull nails.

And Aunt Kay will bring a radio with batteries. There's power now in some St. Bernard neighborhoods. There's running water at her house.

Aunt Kay says: Power and water, what more could you ask for?

Kelsey sits up straight.

Can we go back?
Yes, my girl. But not yet.
—*When*—
Not till May, Kelse. At least.
—*we could live upstairs*—

Kaylen stops her. (Shut up. It's not going to happen. Stop asking.)

Aunt Ellen says: Michael, listen to me. Don't touch my house. Are you listening? Don't touch it. I want it bulldozed.

She looks around at us and nods. She says: I never want to see it again.

There's a trampoline out back: I take off my shoes—I haven't been on a trampoline since I was twelve. Kelsey is jumping and talking to Erin on her cellphone. Claire climbs up with me, and Sean Patrick, and Colin. Then Ryan, still in his Batman costume. He sits on the trampoline instructing the other boys to stop jumping. Maybe he's scared, so I sit down with him and he climbs onto my lap. He's got his arms around my neck; he's saying something like "Jump me," and I bounce with him, sitting. Then I stand on the trampoline and pick him up, he attaches himself to me, he's heavy, I've got him. He whoops and we jump.

CRAIG GIESECKE, *METROBLOGS*

I'm 51! I'm 22!

A scant 90 days ago, I was building a new company. I had clients spread from Jacksonville, FL to Dallas and was on the verge of the greatest season my company had ever experienced. Despite going into monstrous debt and taking a lot of chances, things were coming into focus and, dammit, everything was just about to pop big-time.

This morning, I started my new job at Parasol's up the street, making $9 an hour slapping together po'boy sammiches and scraping out greasy pots and wondering how the hell to reassemble everything that was shaping up so perfectly. I have gone from being middle-aged master of my fate to being a 22-year-old with a new degree in something useless like Asian Prehistoric Topography. TBK (The Beautiful Kim) has resumed her old job, selling overpriced toys to the wealthy on Magazine St.

And, yes—we now have a food stamp card.

But y'know what? It's fun.

My business will be rebuilt and things will get back to normal because it just takes time to do this kinda thing these days in New Orleans. There are thousands of us in the same situation, going back to familiar streets in unfamiliar circumstances. Very unfamiliar circumstances.

Please be patient with your server or your bartender or your chef or the retail help in New Orleans for a while. Many of us are doing things we weren't doing 90 days ago and haven't done in years. And, as fun and rejuvenating as it is, we're also seriously weirded out sometimes by this new reality.

That said, we're glad to be on the train.

GROUND ZERO

MICHAEL TISSERAND, *SUBMERGED: AN EVACUEE'S JOURNAL*

My wife spent yesterday in New Orleans, getting the house ready to put on the market. She woke up at 5 a.m. to drive in with a friend. She cleaned the kids' rooms, hung the pictures back on the walls, stacked the Saturday, Aug. 28, issue of *The Times-Picayune*—the one with the "Katrina Takes Aim" headline—on the pile with the other papers.

I never asked about her trip. Finally, she brings it up. "You didn't say you appreciate my work," she tells me. "You did that for yourself," I say. "I didn't even want you to go. Why should I thank you?"

"We have a house to sell."

"Nobody's thinking about curb appeal. Anyone who wants to buy that house is going to buy it anyway, even if it looks like shit. It doesn't matter. The rules are changed."

I keep on with this stubborn refusal. Right now, being angry feels like the right place for us.

Because I have a secret. All day, I've been carrying around the faxed contract from our real estate agents. It needs my signature to get things rolling. For two days, my wife kept reminding me to pick up the fax at a friend's office. I can't sign it.

Since the storm, our personal limbo has taken the form of two months in a 4-year-old's bedroom, a family of four sleeping in two twin beds pushed together. Our hosts' limbo is that their 4-year-old is back to sleeping

144

with his parents until we're gone. So is their 2-year-old, whose room is now filled with the suitcases and clothes of two evacuated families.

Limbo ends next week. We're returning from our hosts' home in Carencro, La. to New Orleans for the remainder of the year. It's time for us to start reassembling.

But I'm not moving on, even if CNN has. If it's not about Katrina, I don't want to hear about it. Forget movies, forget TV, forget Scooter Libby. I'm still living in that week after the hurricane made landfall.

I keep thinking about how we watched the footage from the Superdome and sputtered at our president's disinterest in our drowning city. Why didn't we get a damn bus, load it with food and water, and go save someone?

Is this survivor's guilt? Or is it something we all should have been feeling a long time ago—the crush of poverty and despair that surrounded us?

Two days after my wife goes to New Orleans to clean our house, I also drive in. The real estate forms are stacked on the passenger 's seat. I tell her I'll drop them off. But that's not why I'm going home. I want to get a haircut from my old barber. See some old friends. Eat at a New Orleans restaurant. I have to do something to get unstuck. So I try taking a pleasure trip.

Magazine Street is a series of shops and boutiques, interrupted by a few boarded homes. Taped-up refrigerators and piles of garbage line the sidewalks, but it's getting easier to overlook these scenes. A lot of the places are open. People are flocking here.

I start with late-afternoon bottles of Guinness at Aidan Gill's barbershop, where a "No Surrender" banner hangs over the front entrance. Supper at Taqueria Corona, which is filled with people I know.

We greet each other with "How's your house?" That's the dividing line here: those who lost everything, and those who didn't.

I am happy to see old friends. But I'm also growing tired of seeing everyone in different places, wearing different clothes, leading different lives. Even our faces look different.

A little farther up the street, a circle of *Times-Picayune* reporters are gathered on a front porch, swapping war stories. Ties are tucked into shirts, sleeves rolled up. I've made plans to join my friend, Tom Piazza, on Magazine Street. We join the reporters' gathering, then decide to head over to Mid-City. Tom wants to see his girlfriend's house. I want to see my old newspaper office. We're going to take a disaster tour.

On the drive down Canal Street, going away from the river, streetlights glow over a desolate thoroughfare. Then the lights stop. Crossing Claiborne Avenue is a plunge into darkness. It's like driving off a cliff.

Entering Mid-City, our headlights flash over the ruined cars, still covered in a crust of dried ash. Up ahead, a yellow, two-story root-beer mug towers before a restaurant, illuminated by a single floodlight. It's the only thing visible for blocks.

As we drive on, our headlights shine on piles of garbage that cast large shadows on houses and school buildings. "It's like being in a sick body," Tom says.

We turn to the side streets, tires rolling over debris. That's it. We get out.

The spell from Magazine Street has dissipated. When we arrive at my house, I pour canned water into two paper cups. We find a chess board among my daughter 's toys. Tom is usually a little better at this game than I am. But now I'm playing the worst chess of my life. I only see one move at a time. I can't find any patterns.

We talk while we play. Tom tells me that he had to see me; over the phone, I was joking about the real estate prices. It had bothered him that I didn't seem to mind leaving. Now he knows better.

One game ends, we start up another. I move a rook into capture. Then a bishop. Tom builds his attack. We start up another game. I lose one after the other. It goes on like this for hours.

The next morning, I roll out of bed. I'm aware that I'm unshaven, wearing the same clothes from the night before, and I still have little cut hairs on my forehead from the haircut at Aidan Gill's.

It feels good to look a little crazy.

After breakfast, Tom and I go to a key store. We're getting keys made to my front door so he and his girlfriend can use my hot water. The cell phone rings. It's my wife. She immediately asks if I've talked to the real estate agents. I say I haven't even thought about it. I say good-bye and hang up.

Then I get another call. I look at the number—it's a 504 area code. Local. I answer.

"Hello?"

It's the real estate agent. And he knows I'm in town.

"How are you doing, guy?" he says.

I tell him I'm doing OK. That I'm at a key store.

"If you want," he says, "I can just come by the house and look it over."

That sounds good, I say. So in a few minutes, I meet him there. He pulls up on my street. Walks through my front door. Looks around the rooms with his real-estate-agent eyes. I like this guy. Just a little more than a year ago, he helped us buy this house. But now I want him gone.

"It looks good," he says.

We go upstairs, check the attic. No damage. I give him a key. He asks about the contract.

"I don't have it," I say.

"All we really need is that first sheet," he says.

"I'll fax it," I say.

He seems to hesitate. The last thing he'd heard, I was bringing the forms into town.

"OK," he says. I see him out.

When I start to think about staying in New Orleans, I can't stop. It's like an addiction. After losing her job as a pediatrician in the storm, my wife found a position in Chicago. It's the city where we met each other; it's a city we both like. So we have a plan. But now all I can think about is the escape hatch. Leaving doesn't seem real. What is our reason? She lost a job? So what? We can stay. We'll figure out something. Isn't this our home? Aren't we happy here?

These questions play through my mind on an endless loop.

Turning off I-10 on the Florida Blvd./West End Blvd. exit, I crest the ramp and steer toward a giant, grey-brown mountain of debris, flecked with red and blue. Chair legs poke out from the top like little trees. Getting closer, I see that it's actually a range that continues on for blocks. A second mountain is all tree trunks and branches. On the next block is another debris mountain. Trucks keep pulling up with more trash. The piles change shape as new households are dumped in.

I pull up to a security guard and ask for directions to the levee breach. It's not an unusual question, he says. A lot of people are coming to visit it.

I drive on dirty roads and finally pull over at the foot of the Old Hammond Highway Bridge. From there, I walk alongside the canal. I'm on an elevated path of fresh gravel. Looking down, I see a truck half-buried in the base of this path. A few giant white canvas sandbags, the size of bathtubs, are piled in a heap; "7,000 lbs." is stamped on the sides.

To my left, it looks as if a train had barreled through and smashed everything in its path. Even the brick houses have jagged holes in the walls. To my right is a calm strip of water.

A short wall runs along the path. Then it stops. A few hundred feet down, it resumes again. Here it is. Katrina was bad enough. It was strong enough to damage homes and kill people. But if this levee wall had held, I'd be back home now. I know I would.

It's just a few hundred feet. That's all. Enough to change everything. "Fuck you," I say under my breath.

A Louisiana State University team of researchers that examined documents obtained by *The Times-Picayune* concluded that the Army Corps of Engineers made a number of rookie mistakes. The levee wall was built on weak soil, and the sheet piling that supports the concrete wall didn't go deep enough into the ground. First-year engineering students would have known it would break. That's what you get for doing it on the cheap.

"Fuck you," I say again.

I'm moving my family out of this broken city. I don't want to, but I am. And I know it's what we need to do.

Fuck you.

I want to shout it. But there's an old couple here, walking around. So I walk over to them. We introduce ourselves.

"Why'd you come here?" I ask.

"We'd seen it on TV," says the woman, who moved to New Orleans from Honduras 25 years ago.

"We lived less than 10 minutes from here," says

the man, who moved here from Chile three years ago, after he met the woman on the Internet.

"It's like a nightmare, and I can't wake up," the woman says.

"All the city is depressed at this moment," he says.

"They didn't want to spend their money," she says.

"All this could have been avoided," he says, waving his hand down at the grey wrecks.

"The first time I came back, there was no color anywhere," she says. "It was like a black-and-white movie. I was driving, and my legs were getting soft. I couldn't drive anymore. I had to stop. My body was like a puppet."

I ask if they're angry.

"Let's not even get to that," she says. "I wish I had a public microphone. I would tell it like it is."

They lost their home. They lost their jobs. They've been living in a shelter in Lafayette. They say they've learned about the goodness of people. Now they're back.

We stop talking for a while. The woman tells me that they drove to the French Quarter earlier today. They were looking for tourists, too. They didn't see any either.

"You know what we'd do sometimes?" she says. "Back before? We'd get some dinner ready; we'd put it in the basket. We'd drive to the lake. We'd talk, we'd joke. We'd go home again."

It's a good memory. "New Orleans has a soul," she says. That's why they're returning.

The sun is now setting over the canal. In the homes across the levee, where the wall didn't break, lights are turning on. A few blocks down, people are lining up for dinner at R&O Pizza Place.

I tell the couple good-bye. I ask them if they're glad they came to the levee breach.

"I think people need to see this," the woman says.

I don't make it home for the children's bedtime. When I walk into the dark room, everyone is piled in the twin beds. My wife wakes up.

"Maybe we shouldn't all move at once," she says. Maybe she should move up to Chicago early. Get started on her job. Find our new home. I can stay back with the kids and finish out our daughter's school year and keep writing here. Lots of families are doing it this way.

I realize that she's been thinking about this all day, ever since we talked on the cell phone. She's working on the next step. That's what she's been doing this whole time since the storm hit, working on the next step. And we—the four people in this little room— needed her to do that.

I sit down and move the sleeping body of my son toward the center of the beds. We'll talk in the morning.

CHEDDAR DISCRIMINATION!

JOSHUA COUSIN, *NOTE FROM THE BOOK*

ANOTHER LIST!

Throughout Our Situation We Found That...

- BREW-Beagles is a Great Company for the Wellbeing of Beagles.

- WARL is a Great Organization & Deserves an award for all the Katrina Animal Rescue.

- WARL is Helping Various Katrina Evacuees Re-Unite with their pets. Even if they don't want them.

- WARL sent ALL beagles to BREW (Cheddar is a beagle)....lol.

- BREW put our dog up for adoption and now he's Nowhere To Be Found.

- OR AT LEAST THAT'S WHAT THEY SAY

- The Petfinders members have been helping my sister throughout this whole ordeal.

- The Media has been on the case also.

- I'm not talking about world news...I'm talkin' about Washington DC's Local news, NBC4.

- Cheddar is Somewhere.

- BREW is trying to prove to us that This Dog is not Our Dog.

- BREW knows it's our dog.

- They don't want to give the dog up.

- WHY??

- We & The People at Petfinders think that it's racial discrimination.

- From what I hear, once BREW found that the owners of The Beagle were Black, they didn't want to help us out.

- They feel that WE aren't good enough to take care of a beagle.

- Cheddar is Black. LOL JK. He's Brown. :)

- We have So Many Organizations involved on this case...it shouldn't even be racial.

- Just give us our dog.

NOV. 4, 2005

A TRIP TO THE DEVASTATED LOWER NINTH WARD

BLAKE BAILEY, *SLATE*

Last week I went back to New Orleans for the third time in a month—this time to meet with my insurance adjuster. With every visit, the city seems a bit more recovered: more people back, more businesses open, more debris cleared. Still, there are signs that all is not well, to put it mildly, and the overall impression is that of a fallen world. On Canal Street I saw an otherwise normal-looking man taking a piss in broad daylight; he didn't seem drunk; people passed him without a jot of dismay.

My adjuster, Danny Wells, was scheduled to inspect my house at 7:30 in the morning, the first of many inspections that day. Tomorrow he'd be leaving for West Palm Beach to get started on Hurricane Wilma. I was running late because I'd stopped en route at a Shell station in Metairie to buy coffee. The place was jammed with rowdy Hispanic recovery workers. Sandwiches were microwaved five at a time then hurled across the store trailing steam; the cash register receded into the distance as workers cut in front of me to join their chuckling buddies. By the time I departed, my coffee was cold and my banana had ripened a bit.

At my house I found Danny Wells picking his way through the debris in my backyard, taking mysterious measurements. "So," I greeted him, "are you going to give me lots and lots of money?"

He chuckled uneasily. "Well, you know, we're checking for wind damage here," he said. He was a wizened man in his late 50s who looked as though he'd seen his share of the world's pain. "You met with your flood adjuster yet?" he asked.

I told him I had no flood insurance, and he began shaking his head. I added that—according to the *Washington Post*—less than one percent of homeowners nationwide have flood insurance where it isn't required. The goddamn FEMA maps, I went on, were *outrageously* inaccurate, and besides, the government has known for *decades* that the whole levee system ..."

"It's a shame," he sighed, and consulted his clipboard. "OK, here's what we got so far. This part of your house will have to be re-sided. Been on the roof and found a few shingles missing, plus a left-front patch needs to be replaced." He peered at his clipboard as if hoping to find more. "I can get you $500 for debris removal." He looked again, but that was it. "Want to go inside now?"

Inside he took photos and sighed from time to time. Finally he sighed deeper than ever and said, "Is that a new fridge?" We looked at my brand-new Sears refrigerator, which appeared to be sweating maggots.

"Yes," I said.

"A tree fell on your roof and cut a power line," he said, making a note of it, "and I'll say that's what broke your fridge. Otherwise"—he indicated the moldy walls, the buckled hardwood floors, the sodden furniture, everything—"I'm afraid it's all flood-related, you know?"

In need of perspective, I thought I'd take the Gray Line bus tour of the Lower Ninth Ward, next to the Industrial Canal, where flooding had been the worst. The idea behind the tour was to give former residents a chance to say goodbye and come to terms with their loss. (Closure was a word I heard again and again that day.) The National Guard was blocking residents who tried to return on their own because it was too dangerous: Houses that were still standing might collapse at any moment, and bodies were still being pulled out of the rubble (another corpse had been found the day before). Also, they worried that people who were psychologically unprepared, and alone, might commit suicide.

Though I'd spent most of my adult life in New Orleans, I'd never knowingly set foot in the Ninth Ward—pretty much terra incognita to middle-class white folks. I knew it was somewhere along the canal, but that was about it. Finally I stopped to ask for directions from two black women who stood chatting outside a sagging clapboard house.

"Well, this here's the Ninth Ward," said the younger of the two—the older woman's daughter, it turned out. She explained that the *Lower* Ninth was on the other side of the canal, by way of the St. Claude Bridge. Her name was Sheila Jackson and her mother's was Johnnye; they, too, had just met with an insurance adjuster, and they invited me to have a look inside their house. The walls were mottled like rinds of rotten gorgonzola. "And look here," said Johnnye Jackson, her voice muffled by a gas mask. "Just *bought* this fridge." It was a big expensive chromium model—much nicer than mine—lying flat on its back, covered with silt. We went back outside.

"I grew up in the Lower Ninth," the daughter told me. "It was a great place to be a child—like your whole block was an extended family. Real sense of community. But that's just gone now...Mm!"

Where would they go next?

"Thinking about Boston," she said, and laughed. "What about Boston, Mama?"

"Long as it ain't here, baby."

Bus tours of the Lower Ninth began in the parking lot of a church on the west side of the canal. The buses left at intervals of a half-hour or so, and each contained two counselors from the Department of Health and Human Services as well as the odd Salvation Army volunteer. Most of the passengers were elderly and tended to gaze out the windows in a sort of brave, impassive way. Our driver was a brassy blonde named Shirley Rolko who kept up a steady, blasting patter over the PA: "You feel like laughing or crying or screaming you should just let it go, folks! ... *Nothing* I have ever seen, folks, prepared me for this. The West Bank is bad, but this is *horrible*... You see something and want me to stop, just yell STOP!" Shirley wasn't overselling it; it was horrible all right.

The larger brick houses along the main thoroughfare, Caffin Avenue, were relatively intact ("R.I.P. Fats
You will be missed" somebody had spray-painted
across the candy-colored compound of Fats Domino—
who's alive and well and plans to rebuild), but once
the bus turned onto a side street, there was a low
collective groan.

Frankly, I'd rather avoid any heavy figures of
speech (*It looked like the end of the world*), so a few details
will have to suffice. Mostly there was the rubble, and
caught high among the power lines and branches
of dead trees was a lot of random detritus: bits of
furniture, toys, tires, garbage, and dead animals. Cars
and large appliances were smashed on top of collapsed houses, as if flung there by giant angry babies. A
few houses had remained intact by submitting to the
water and simply floating away, and now they rested
pell-mell in the middle of streets, athwart other houses
or mounds of debris. Everywhere the ground was
caked in a foul, suncracked mud, like the desiccated
bed of some prehistoric ocean. Bloated flies swarmed
lazily around the bus.

An old woman yelled "*Stop!*" on the corner of
Derbigny and Lizardi. The bus pulled over, and the
trailing police car stopped, too. The woman got off
and hobbled down Lizardi with the help of an
HHS counselor. Her husband stood watching her
go; he was nodding slightly, but his face was a
blank.

"Is this where you lived?" I asked him.

The man explained that he and his wife had both
grown up in the neighborhood, though for many
years they'd lived in Gentilly (not far from my own
house). They'd evacuated to Pritchard, Ala. His name
was Cephus Peavy, which he patiently spelled for
me.

"May I ask why your wife wanted to stop here?"

"You may," he said. "That's where my brother-in-law and sister-in-law and niece lived." He closed his eyes and pointed. "They passed away there."

A few minutes later his wife came back. She could barely walk now; some other passengers huddled around her. After a few minutes she was lifted sobbing onto the bus, and her husband, who'd stood off to the side with his arms folded, followed with a meditative look.

At first I'd thought Shirley Rolko's braying patter was a bit much, but I began to feel grateful for it. "Anybody want a Sno-Cone?" she boomed, as we passed an upended Sno-Cone stand. "Look at the ho-ho! Look at Santa! He looks lonely there … " A forlorn plastic Santa reclined in the mud. "You gotta laugh or cry, folks," she'd say, whenever she suspected one of her quips was in doubtful taste. "You gotta laugh or cry. You folks are looking at one of the greatest disasters in history! And you survived! You folks are all *survivors*."

It was a heartening thought, and everybody hugged her when they got off the bus some three hours later. I did, too. This experience, finally, had felt like closure.

NOVEMBER 10, 2005

A TOPOGRAPHY OF NORMAL

DAVID OLIVIER, *SLIMBOLALA*

When I talk to my friends and family who are elsewhere, they ask "what is the city like now?" And the answer is, "it's very hard to say." The forces that have made New

Orleans what is right now are so distinctive, so unlike anything that happens in normal life that there's really no meaningful comparison. The city has taken on a very strange shape, a widely varying topography of normal, which is strongly correlated to the physical topography of the city:

Normalish: Areas of the city which didn't flood, a band about 10 to 15 blocks in width running along the river from the Industrial Canal to the Jefferson Parish line, are moving forward rapidly. The contrast from when I was here a few weeks ago is startling. Then it was a semi-ghost town under military occupation. Now it's busy. There are people everywhere. Many, many businesses are open. Life looks something like it did in the old days. Although when I say "normalish" let me make clear that I really do mean "normalish." Traffic lights flash. Every intersection is a four-way stop. The neutral grounds are filled with signs advertising demolition, mold remediation, hauling, etc. Moving trucks are everywhere. "For Sale" signs are everywhere. Refrigerators are in the street. Houses have giant graffiti scrawled across the front. People hug and cry at the drop of a hat. Life is definitely back, but it's still pretty weird.

Borderline: Further away from the river are the neighborhoods that got from one to three feet. Because most houses are elevated, many homes are essentially fine. But the utilities are dodgy. The grass is dead. And some people did flood. Less people have returned. It's quiet. Where we are staying now is in one of these neighborhoods. Flooded. These are the neighborhoods, like ours, with several feet of water: four, six, eight feet. Everything flooded. Nobody is living here. No traffic lights and few street lights work. At night, they're pitch black. During the day there is some activity, but it's not regular life. It's demolition and construction crews. Every house is either dormant or a construction site. The curbs are lined with heaps of rubble. It will be many months before these areas are alive, but they will come back.

Devastated: Lakeview, Gentilly, New Orleans East, the Lower Ninth Ward. The destruction here is of an entirely different order. To see them, it's hard to imagine anyone ever living here (even though much of it will some day rebuild). On West End Boulevard in the neutral ground, formerly a large grassy expanse where people jogged and walked their dogs, there is a massive trash heap three stories high, extending out of sight down the street. I stumbled upon it unexpectedly the other day and it took my breath away. I've seen plenty of trashed homes now, but the scope of this was different, huge, thousands of lives in a pile. It's awful.

So there really is no one answer. The city is all of these things right now, and trying to find some simple way to make sense of and encapsulate it in one single summation is impossible.

NOVEMBER 16, 2005

NO LOSING US

CATHERINE JONES, *FLOODLINES*

Today my mother called me to say that a family friend, a well-respected doctor, had killed himself last night. He had lost most of his patients after the storm and was struggling to rebuild his practice. Everyone knew he was depressed. I played with his kids when I was little: I remember rolling Hot Wheels through their kitchen, grabbing CapriSuns from their overflowing pantry. He hanged himself in their house. All those closets we used to play hide-and-seek in.

He hanged himself. After my mom told me that, I couldn't breathe. I sat down on someone's pale blue steps in the middle of Dauphine Street and I couldn't even cry.

He was a good person and a good doctor. He will be missed.

Fittingly, perhaps, I went to the All-Saints' second line this afternoon. Irvin Mayfield was playing trumpet and, as expected, lots of tourists and media showed up. At the beginning I had that "where are all the locals?" feeling that still marks so many of our cultural events. Where were we, in the midst of all those TV cameras? There are so many cameras marking our lives these days, it is hard to tell where we are sometimes. It was a little too much for me. I went into the St. Louis No. 1 and walked alone among the graves, the evening sun turning all those decaying tombstones silver.

Then the music started and I walked back out onto Basin Street and then I could see us. There we were! Suddenly I felt so silly: there is no losing us, even amongst all these strangers.

There is no losing us.

The sun hung low over the empty Iberville projects and the St. Louis No.1, and the music started, and all the New Orleans people started dancing like we have for centuries. The way we move our feet, even the streets know it's us.

Here are my people: Mostly, we are not the ones with video cameras. We are not wearing Mardi Gras beads. We are not the ones not dancing. We do not say to each other, "Irvin Mayfield is a really good trumpeter." We do not say, "Such a shame, all the devastation," or "Martha will be so sorry she missed this."

Here are my people: the ones who did not have time to change after work. The ones who have come to the second line in coveralls and scrubs, and chambermaids' dresses and hardhats, and Burger King T-shirts and security-guards' uniforms and cook's pants and even some people in all-white hazmat suits. The ones who are back, the ones who never left, the ones who are here. The mothers carrying babies and groceries. The friends embracing wildly on corners saying, "how'd y'all make out?"

This is what we say to each other:

"I didn't get any water but my mama, she got about six feet of water."

"Girl, I never thought I'd see you here!! I thought y'all went to Dallas!"

"Everybody's over by my sister 's house and she about to kill us all."

"I lost my house and my job but I'm ok. How you doing?"

"Baby, this is my first second line since the storm. I'm all right!"

Here are my people: the ones shivering on this first cold day; we are the ones who bundle up when it becomes 54 degrees out. We are the ones drinking 40s out of paper bags, the ones who know all the words to all the songs, the ones who know how to dance and walk at the same time. The old people pushing walkers and still keeping time!

Did I say there is no losing us? Even amongst all those strangers, all those cameras, all that water? Even amid all that distance? Even though we have been scattered to the four corners of this huge planet, even though I have seen so many of you for the last time? Did I say there is no losing us? Even with everybody's baby pictures decaying on the neutral ground, and all our refrigerators standing out on the curb with the magnets still on them, and all the trophies and trumpets and graduation suits warped and stiff and moldy, piled on sidewalks for miles and miles and miles?

NOVEMBER 16, 2005

CLOSE TO HOME

WADE RATHKE

Wade Rathke founded ACORN in 1970 and was its chief organizer until 2008.

We were raised in a neighborhood in Gentilly called Oak Park for no especially good reason. When my dad's company transferred us from an old field in Irvine, Kentucky to New Orleans, we first lived on the West Bank, but then we became one of the first families to open up this area, filled in from the swampland hardly a mile from Lake Pontchartrain and only a few hundred yards from Bayou St. John. Our early pictures from the '50s show one or two houses on our block with sand all around the lot and not a blade of grass or tree in sight. Gradually, the blocks filled up with houses all up and down Burbank Street and the whole neighborhood.

People would come and go, but mostly they came and stayed. Around the early '60s, a family moved in across the street. The daughter was older than me, and off before we knew it. The son was my brother's age, and we knew Mark relatively well, and over the years would run into him in New Orleans where he worked at the Maple Street Bookstore and then on his own near the Ice Rink for many years, and he died in the Bywater several blocks from me several years ago.

Walter Zumpe was the old man. A gruff-talking but friendly enough sort who one didn't exactly get to know, he kept to himself for the most part. I would see him from time to time, but not much. I dropped out of college and came back full of piss and vinegar to organize in New Orleans against the war in 1968 after some brief training by the Boston Draft Resistance Group following the March on the Pentagon. God knows what I thought I could really do, but I was full of rage, ideas, passion, and ready to go wherever! I got an apartment uptown a couple of blocks off of St. Charles Avenue for $40.00 per month on 4th Street. I was making it on Kraft Macaroni and hotdogs for dinner, grape nuts for breakfast, and peanut butter and jelly for lunch. I had to work of course and that was a harder proposition. I did a couple of weeks as a print dryer in Kenner. Struck out trying to work for a hoist company for reasons I never understood. Managed to get as far as meeting with the publisher of *The Times-Picayune* with a proposal that I write a column on the youth culture, but he was probably just trying to give advice to someone not listening, and I was years ahead of my time.

Finally, Walt Zumpe gave me a job on the shipping deck of the Luzianne Coffee plant way out on Chef Menteur just past the Industrial Canal. In the beginning, I was a 19-year old shipping clerk working under the shipping and receiving clerk, a fellow who lived in the Irish Channel called Russell who was a piece of work. The only real pleasure in the job was driving a lift truck and learning how to load the pallets up 3 and 4 levels. I would make the orders for the trucks, and run the machinery right into the bed of the delivery and 18-wheelers. I would call the trucks at 7 AM sharp at the beginning of the shift. I would take the inventory in the plant at the end of the shift. We got all of the thick, black coffee and chicory we could drink in the plant cafeteria, and we needed it. I would catch a streetcar in the dark, transfer on Louisiana at the funeral home to a bus, and stay on until the stop up the road from the plant, and somehow make it on time no matter what time I had rolled in the night before. A salesman, Peck, would flip me a one-pound bag off his truck every week, and from that time on I was hooked on coffee and chicory for life. I didn't see Mr. Zumpe. He was the plant manager. I had to carry my weight. At the end of the summer when it became clear I was not just a college kid with a summer job, they moved me from the shipping dock on 7-3 to working the 11-7 driving a lift truck on the back of the tea line. The tea ladies would fill the boxes with bags, kid me while I waited, and then when a pallet was full, I would drive it out to the warehouse. I would sit on the lift truck reading a book or something to pass the time and stay awake. After a couple of weeks on the line, newly married, I simply quit. I went up one morning to thank Mr. Zumpe for the opportunity, but mainly for the job and the experience. He was there early. It was no problem, and it was done.

I didn't see any of them much. My folks had moved to another neighborhood after we left high school, so it would be happenstance at the most. I was off on my way in another direction.

Walt Zumpe stayed in the house across the street —stayed too long, as it turned out. *The Times-Picayune* is now running a daily story, much like *The Times* did after 9/11, where people remember each day one of the more than 1000 who died from Katrina. Mr. Zumpe's granddaughter reminisced about him in today's paper. She remembered him hard and stubborn, which seemed right. Turned out he was a WWII fighter pilot, who had been shot down and captured by the Germans 60 some years ago when he was 25. He had a fine voice and had once aspired to the opera and his granddaughter said his captors would sometimes make him sing for them. He won the Distinguished Flying Cross and a handful of other medals. His granddaughter couldn't get him to leave the house even after his wife evacuated quickly. She said he told her he had "gumbo" and "coffee" and would be fine. She asked him what he would do if there wasn't enough water. He reminded her that he didn't drink water, and that rang true as well.

Oak Park took no less than 4-5 feet of water everywhere. I ran into a PICO organizer, Joe Givens, who used to live in the same neighborhood, but closer to St. Francis Cabrini High School, which was wiped out a couple of blocks away.

Mr. Zumpe's family speculated that he came down from the attic at some point, where he had been holed up with pictures of and by his family members, to see what was happening downstairs. They guess that while he was there the floodwater was probably too strong for legs now frail. He drowned. They found him in the den. They buried him in Indiana where he was raised, far away from the water, even though he had been gone from there for more than 50 years.

CHEDDAR IS BACK HOME!

JOSHUA COUSIN, *NOTE FROM THE BOOK*

I've uploaded the video of Cheddar's return home. You'll see it real soon. But in the meantime, we all want to thank:

> Eric for all of his Hard work & Getting this dog
>   back to us
> Washington Animal Rescue League
> NBC4 News in DC for their cooperation & having
>   Chat's face highlighted :)
> Uhh...Them Beagle Folks...

I don't know. We have to thank everybody involved. You know who you are!
  Especially the members of The Petfinders Network.

NOVEMBER 23, 2005

THE LOVE, AND THE RECIPES

CATHERINE JONES, *FLOODLINES*

Yesterday I got back from Washington, DC. It was the first time I'd left Louisiana since I'd returned here, about five days after the storm. I was strangely apprehensive about leaving. I know this storm has made us weird down here: I am used to people cooking huge pots of red beans for strangers on the neutral ground; I am not used to eight different kinds of toothpaste in Walgreens. What would it mean for me, I wondered, to go to a place where people take the subway to work, and don't talk to each other, and then go home, or maybe stop for groceries or a beer on the way? Could I function in a place that wasn't so marked, as we are here, by such deep collective grief?

And of course I had those moments of culture shock: looking at my friend's enormous pile of junk mail in her entryway; being amazed that I could recycle my Arizona tea can at a party; getting snapped at by a shop worker when I pocketed a tiny perfume bottle that I'd really assumed was free. (In New Orleans right now, you can find huge crates of bottled water, and dry food, and hot meals, and cleaning supplies, and toiletries, and blankets and coats and pants and baby clothes and diapers, almost anywhere. I kind of forgot that in the real world, if there's stuff in a big bin, you can't just walk up and take it.)

And of course there were all those reminders that DC is a functioning city: garbage, for example, does not consist of furniture and electrical wire and sheetrock and decaying animals. It can fit into cans that people organize neatly on their curbs. And it doesn't get picked up by tractors and bulldozers, but by garbage trucks. And every single billboard has an advertisement on it. And every single streetlight works, and the mail comes, and there are no 1-800-GOT-JUNK? signs on the telephone poles, and the powerlines don't lean down over the sidewalks like nooses. But I knew about all that. I had been expecting it, and it was somehow less weird than I'd thought it would be to see so much intact-ness.

Here's what I wasn't expecting: the love, or the recipes.

I'd decided to take a train, partially because it was so much cheaper than flying, and partially because I wanted to look out a window for 24 hours and watch the land change. I had all these visions of myself sitting alone on a train gazing out of a window for hours and hours, not doing anything, not thinking anything. I knew it would be exactly what I needed.

Here's what really happened on the train: 20 minutes after pulling out of New Orleans, my whole car started talking. Everybody. About the storm, obviously: it's become a sort of dysfunctional security blanket for us. It gives us definition and purpose. We don't go anywhere without it, tucked, barely visible, into our back pockets.

But not only about the storm, not only about houses, jobs, relatives, schools. Not only about jail and being evicted and not being able to find the doctor. No, not only about those things. We talked about grandparents, holidays, the games we used to play as kids. We talked about cooking for about three hours. We got into arguments about how long it takes to learn how to make good red beans. A 23-year-old cook was going back to Pittsburgh, where his fiance and three-week-old son were waiting for him. He'd found a job in Pittsburgh restaurant, where he'd convinced them to let him cook "real New Orleans" food. Now the restaurant is making all kinds of money.

"Yes, indeed," the 90-year-old great-aunt across the aisle kept saying. "Yes, indeed. But I bet it's cold up there."

"Baby, it's cold everywhere," the old man said in front of her, buried in his jacket.

Once people found out I was in medical school, that was it.

"Congratulations!" people told me. The seat next to me was never empty again. "But I'm not a doctor yet," I kept saying over and over again. "I don't care, baby!"

everybody said as they showed me their rashes, told me about allergies and headaches.

Then I started speaking in Spanish with a construction worker from Panama. He had gotten on the train with paint still drying on his clothes. He was going up to Atlanta to get his truck and his five roommates to come down here to work. After that all the Spanish speakers on the train made a little corner in the lounge car. Deep into the night we drank hot chocolate and talked about food and kids and immigration policy and how to fix cars.

No alone time on that train. That was ok. Privacy might be nice sometime, but I guess now's the time for us to be together. *This is what's happening to me now*, I thought, surrounded on that train by so many beautiful people. *I am so, so grateful.*

NOVEMBER 28TH, 2005

RANDOM ELECTRONIC SQUAWKING

BART EVERSON, *B.ROX*

Been too busy and too preoccupied to post, so here's a random grab-bag update. My apologies if this seems somewhat haphazard or disjointed.

We continue to chip away at basic clean-up tasks. I bought a pressure washer.

The electrician was supposed to show up today, but he didn't. The insurance company was supposed to call today, but they didn't. I was supposed to meet the plumber today, but I didn't. He showed up, but I wasn't there, and I felt like an idiot when he called me.

We have not moved back into our house permanently yet. Tonight will be our third night here. It has been unseasonably warm, but when the cold front comes through tomorrow it might be a bit chilly without some form of heat.

Xy and I were speculating on what happened to a certain young thug from our neighborhood. Lo and behold, shortly thereafter we passed him standing on the corner of Gayoso and Bienville, in front of Adam's Grocery. This is where he always used to hang, and there was something funny about seeing him there again even though the place was flooded and remains closed. Xy waved and he waved back, all smiles.

We stopped by Xy's old school, which is still being used as a SWAT/SOD headquarters. Xy got a look at her old classroom, which is basically intact. There are still instructions on the chalkboard from the Friday before Katrina.

As for Xy's job, I hardly know what to say. Her school was designated as a charter, but now it's been taken over by the state, and we have no idea what's happening. I hope to have more news soon.

Lucy finally caught a mouse, after several days of stalking. Speaking of rodents, a few days ago we found a dead rat lying on the sidewalk in front of the house next door. Today I picked it up—carefully, with a shovel and gloves and a plastic bag—and threw it in the dumpster down the street.

One of the more revolting things I've ever done.

Speaking of revolting, we re-potted a big plant that Michael and I had jury-rigged in a trash can a couple months ago. (The original terra cotta pot had been shattered by the hurricane.) As we grappled with it, a quantity of fetid water was disgorged on my leg, and the smell brought back memories of sorting through our flooded possessions. I'd hoped I would never smell that smell again.

We've been eating well: Thai at the Basil Leaf, Caribbean at Mango House, sushi at Sake Cafe, pizza at Slice, and some excellent home-cooked meals (at David's house, since we still have no power). The home-cooked meals have been cooked by Xy. I have not been in the mood to cook much since Katrina. We've also had a number of hot lunches from the American Red Cross. They have trucks roving through Mid-City. Not gourmet fare, of course, but free and deeply appreciated.

Food and drink have been a source of immense comfort, and I'm glad to see more restaurants re-opening everyday. Whatever else happens, we won't starve.

Tonight we discovered there are streetlights burning at Jeff Davis and Canal! Still none at Salcedo and Canal, but they're getting closer.

As you walk through our neighborhood, you hear random electronic squawks coming from deserted houses. These are smoke detectors, dutifully alerting the absent residents that their 9-volt batteries are running low.

And, finally, I would note that a general consensus seems to be growing here, a mood that I would describe as a mix of desperation and determination. The feeling seems to be that the rest of the country has forgotten about us already, and that even those who have not forgotten cannot truly appreciate the devastation without seeing it firsthand, but that somehow, someway, we have to make our voices heard.

"DIDN'T HE RAMBLE"

JUSTIN LUNDGREN

In late 2003 I started collecting obituaries from the Metro section of the local New Orleans newspaper, *The Times-Picayune*. The single criteria for inclusion was that the deceased must have a nickname of distinction, something capable of eliciting a giggle or a frown or a raised brow. Admittedly, it's an odd thing to collect, and in its mounted form on my kitchen wall, the hundreds of pinned clippings would often serve as a point of conversation and, occasionally, disapproval. I never felt that the collection was disrespectful to the dead or to their families. The people of New Orleans are death obsessed, and for better or worse, I suppose that I am too.

I liked these obits because they captured snippets of lives that are a reflection of the community I love. New Orleans in the pre-Katrina world was full of characters that you'd sooner expect to read about in a Flannery O'Conner short story than meet in real life. These scraps of paper survived Katrina in my beaten up Mid-City home, and as I gaze on them now, they are a poignant reminder of what's been lost. Infrastructure can be rebuilt with money, sweat and time. Social structure is a more complicated endeavor.

With eighty percent of the town still in forced exile a full 3.5 months after Katrina, I wonder how "Tangle Eye" would have done in Salt Lake City or how Mr. "Dolomite" would have been received in Minneapolis. I imagine "Rabbit Carwash" working as a detail technician in Bose, Montana and I fear for his life. And what about the next generation of "Puddins" and "Stumpies" and "Mumbles" and "Roundheads"? How are they making out right now?

As my friend Ian McNulty recently confessed to me in a moment of clarity, many of us live in New Orleans not by choice but because we can't function anywhere else. The reality is not that extreme. The pre-Katrina city was unique because it allowed people to be their true eccentric selves. A lot of the New Orleans evacuees will certainly succeed in moving on and finding jobs and creating successful lives in other cities, but will those cities allow them to be "Snake" or "Baudy Man" or "Betty Boo"?

I have my doubts.

LEROY JOSEPH 'TANGLE EYE' 'BUCKIEMO' WILLIAMS SR.

Leroy Joseph "Tangle Eye" "Buckiemo" Williams Sr., a retired cabinet maker, died Friday of cancer at Memorial Medical Center. He was 73. Mr. Williams was a lifelong resident of New Orleans. He was an Army veteran. Survivors include his wife, Dorothy Hester Williams; two sons, Rodney Richardson of Sacramento, Calif., and Leroy Williams of Atlanta; a daughter, Monique Williams of Atlanta; a brother, Lawrence "George" Williams; four sisters, Melba Dean, Eunice Battiste, Claylee Williams and Yvonne Weathersby; and four grandchildren. A funeral will be held Wednesday at 10 a.m. at Historic Haven-Trinity United Methodist Church, 1238 Joliet St. Visitation will begin at 8 a.m. Burial will be in Green Street Cemetery. Majestic Mortuary handled arrangements.

W.T. 'WHITIE' WHITEHEAD

W.T. "Whitie" Whitehead, a retired seismologist for Apache Oil Exploration, died Friday at West Jefferson Medical Center. He was 94. Mr. Whitehead was born in Camden, Texas, and lived in Lafitte for the past 60 years. He was owner and operator of the former Whitehead Sales and Service Co. A Mass will be said today at 11 a.m. at St. Anthony Catholic Church in Lafitte. Visitation will begin at 9 a.m. Mothe Funeral Home is in charge of local arrangements. Burial will be in Livingston, Texas.

JOHN 'BOGGIE RED' MILTON

John "Boggie Red" Milton, a retired drywall hanger, died Wednesday of cancer at Charity Hospital. He was 65. Mr. Milton was born in Hardwood and lived in New Orleans for the past 12 years. He was a graduate of John Dawson High School. Survivors include three brothers, Roy and Donald Milton and C.W. Milton Jr.; and 10 sisters, Thelma Meaux, Barbara Tillman, Dorothy Mamon, Patricia Sterling, Ethel Rucker, Beverly Bell, Alice Hayes, Gwendolyn Hughes, Tara Askin and Veronica Milton. Visitation will be held today from 6 to 8 p.m. at Majestic Mortuary, 1833 Oretha Castle Haley Blvd. Burial will be in Hardwood Cemetery, Hardwood.

ERNEST 'DADDY BOY' 'COON DOG' ROBERTS

Ernest "Daddy Boy" "Coon Dog" Roberts, a self-employed painter, died Sunday of a stroke at his home. He was 61. Mr. Roberts was a lifelong resident of New Orleans. He was a member of the Fashionettes and Gents Carnival Club. Survivors include his wife, Theresa Mitchell Roberts; two sons, Ernest Roberts Jr. and Isiah Mitchell; two stepsons, Edward and Kurt Mitchell; two stepdaughters, Sheweka and Veresa Mitchell; four sisters, Delores Rolling-Williams, Thelma Forster, Kate R. Williams and Audrey Bryant Tolliver; and 12 grandchildren. A funeral will be held today at 9:30 a.m. at Tilly's Funeral Home, 2831 St. Claude Ave. Visitation is at 8 a.m. Burial will be in Resthaven Memorial Park.

GRRR.

ARIANA FRENCH, *LEVEETATION*

It's getting really hard to hang on...just in the sense that daily life isn't life so much as it is a collection of distractions, none of them terribly real, or gratifying, or sustainable.

It's hard for me not to resent the hell out of this city, this whole situation right now. Yeah, I love New Orleans. Yeah, I love its quirks, its human gumbo, its flava. But this is getting fucking insane. I am annoyed. Sometimes post-K life is like this little mosquito in my ear, an incessantly buzzing mosquito in my ear that I want to kill but I know that trying to kill it would mean hitting myself in the head in the process.

And then other times I think, well, at least life is interesting. I find comfort in the company of friends though, usually. Which is very, very good. We get together and laugh about the way our memories are shot through...I find myself increasingly ineloquent. The other night I couldn't think of the word "excess." I kept trying to say "excellent." And I wasn't even drunk.

Promises out of DC today to build the levees "better, stronger," but not neccssarily Cat-5 strength, mean jack shit. Fucking lip service, but who cares? Did Nagin or Blanco call bullshit? No, there was a lovely photo-op and I'm sure Shrub made up a cute nickname for Nagin, like Sugar Ray or Ray-Ray or Nagles, and there were back pats and everyone stood on the appropriate marks in the carpet for the nice camera lady. And Nagin says, the nice man in the big

White House said it'll all be okay, so everybody come on back now.

DECEMBER 6, 2005

REFUGEE OR CONCENTRATION CAMP AT I-10 AND CAUSEWAY?

MICHAEL HOMAN

On September 2nd-3rd, the night after I evacuated my house in New Orleans, I spent several hours inside this massive encampment of suffering people at the intersection of Causeway and Interstate 10. There I saw the most horrific scenes that I have ever witnessed. I estimated that I saw twenty thousand people. A few were corpses, many were elderly and in bad physical condition. I saw many people with Down Syndrome, and casts, catheters, wheel chairs, all sorts of stuff. They were almost all people of color, except for the National Guard and police, who were almost all white.

The National Guard and police were not letting people out of this area. Total disorder reigned on the ground inside the camp. I was glad I had my dogs with me, as that place was anything but safe. People inside the camp told me that they had been there three days. They were sitting outside without food and water in near 100-degree heat just waiting for buses. Every once in a while a bus will show up and there would be a mad rush of people to get a few seats out of that hell. I never saw this, as apparently only a few buses showed up in the daytime. I later learned that once you were on the bus, you couldn't get off, and they would later tell you where you were going. If you lived in Jackson but the bus was going to Utah, they wouldn't let you off the bus as it went through Jackson. You had to wait. And friends and family couldn't just come and get you out of this camp. There were barricades set up blocking the I-10 at LaPlace, about 20 miles away. I still get very angry at this country when I think about those suffering people in that camp. I think about what if my mother or children had to see such sights, and I get furious.

Five African American residents of New Orleans, Katrina survivors, testified before Congress today. Many members of Congress didn't believe what they heard. Four of the five citizens claimed race played a big role in the lack of recovery immediately after the flooding and even now. Some claimed that race played a role in the flooding to begin with. They said that if the stranded people were white that the government would have done more to help them. They said that National Guard troops pointed guns at their toddlers, and they were treated like criminals. Personally I believe that class had much to do with the situation as well, but I still believe that race played a major role. I saw it personally. These National Guard troops were scared to death because of race. They were mostly from rural areas and for them their knowledge of African Americans comes from TV shows like *Cops*. They pointed guns at many people, and there were plenty of racial slurs from both white groups and black that I heard driving around the city in a boat, as well as inside the camp. Another blogger who saw the same camp at Causeway and I-10 describes it as well.

I thought in the Congressional testimony today, the most interesting moments came when Leah Hodges claimed that "people were allowed to die" and likened what happened to the black residents of New Orleans to "genocide and ethnic cleansing." Rep. Jeff Miller, R-Fla., asked Hodges to stop referring to the camp at I-10 and Causeway as the "Causeway Concentration Camp." He then asked Ms. Hodges if she knew just what happened in the Holocaust. Hodges retorted "I'm going to call it what it is, that is the only thing I could compare what we went through to."

Miller kept asking her to stop with the analogy, and said that "Not a single person was marched into a gas chamber and killed." Hodges then said that the people "died from abject neglect" and "We left body bags behind."

I, of course, admit that nothing that happened in New Orleans was as bad as the Holocaust. And comparing tragedies and arguing about which was worse helps nobody. But I feel that New Orleans is on its own. And I believe that none of this would have happened in Connecticut.

DEC. 7, 2005

HOMESICK FOR THE HOLIDAYS

CLIFTON HARRIS, *CLIFF'S CRIB*

There has to be enough refugees in this area for the Hot 8, Lil' Rascals or the Newbirth Brass band to come here and just parade around the block a few times. They only have to do a few songs and I will have my fix. I don't want to go home and see a second line in the French Quarter because that will only piss me off. I need a good ghetto second line that involves grandmothers shaking things they haven't in years, pitbulls without muzzles, big girls wearing clothes that are way too small, someone getting shot along the way and that dirty, strange white dude with that nappy beard that shows up to every second line no matter how dangerous the neighborhood is and always has more fun than every person out there. If you don't know what I am talking about then I can't explain it. If you do know what I am talking about, I hope you are not homesick for the holidays like me.

DECEMBER 7, 2005

LOOK AND LEAVE

DAR WOLNIK, *HAGAN AVENUE PEOPLE*

So, I came back to town and opened my front door to see. Feels like a burglary happened, but the burglar was a ton of water pushing its way around your stuff, throwing the t.v. on the floor, moving the bookcase.

The water only got about a foot high at rest, but trust me, that is enough. Everything smelled of mold or looked moldy and kind of grey. I was able to keep about six boxes of stuff; no clothes, no shoes, sheets, towels. I stuffed my financial records in a large plastic bag so that I could give the IRS a wad of papers if they ever ask. Let them try to peel them apart.

My stepfather, Jerry, helped me throw out furniture and other stuff. I actually could have saved some of the furniture if I had a place to store it. No storage spaces were left in the region, so out it goes. I know folks will come by and take most of it before the garbage pick up, cuz that is how New Orleans is; we just move the stuff around....

As I was throwing out my home, Veda and Musa were already starting the stripping of the Laid Back shop and making their plans for the future. They had put up a sign the day they came back that said "We're Still Here Ya Bastards." The sign is for looters and city hall they say. People drive by and take pictures of the sign.

Their friends, Andrew and John G., were in there helping. Andrew is their mechanic and John is a friend who also volunteers at Plan B, which is a non-profit that helps build low cost bikes. John and Andrew are great guys who I have worked with at Laid Back Tours when the shop has a large group and needs extra guides.

Parkway Bakery's owner, Jay Nix, was also already hard at work after sitting at Musa and Veda's the week before trying to decide whether he should rebuild. They obviously helped to convince him along with his nephew, who is always hard at work at the shop. Jay is in construction by trade, so he has the skills and ability to get it done. He has room for a trailer in his lot, so he will live there while fixing it. Jay added the shop to the neighborhood in the past few years, and in doing so, revived an old place that even my grandfather remembered.

My next-door neighbor, Bill, was in his apartment, and the neighbor at the end of the block, Lynn Borsodi, was also there. They were not in any hurry to clean out their houses; our landlady, H.L., had not contacted us yet, so I think they were unsure of what to do.

Of course, the second thing I did was to go to the fair trade coffee shop, Fair Grinds. Robert and Elizabeth are good friends who I had text messaged in early September to make sure they had got out. They actually had evacuated in time, which is amazing for them. They never leave—usually.

The coffeehouse had water in it, but not a lot. Enough to need to pull the sheetrock out and let it dry out for a while.

Robert decided to do a little remodeling while in construction mode, so he is probably reopening in January, but, of course, still acting as a center by giving away free coffee every day, hosting a free store (reminiscent of the Digger stores in the '60s) and holding court for all to come and be in his kind presence.

He gave me some mildewcide to spray in my apartment, which should keep the mold from spreading. I stayed at my parents for the first two days in the Quarter and then moved Uptown to stay at my boss's house. Richard and his wife Bonnie have been great to many of us needing a place. They are in Houston so that their daughter can attend school. They will be back at the beginning of 2006 like so many others.

DEC. 7, 2005

CLIFF'S X-MAS WISHLIST: #11

CLIFTON HARRIS, *CLIFF'S CRIB*

A bucket of Patton's Hot Sausage. Why is the rest of the world sleeping on the greatest food of all time? I mean you just can't buy it anywhere North of Hammond, East of Baton Rouge and West of Pearl River. If Mayor Nagin wants people to return home, he should pass an ordinance that Patton's Hot Sausage can only be eaten within the New Orleans city limits. He will assure at least all of his former residents will at least visit five times a year for their fix. I can feel my arteries closing just from the thought.

DEC. 19, 2005

GREG PETERS, *SUSPECT DEVICE*

Last night's *60 Minutes* episode about the Gretna bridge crossing incident—where Gretna police turned away New Orleanians who had walked out of the ravaged city seeking help—crystallized a couple of things for me.

First, after reading a spectacularly idiotic discussion on another site, I've come down firmly on the "never go to Gretna or give them a drop of business again" side of the argument. The People of Gretna have applauded the heartless and bigoted actions of the police department and continue to rationalize the action as "protection." Well, I've had enough of this "protecting your communities" bullshit: they were trying to keep out citizens of the state of Louisiana, who, like all citizens, have the right to travel freely between any and all points. There was no lockdown or state of emergency that would enable the Gretna border to be sealed. No, they just wanted to keep the niggers out, and the yard signs and applause of Gretna citizens sends a clear message to the rest of the country, and please do not insult my or anyone else's intelligence by trying to claim otherwise. If there are good people and worthwhile businesses in Gretna that don't follow the racist party line, then bully for them: urge them to speak up and assure them you'll be back when they do.

Second: here's the message that really bothers me. In the midst of trying to convince the rest of the country to remember us, and to take seriously the near-total devastation of a major American city, here was yet another primetime exhibit of Neanderthal assholery and smugly ignorant bigotry. If Louisiana wants the rest of America to take it seriously, and if Louisiana wants the federal Government to pony up 30 billion dollars for recovery, then it better stop acting like King Ripple of the Hobo Jungle and start acting like a grownup.

I mean more than just keeping the legislature from their usual smash-n-grab budget and bribery tactics, and more than just keeping the culture of corruption gagged and tied up in the trunk next to the hooker. I mean putting an end to the centuries-long idea that Louisiana is a place separate and distinct from America and resigning our role as America's Court Jester. The pride at our petty political corruption, the willingness to be seen as drunk and uncontrollable, the kingdom of misrule, all make the calls for help and the demands to be taken seriously ring a little more hollow. Why should the rest of the country take us seriously when we've insisted for two hundred years that they do no such thing? Why should we be considered part of America after insisting for generations that we are not? Even now, I hear angry contradictions from Louisianans: Anyone not in New Orleans or the affected areas should have no influence over where and how to rebuild the city, but they should pay for it since New Orleans is, after all, a part of their country. Hey, we need your money to recover from this unfair blow, and we deserve it, oh, and did you see how them jigs ran off the bridge when I fired the shotgun over their heads?

Well, we are a part of America. And the rest of the country needs to help us rebuild just like we should help any other part of the country in need. But we need to stop this circus of dipshits we've let rage for three hundred years: the state bond commission needs to be told, one way or another, that their back-home pork projects are off the table while the state's available recovery funds are properly allocated—and if we need to bring in some grownups to do it, just like we had to bring in grownups to try and sort out the galactic clusterfuck created by the NOLA school board, then that's what we have to do. The citizens and police of Gretna need to face loud, public, and universal condemnation until it can be driven into their little white heads just why what they did was wrong. Those people who need FEMA trailers should be able to move into a temporary park without more hooting and rock throwing from the locals. Maybe Mardi Gras should be scaled back a little this year. Maybe the fucking Cotillion of Dolts needs to take a back seat for a change.

Anger is called for, yes, true. Human incompetence and error helped turn Katrina (and Rita) from a mere disaster into an apocalypse. Be angry. But remember that the tinfoil crown doesn't really make you a king, of misrule or anything else, and if you think the rest of America isn't taking you seriously, reflect on two hundred years of concerted effort to be taken lightly, and the inevitable consequences.

MEN IN TRUCKS

DEDRA JOHNSON, *THE G-BITCH SPOT*

Our hotel/restaurant/retail economy has become a men-in-trucks economy: 1 man or 2 men or 5 men in Dodge Rams, old Toyotas and Nissans, dump trucks, Ford F250s and F350s or F450s with massive trailers, all garbage-hauling, house-gutting, tree-removing, rewiring, fumigating, inspecting, roofing, reconnecting gas and cable and electricity, everything.

They were a novelty until I had to drive with them—too fast, then too slow, vague and contradictory turn signals (if any at all), near sideswipes, speeding around me to cut me off or crowd me out of the lane on their way to the next job or to wait in line with the other men in trucks at Wendy's, Popeye's, Subway, McDonald's, or to Baton Rouge or the French Quarter running on men in trucks' $5, $10 and $20 bills. They run red lights and stop signs and turn in front of you like you're not there. They have no use for civil society.

I'm glad they're here—a nice pair of them gutted my mama's house—but I can't wait 'til they're fucking gone.

NEW YEAR, NEW LIFE, NEW ENERGY

CLIFTON HARRIS, *CLIFF'S CRIB*

There will not be another sad, sentimental post about the holidays. Anyone that reads this blog knows what has went on in my life for 2005 and we don't need to go over that again. Things will never be the same and that's a fact. With this being my last post until the New Year, I thought I would just think about what 2006 will have to offer.

I don't make resolutions because I have never came close to keeping one. Plus when you make resolutions you are admitting that something about you needs changing and I am much too in denial to ever admit to needing some change. There are some things I want to try and do for myself in the next year and beyond.

The first thing is that I want to start reading more books beyond *King Magazine* again. I looked at all the books I owned at home and realized how long it had been since I actually opened one of them and read more than a paragraph. I purchased my first new book, *The Michael Eric Dyson Reader*, for Christmas, and I am going to start with that one. My attention span is short so I am setting a goal of 12 books by the end of the year. That's one a month. I think I can do that.

The second thing I want to do is take better care of myself. I was doing OK before that event in August. I had started playing ball again and was feeling good. The last few months I have been eating and drinking in a mixture of boredom and depression and I am slowly starting to resemble a pear. I will never be small. I have never been since a kid. I can be in shape and feeling better however and that's what I am going to do.

The third thing is try to figure out where the next five years of my life will be spent. I don't like moving and being unstable. I have decided that New Orleans gets one more shot to get their act together. Love and history will take me back there before the end of the year and we will see how things start working itself out. If things appear not to be moving in the right direction, I may have to roll out for the sake of my children's future.

I was always willing to put aside certain profess-ional goals for the sake of staying home. I always figured being around family and friends was worth the aggravation of hearing other friends and family tell you how good it was in other places. Now, the friends and family are gone and the recovery is going so slowly that it's anyone's guess when they will be coming back. That means if an opportunity presents itself in another place I can stand, I may have to explore it. My main wish is to go home and help the community recover and prepare for the influx of people once FEMA cuts the cord. That will give me the most satisfaction. If it doesn't work out that way, it won't be because I didn't try.

To all my friends and people who read this blog, I hope you have a great and prosperous New Year.

To all my people from New Orleans...We can't pretend that what happened didn't happen. I don't know the right way to fully move on so I won't offer any. We'll just take our new lives one day at a time and make them as good as they can be.

To my family and loved ones...We are all going to be OK. Things will work themselves out with time.

Rest in Peace to Walter Harris Sr. 1916-2005. I miss the stories and the perspective. To my grandmothers Mildred and Geraldine, I miss you both and hope to see you again soon.

2006

SERVILITY WITH A SMILE

TARA JILL CICCARONE, *NOLAFUGEES*

It's late October and in a small Marigny restaurant, the cooks are grilling dozens of burgers on propane grills. Without a functioning hood, the dining area fills with smoke so we almost forget the flies. There are hundreds of them. It seems like there are hundreds of customers too, belligerent drunk contractors screaming for roast beef on French (we don't have any roast beef or any French bread) and 22-year-old National Guard soldiers who are not allowed in the French Quarter because of their bad behavior. Everyone is ordering food to-go.

"You got that? It's to-go," they emphasize, even though all the food is served in Styrofoam containers because we don't have a dishwasher (the machine, or the person to operate it).

A group of women with gold teeth send back their meat because it is not well-done. There is no sign of pink, but they want well-done burgers in 5 minutes. They want new burgers, and we'd better not put these same ones on the grill. One of them rushes into the kitchen to scream at the cook. Sweat drips down my neck as I explain that we don't have any cold drinks because the power has been out for 16 hours. We have lost $2,000 worth of meat.

A middle-aged woman asks me for some ice for her tea and I tell her to go to Uptown, where they got power. A gay man tries to argue with me that we obviously have power because he can see lights in the kitchen.

"Do you know what a flashlight is?" I ask him.

I fantasize about making a test the customers have to answer before ordering. This would involve a multiple-choice test on the menu and some short-answer questions like, "If the restaurant does not have power, one cannot expect the following items and should not complain about their absence."

That was October. Since the New Year, the Marigny has managed to maintain an almost constant stream of electricity, so the drinks are cold again. We now use plates, and I, the waitress and bartender, wash them myself. When it gets too busy I use Styrofoam and say the machine is broke. Nobody is willing to work as a dishwasher, not for six dollars an hour.

The cook, an illegal alien, constantly begs me to marry him so he can get his papers and work at McDonalds. He's in love with that signing bonus. I tell him that, no matter what, they really need to open a McDonald's around here soon. Maybe a Burger King would be good, so everybody can have it their way and leave me the fuck alone about the temperature of the meat and the amount of pickles they get.

No matter what we order, the beer company is always a day late, and the owner eventually shows up in an unmarked van stocked with a bunch of cases of some beer like Rolling Rock, which nobody wants to drink.

However, these problems are banal compared to the chaos caused by the influx of crazy people who now, without their medication, loiter around. The restaurant doubles as a Laundromat and also offers video poker, as well as a small grocery section, so it is easy for displaced lunatics to linger about endlessly like students hollering in the halls and skipping classes while receiving student loan checks. One mad-man is constantly showing me his belt, his shoes, his socks, his pants and wallet when I walk by the poker machines. If I don't comment on each article of clothing every time, he attempts to follow me around the restaurant—"You like this belt? You like these shoes?"—until I want to smack him.

Then there was Oink man, the obese elderly gentleman who cannot speak, but instead oinks like a pig. He started coming in for coffee and oinking in my face. I would offer him half-n-half, milk, sugar, and sugar substitutes, but he could only oink, over and over even after I walked away. He could usually be found outside at one of the sidewalk tables, oinking to himself for the whole world to see. A few weeks ago, Oink man tried to steal a Diet Coke and the owner yelled at him to put it back. Oink man proceeded to hurl a bottle of Chardonnay at the owner 's head. He grabbed more bottles and ran out onto the sidewalk, oinking furiously. We told him we'd called the cops and expected him to do what any normal assailant would do, run, but instead he oinked in the doorway for the 20 minutes it took for the cops to show up.

One morning, a sweaty woman came in, her shirt soaked and reeking. She wanted to use the phone and I let her after she explained that her phone lines weren't working. I even dialed the number for her because her hands were shaking. Then I eavesdropped. Her diatribe went something like this: "You've got to call David and tell him they're after me again. They're getting the cops after me and I can't go to jail here now. I'll never get out. I'm going home and I'm not turning the lights on"—I doubt she had power—"or answering the phone. Tell David to leave me a message at Smitty's. They're hunting me. They're hunting me down again." When she hung up, I asked if she was okay. "It's just my family trying to have me killed. It's no big deal, one of those things that happens to everyone," she assured me. Yes indeed, ma'am, I believe it is.

Some twenty-something-year-old hippie kept getting grabby with me, so I told him to keep his hands off. He came back during the lunch rush and began sobbing inconsolably, real tears and his shoulders shaking, his voice trembling that he was so, so sorry. He obviously had some sort of horrendous eye infection. He, too, wanted a well-done burger to go, extra mayo, light mustard, only one tomato, no lettuce, extra pickles, and onions on the side.

Will somebody please open a Burger King or a Free Mental Health Clinic in this area soon???

JANUARY 5, 2006

MELTDOWN TOWN

DEBORAH COTTON

First of all, let me apologize for my unceremonious checkout. To be honest y'all, I had a meltdown.

December approached our fractured city, bringing the much-coveted but shockingly tiny FEMA trailers along with media stories pronouncing New Orleans as dead, dying, or in need of an organized pullout, while we continued to gut 200,000-plus soggy houses in the now cold, gray weather.

And without warning, a depressed hush descended over Bethlehem-South so pronounced and unprecedented in this 24/7 party town that you could go a full day without hearing so much as one person laugh. Try then as I did, I could not write anything worth reading, except for the embarrassing three-paragraph crying jag I emailed to editors who were patiently waiting for overdue articles.

My dear editors, probably feeling grateful as they scanned through my pitiful account of life at Ground Zero that they lived anywhere but New Orleans, gave me a reprieve, told me to take care of myself, and write when I could.

So I closed the laptop and flew west to Sunny California to get some Mommy and Daddy pampering, enjoy a civilizing pedicure, drink a mimosa on Melrose, and pretend, for a week anyway, that everything everywhere was sparkly, clean, and fabulous again.

There were, of course, the predictable questions from family and friends: "What's it like there now?"

Like I said, I'm out of words to describe our city right now. Melted...? Melting down...? The only thing most of us in town can relate to these days, besides public emotional outbursts, is the newly created catastrophe lingo like Dr. John's "traumacalized" or phrases like "I never had water before. Now I have water." If you don't live here, it wouldn't make sense. I live here and it still doesn't make sense.

And then, of course, the predictable next question: "So you're sure you wanna stay there?"

To quote our local savior-scribe Chris Rose, "The only thing worse than being in New Orleans these days is not being in New Orleans."

That's my truth and I'm sticking to it.

Okay, it was nice, unusual even, to be in an environment where every business was open, where everyone could get everything they wanted, and where there was no group tragedy bumming us all out. But truth be told, even with the reasonably priced pedicures and fully stocked Trader Joe's, I found myself longing for home.

On New Year's Day, *The Times-Picayune* reported that evacuated New Orleanians, having calmed down from the initial trauma that led many in the days immediately after the storm to say they weren't coming back, are returning faster and in larger numbers than had been predicted. Now why is it, after watching the weeklong blow-by-blow horror movie on the news of our city being plunged under water, we'd be flocking back daily by the thousands? I'll tell you why: it's because once New Orleans is in your blood, no other city, no other love, no other brand of good time or neighborly exchanges or local annual events will do. We are strange birds, wired to weather all sorts of elements, to get back home. And so, like the many thousands of other returning New Orleanians, I said goodbye to my family in Los Angeles on New Year's Eve, got on a plane and flew back home.

Within 30 minutes of being back in New Orleans, the violin music ceased. I witnessed two public meltdowns in Louis Armstrong Airport, both over lost luggage, both involving the police, both within 10 minutes and 100 feet of each other.

One guy was arrested by two cops for disturbing the peace. Bad scene, another article for another time.

The other guy actually was a cop, there to pick up his wife and toddler, clearly tired from having lost so much already and from living squeezed together in dorm-like rooms on a cruise ship where essential city workers who lost their homes currently live, and now having their hopes of starting a new year with a night out dashed because all she had was the black velour tracksuit she'd worn on the plane.

Well, the po-po lost it right there in baggage claim, fully fitted in motorcycle knickers and Village People-style black boots, yelling at the lost baggage agent that the missing suitcase contained all the clothes his wife and child had in the world. The truth of this statement was enough to make his visibly tired wife begin to cry, which caused the baby she was holding to cry, which triggered the agent's tears, which domino'd me into tears as I stood there waiting to file my own missing luggage report.

Dammit! Can I get my *other* foot in the door first before we commence with the group nervous breakdowns?

Spontaneous crying jags are the new New Orleans pastime, up there with eating oysters and pulling for the Saints. At any given moment and without warning, you start to lose it right there on the spot, crying like a four-year-old. There's no avoiding it, you can't outsmart it. It's bigger than you—it's a hurricane really. And when it comes all you can do is stand there, quaking and blubbering till the storm passes. Everyone understands. Everyone is patient and quiet, knowing they're just one Xanax away from wailing right alongside you.

Some triggers are predictable: a drive through the dark, lifeless, melted parts of town. Locals have dubbed it the "Disaster Tour." Or it could be an unexpected frustration like misplaced luggage or when the bank teller informs you that your account is overdrawn or when the film processor at Walgreens mixes up your order, just to cite a few recent scenes in my neighborhood.

Anyway, our town's mood is brightening these days as more of our people are returning home. The antidote, it seems, to our emotional meltdowns over New Orleans being broken...is to be back in broken New Orleans. Cause really, once you've had a life full of sweet nothing exchanges with total strangers who call you "baby;" spicy seafood feasts at every meal served with wine, rum and whiskey; cottages, cathedrals, and faded saloons with candles and lanterns lighting your way home at night; brilliantly beaded Mardi Gras Indian war-birds; your very own peculiar language filled with phrases like "spy boys," "king cakes," "Zulus," and "momma nems;" brass bands dancing your dead to the other side and a town full of people who will cry with you through the bad times just as hard as they party with you during the good....

When you've got all that, you realize that gutting and repairing 200,000-plus homes, fixing some levees, and rebooting the city's power system is a hell of a lot easier than trying to recreate all our good stuff someplace else.

Or worse, trying to do without it.

JANUARY 20, 2006

CHOCOLATE CITY

DEDRA JOHNSON, *THE G-BITCH SPOT*

Part of the flak over Nagin's Chocolate City comment (he said it when he testified in front of Congress and no one seemed to notice though that time he did smile as he said it) is that no one has a sense of humor when they are looking for a fight. No one seems to know about the Funkadelic song or that other cities (DC and Detroit especially) have also been referred to as Chocolate Cities and there were no white riots. The only commentary I've seen that even slightly understands the humor and truth and joy in being a Chocolate City is Sam Smith (at *Counterpunch*). My favorite part:

> But to this white DC native, Nagin's worst offense was to try to rip off our nickname.

Having lived much of my life in the real Chocolate City, I find myself far more bothered by people who become irate at the impolite subtexts of those who haven't done as well as they in the American system, and who not only regard the suffering as inevitable but believe it should be endured with silence and gentility.

There is a curious connection between NOLA and DC. They are both cities that early had an unusual number of free blacks. Segregation operated under local ground rules, sometimes at odds with the larger southern standard. There were an atypical number of black Catholics. Class distinctions intermingled with—and sometimes surpassed—ethnic ones both within the black community and its relations with whites. There was an atypical number of whites who grew up with cross-cultural experiences and an atypical number who found it part of the pleasure of the place...

...The plagiarism aside, Nagin's comment seemed to me perfectly normal. It was the sort of thing I had heard in DC for years. And I didn't mind it because it was my Chocolate City too. It still seems odd to many whites, but you really don't have to be in the ethnic majority to love a place.

The whites who live in New Orleans proper, not the suburbs, love this city just like that, without having to be the majority and able to appreciate and mingle and second line and eat red beans on Monday and take down Christmas decorations on January 6 and only eat king cakes between King's Day and Mardi Gras. Few whites that I have talked to, who really love the city, who really live in the city, who really appreciate the city, took offense. Most nodded, many smiled and kept trudging through the New Normal. New Orleans IS different. That's why I moved back 9 years ago, that's why I came to Jazz Fest every year when I didn't live here, that's why I lived New Orleans even when I wasn't in New Orleans.

Instead of giving Nagin shit when he's trying to counteract some of the bullshit the New Orleans diaspora hears and trying to tell folks to come on home, it's still home, people need to ask the Red Cross where all that money they collected is, ask why Mississippi has gotten more money, trailers and insurance payouts than Louisiana, get the men in trucks back to work. No offense but people not from here who can't get with the program need to stay the fuck out.

JANUARY 23, 2006

DEADWOOD-SALAMI FEST

NIKKI PAGE, *NOLANIK*

When I lived in New York, whatever mood you're in, no matter how dowdy you look, if you walk down a street alone as woman, there is the inevitable catcall. Some comments are VERY descriptive and at times threatening (some bad stories, I tell ya). Being the kind of person who walks around in La-La land, these can interrupt fantasy world with a screech, to say the least. Of course, there was the friendlier, more polite comment once in awhile. And that was nice. My husband never believed just how rude the comments could get, so I made him follow behind me one day at a distance far away to suggest we were not together, but still within hearing range of the comments. Let's just say he never doubted again.

In New Orleans, the comments are more polite, for the most part. Example: Last year, I had put on a few New Orleans pounds and was going to the gym (so I wouldn't die of a heart and lung attack on the soccer field). As I was crossing Rampart, these two men ran in front of the gym's doors, blocking my way and begged me not to go in, claiming that I shouldn't change a thing, it would ruin it all. Well, that was nice as it was done with humor and flair.

Now:

I had been warned by a bartender friend of mine that venturing out into certain Uptown bars is flat out advised against for women. But I thought, pish-posh, I ain't ascared of no boys. However I went into one after soccer practice with a few male members of the team. I was one of two or three women in there, max, with one playing video poker in such a way that she didn't count.

You know that feeling when you are in a restaurant and there is someone sitting in your "thinking view" (When in conversation, when thinking or listening, I often look over to my right, and in public situations, this often creates unwanted eye-locking moments with the same person over and over again)? Well, it was like my thinking view was panoramic, because if I looked anywhere but in the faces of the two guys I was chatting with, I locked eyes with a man. Then I realized that it was because every man in the room was actually staring at me.

A compliment? Can't say it was. My friend, the bartender, says that if a woman walks into his bar (which he now calls a salami fest, post-K), where all the contractors and guys who came into town to work hang out, she is zoomed in on in this competition-like survival of the fittest—who can get in a conversation first. Yeesh. I did not realize that it was actually giving me the creeps until I went to go use the ladies' room and felt really weird. I expressed this to my friends and one said that if they weren't there with me, as a "protective shield," if you will, the whole bar would close in.

It's freaky, but really sad for those lonely guys. It's not like I feel threatened, just ogled to the max.

I can say, however, that it is not like that in the Bywater bars or the Circle Bar. I haven't been back to the Saint yet.

FEBRUARY, 2006

KATRINARITA GRAS

WILLIAM JOYCE

My wife was going to a 12th Night party dressed as Hurricane Katrina. This was soon after the storm. Her hair was styled in great swooping whirls. Her dress was a hoop skirt wrapped in black netting and cluttered with dozens of tiny houses, cars and other stormy ephemera.

A friend of mine (whose whereabouts since the hurricanes I was unsure of until I saw her on Christmas Eve) explained that it's generally accepted that people in New Orleans will burst spontaneously into tears during even the most cursory conversations.

"Any little thing will trigger it," she said. "I mean you say hello and you'll get sobs. But everyone knows to just be quiet for a minute and it'll pass." Then she added with that cheerful, attractive insolence so common to New Orleanians. "I add 15 minutes of 'cryin' time' to everything. Goin' the grocery store takes forever. There are more tears than in Tolstoy."

Like my wife's dress this line got a laugh. It had to.

It's a glad/sad time down here. Glad you're alive. Sad about everything else. If you can't laugh about it, you are toast.

There's been some controversy about having Mardi Gras this year. That it is somehow inappropriate given the scale of the recent tragedy and disaster.

The punchline to that misguided sentiment is that Mardi Gras is a celebration actually devoted to being inappropriate in a community that has courted disaster since the day it was founded.

You don't build a city on land that sits below sea level and is surrounded by water and not expect to get soggy at some point. It is a geographical crapshoot well understood by New Orleanians and Mardi Gras is part of their gallant disregard for that unpleasant reality.

It's one of their ways of laughing at doom.

The history of Mardi Gras is so deep, vast, and strange that it's difficult to encapsulate. Starting hundreds of years ago with the shepherds of Arcadia and detouring through most of the more interesting cities in history, it has always been steeped in sin and redemption.

The Romans. The Greeks. The Catholics. They've all put in their two bits of paganism or piety.

But it's fitting somehow that much of Mardi Gras pomp and plumage would evolve from the carnivals of Venice, that other impossible city at odds with time and tide.

And for all this historical pedigree, there's still something very childish about Mardi Gras.

If you are exposed to it as a kid, you will never be quite like other people. How could you be?

You've watched an entire adult population—your parents, your aunts and uncles, your teachers or your school principals, all your authority figures—suddenly transform into Poseidon, or Mae West, or a cross-dressing Santa Claus. Everyday life becomes an overnight Technicolor fever dream. Schools close. The daily schedule is thrown out for a new schedule of parties and parades that become an unending delirium. It's not inconceivable but in fact highly likely that you will look out the den window and see several dozen men and women dressed as Yogi Bear drift nonchalantly by in a papier-mâché galleon. Or go into a neighborhood bar and find everyone dressed as bumble bees.

It's like somebody knocked over the TV set and cartoons came spilling out.

For those of us who grew up in Louisiana, *The Wizard of Oz* was like a documentary. Dorothy left Kansas and simply went to Mardi Gras. Talking trees and wicked witches seemed perfectly normal if you've seen your librarian walking down St. Charles dressed in a gorilla suit and a set of woman's breasts complete with blinking neon nipples.

As a result we tend to grow up with a keen sense of life's absurdity and a healthy regard for the curative potential of fun.

And there is no fun quite like a Mardi Gras parade. Its epic silliness can be very seductive. It is one of the marvels of nature that the quest for giving or catching cheap plastic beads can lead people of every temperament to engage in behavior that is singularly, perhaps historically ridiculous.

Not that I'm a pillar of normalcy but I do pay taxes and manage to mingle in polite society occasionally, yet I once led an organization, called the Mystik Knights of Mondrian's Chicken. In homage to the great painter, we rode in a giant cube shaped chicken, wore costumes the color of yolks and threw egg-shaped beads, while white helium balloons were periodically released from a hole in the chicken's ass.

After three years with this same float, we were told by the parade organizers we would have to change our design. The novelty of our cubist chicken had apparently worn off. It just wasn't weird enough anymore.

There are people, ordinary both-feet-on-the-ground people, who during Mardi Gras sport titles like "The Lord of Misrule" or the "Abbot of Unreason."

It's all so perfectly foolish. And essential.

It fills some vast human need to, however briefly, be something else, a satyr, a god, or anything deliciously forbidden. You simply don a mask and give in to enchantment, desire or foolhardy joy.

This year's Mardi Gras will be the most surreal of all. Never has the gaiety confronted so grim a reality. The walls of rubble, the vanished neighborhoods, and the memory of the city from before the storm haunt every street.

But Mardi Gras has had troubled times before. One newspaper wrote in 1851, "The carnival embraced a great multitude and a variety of oddities. But alas! The world grows everyday more practical, less sportive and imaginative. Mardi Gras with its laughter-moving tomfooleries must content itself with the sneering hard realities of the present age."

The streets of the city are in black and white now. Like Dorothy's Kansas. A thin coat of grayish dust covers entire neighborhoods since the flood.

Maybe this will make the traditional green, purple and gold colors shine out even brighter.

New Orleans is a "let's face the music and dance" town. It always has been. Try as they might, the sneering hard realities cannot keep it down.

But it'll be harder to catch the beads this year. Those spontaneous tears will make it tough to see.

DICK CHENEY SHOT HIS FRIEND BUT HE KILLED OUR COVER

WILLIAM JOYCE

I was asked some months back to do a *New Yorker* Cover depicting some aspect of how New Orleans was dealing with Mardi Gras in the post-Katrina world.

I've done occasional covers for the *New Yorker* since 1994 and since I am a native Louisianan and still live here, they hoped I'd have an informed perspective on the tragedy and its aftermath.

My schedule has been crazed. The movie business demands all you've got and more. But this was a labor of love and something I felt I had to do.

Coming up with a concept that tempered my rage with some hope was not easy, but I got inspiration from an old photograph of Mardi Gras in the '30s by J. Guttman, called "The Game." It's a wonderful, eerie image of New Orleans and its curious magic.

The editors were very pleased with the results. The proof looked great. Some friends cried when I showed it to them.

The image did what I'd hoped. It made people from here sad and proud at the same time.

I was hoping it would, I don't know, somehow help. Help call attention to our plight. Help people understand us.

Then Dick Cheney shot his friend instead of a bird.

A more topical cover was cobbled together. A clever twist on Cheney's folly. I've had covers at the *New Yorker* bumped before. That's just part of the game. But this one really mattered. The hurricanes have turned the people of Louisiana into activists. We no longer have the luxury of emotional distance with this story.

Louisiana had received its share of coverage lately I was told. They tried to find a place for it inside the magazine. Everyone said they were sympathetic. But nothing happened.

So we've been shunted aside again.

Our collective sorrow and tragedy mattered less than a single hunting accident.

I really had hoped that compassion would win out over clever.

Mr. Cheney's friend is thankfully alive. Meanwhile we're still finding bodies in New Orleans.

Here's the cover. I hope you can use it to keep the story of our troubles alive.

MARCH 22, 2006

THE DAY I REALIZED I WAS A PART OF NEW ORLEANS PUBLIC SCHOOLS' GREATEST ORGANIZATION

JOSHUA COUSIN, *NOTE FROM THE BOOK*

When I was in Kennedy's band, I went through most of my first year fine, but I never realized that I was a part of one of NOPS's greatest organizations, until Parade Season '00 (I was still an Underclassman).

We were marching up St. Charles Avenue Bacchus Night & I was on my horn playing song after song after song. But then, Big Joe (my Section Leader) asked me for the horn so that he could play (we were alternating)

...yeah I was on the Back End that day, lol (12 tubas, 24 bones, a 12-man front...lol).

Anyway, I gave Joe the horn and stood aside, walking behind the band in full uniform. Then after that the whistle sounded off and the band started to pay the songs "Stay" & "Believe In Me," eventually I got the chills. Then in my head I said to myself, "Man, I march for The K—This is Wild."

Although I didn't get to play on the horn until we reached Canal Street, I was smiling the whole time because I felt like I was a part of the Best Band in the World at that moment. For me, the songs "Stay" & "Believe in Me" were classics. Because I remember the band of '95 & '96, when my sisters were marching. The band played those songs and the sound was Beautiful. Just imagine, I was in the band & I Felt it, the classic JFK sound (to me) was THERE in my face & I was A Part of It All.

It was like this: I marched, but it never dawned on me until that day that The K was the greatest.

When I was younger, all I knew of Kennedy was the fact that my sisters, cousins & bro-in-laws marched for them. I used to go to City Park to the watch the girls practice...them & the dudes used to come to my house with that Classic K logo in their chests. Other than that I had no musical ear to know that they were just that great. At that time I didn't even know who St. Aug was...I was in 6th grade in elementary school & the only other band I knew of was John McDonough.

Other than that, I didn't know anything of the K but a few members & some band tapes.

To Me, Walter Harris was just the Man who came to get instruments from Phillips Middle School. I didn't know he was Kennedy's BD until I experienced The Wrath of Doc (just kidding). Actually he came around often in '99 & '00. Dude was retired, but his presence was felt in that band room.

Speakin' of Doc: There are some Old School alumni who still get that same feeling when speaking to Doc—they have to straighten up their act (like puttin' their shirts in their pants or taking earrings out or whatever).

That was Fear, man. Lol.

APRIL 28, 2006

GREG PETERS, *SUSPECT DEVICE*

This is an American city:

"It's hard not to look away. It's hard to know what to compare this to. It's seldom that a music that once thrilled you now repulses you. We move on to the Industrial Canal and beyond. There's the grainy, long-ago newsreels of WWII Stalingrad, bombed-out, shelled-out buildings, block after block, fallen or even more, half-fallen where they stood, ruined but not yet destroyed, shattered but not yet abandoned. Along St. Claude Avenue, some of the shells are again occupied by a half-hidden army, moving in the inside shadows of generator light, sniping at the enemy. They'll have to be rooted out of the rubble, house by house…"

These were American citizens. Two thousand of them died.

And you're bored with it, and us.

New Orleans has been a major city for almost three hundred years. It's the birthplace of American culture, period. Despite the crime, despite the poverty, despite everything, New Orleans bred a fierce bond with its people. They loved New Orleans like a lover, a physical being so deeply tied to their souls that they could never give her up, even if she was bad for them.

The citizens of New Orleans had families, jobs (they really did), dreams, tragedies, hard times. They were alive, more alive than any of the zombies you see walking the streets of Atlanta or the ghosts hiding in the corners of Detroit. Despite the crime, despite the poverty. They were living in the truest sense of the word.

And then the hurricane came and took it all away.

Took away the homes, the lives, the dignity, the dreams, everything. You'd really have to see it to understand: it's not just water damage. It's not a ruined house here and there. It's bad. People died, people fled, the proudest and most vibrant and most alive city in America was hammered, knocked to its knees and left for dead.

But you're bored.

People are coming back. The city is slowly being rebuilt by people who can't live anywhere else or do anything else, who won't abandon their lover when she's hurt and sick, maybe dying. No one knows if it will work, if New Orleans will live again. Or if Cameron Parish or Vermilion Parish, blown to smithereens by Hurricane Rita, will live again. But we haven't given up.

You've given up on us.

You've given up on us because we're poor, black, Southern. We're clowns, partying all day, drinking all night, and running a banana republic government on graft and free drink tickets. Deep in your hard little hearts, you think we deserve this. Had it coming, carrying on like that. It's as if we had been daring God to put a stop to the nonsense, and he finally did.

Besides, black people, poor people—do we really want to build new nests for them? Shouldn't we accept their dispersal as a gift, a way of diluting the concentrated oil slick of beastly black faces and exasperatingly poor white ones? Mostly Democrats, too, if I recall. Maybe if they're far apart they won't breed. If they're scattered, they can't organize, either, so its win-win, right?

See, it's all worked out, so will you whiners just drop it?

We're not going to go away. We are going to keep staggering along, demanding attention, pulling on your sleeve like some scabby beggar who knows you from another life. We're going to come to all your functions and introduce ourselves, the legless one-eyed veteran, the black sheep of the family who mortifies the guests, even as they can't stop gazing into that sightless, empty socket, at the red, raw stumps where legs used to be.

We are not going away. And if we go down, we're going to take you down with us.

PETER KING, *SPORTS ILLUSTRATED.COM*

I know you come to this column to read about football, sports, and other things. I'll get to the regular Tuesday fare, your e-mails, in a few paragraphs. First, there's something a little more significant to discuss.

I sense that we in this country have Katrina fatigue. *The New York Times* reported as much recently, saying that people in some of the areas that welcomed Katrina evacuees last September are sick of hearing about the hurricane, the flooding, and the aftermath.

Well, my wife and I were in a car last Wednesday that toured the hardest-hit area of New Orleans, the Lower Ninth Ward. We worked a day at a nearby Habitat for Humanity site on Thursday, and we toured the Biloxi/Gulfport/Long Beach/Pass Christian Gulf Shore area last Friday. And let me just say this: I can absolutely guarantee you that if you'd been in the car with us, no matter how much you'd been hit over the head with the effects of this disaster, you would not have Katrina fatigue.

What I saw was a national disgrace. An inexcusable, irresponsible, borderline criminal national disgrace. I am ashamed of this country for the inaction I saw everywhere.

I mentioned my outrage to the mayor of New Orleans, Ray Nagin, on Thursday. He shook his head and said, "Tell me about it." Disgust dripped from his voice.

What are we doing in this country?

"It's been eight months since Katrina," said Jack Bowers, my New Jersey friend and Habitat for Humanity guide through the Lower Ninth Ward, as he took us through deserted streets where nothing, absolutely nothing, was being done about the wasteland that this place is.

"Eight months!" he said. "And look at it. When people talk to me about New Orleans, they say, 'Well, things are getting back to normal down there, aren't they?' I tell them things are a long, long way from normal, and it's going to be a long time before it's ever normal. And I tell them they've never seen anything like this."

Our Mississippi guide, Josh Norman of the *Biloxi Sun-Herald*, put it this way: "People outside of here are tired of hearing about it. They've moved on to the next news cycle."

How can we let an area like the Lower Ninth Ward sit there, on the eve of another hurricane season, with nothing being done to either bulldoze the place and start over, or rebuild? How can Congress sit on billions of looming aid and not release it for this area?

I can't help but think that if this were Los Angeles or New York, that 500 percent more money—and concern—would have flooded into this place. And I can't help but think that if the idiots who let the levees down here go to seed had simply been doing their jobs, we'd never have been in this mess in the first place—in New Orleans, at least. Other than former FEMA director Michael Brown, are you telling me that no others are paying for this with their jobs? Whatever happened to responsibility?

Am I ticked off? Damn right I'm ticked off. If you're breathing, you should be morally outraged. Katrina fatigue? Hah! More Katrina news! Give me more! Give it to me every day on the front page! Every day until Washington realizes there's a disaster here every bit as urgent as anything happening in this world today— fighting terrorism, combating the nuclear threat in

Iran. I'm not in any way a political animal, but all you have to be is an occasionally thinking American to be sickened by the conditions I saw.

The Lower Ninth Ward is a 1.5-by-2-mile area a couple of miles from the center of New Orleans. It is a poor area. I should say it *was* a poor area. Before the storm, 20,000 people lived there. Fats Domino lived there. So, formerly, did Marshall Faulk. And now you drive through it and see nothing being done to fix it or tear it down, or to do anything.

In Mississippi, we drove through one formerly thriving beach town that has two structures left. We drove past concrete pads with litter and shards of wood around them. Former houses. The houses, quite literally, have been eviscerated. Hundreds of them. This is what nuclear winter must look like, I thought.

I'm a sportswriter. It's not my job to figure how to fix what ails the Gulf Coast. But the leaders of this society are responsible. And they're not doing their jobs. I could ignore everything I saw and go back to my nice New Jersey cocoon, forgetting I saw it. And I know you don't read me to hear my worldviews. But I couldn't sleep at night if I didn't say something.

On Saturday, at the Saints' headquarters for the draft, I watched the day unfold with a friend of the team, New Orleans businessman and president Michael Whelan. I told him what I'd seen, and asked him what he thought.

"We spend all this money on the war in Iraq and we can't take care of our own cities?" he said. "You get out of downtown, and it's like a war zone in a lot of neighborhoods still. The government has been a huge letdown. I've heard billions of dollars are going to be sent here. Where are they? Nothing is taking place. I certainly think that now it's back-page news; the government is sweeping it under the rug."

In early 2006, much ink was spilled in the national media about the "appropriateness" of celebrating Mardi Gras in New Orleans when so many residents were suffering and tens of thousands were unable to return to their homes. By April, the return of Jazzfest was considered a foregone conclusion.

MAY 3, 2006

AN ICON CAME FORWARD

SEAN NELSON, *THE DESIGNATED MOURNER*

I'll begin with a blunt confession: I've never liked Bruce Springsteen. It's not that I've hated him or anything, but there are two kinds of people in this world, and I've always been the kind who didn't care for Bruce. This is why the news that I'd missed Springsteen and The Seeger Sessions Band's 8:30 a.m. sound check didn't really faze me.

My fellow Jazz Fest-goers on the webcast crew assured me that the morning rehearsal was something to behold, but people have been telling me that about Bruce Springsteen all my life, so I didn't put much stock in the news.

The real excitement promised by Sunday's lineup was Allen Toussaint's set, which would feature a special guest appearance by Elvis Costello. Everything else was filler as far as I was concerned—strong filler, to be sure, but still filler.

Never mind that both John Mooney and Sonny Landreth offered up master classes in New Orleans' songcraft, or that the mighty Hugh Masekela was being interviewed live at the grandstand. Masekela held forth on his storied career as a dissident South

African musician who found glory and fame as a California transplant in the '60s. He talked about playing at Monterey Pop and befriending the likes of the Byrds, Jimi Hendrix ("a very gentle soul"), Jefferson Airplane, Big Brother and the Holding Company and the like, all of whom impressed Masekela with the "forthrightness" of their opposition to the Vietnam war. He also answered questions about his work with Paul Simon on the *Graceland* album and tour and about the parallels between New Orleans' path to reconstruction and South Africa's rise to freedom from apartheid 12 years ago. "Patience and forgiveness," he advised, are the only roads toward rebirth.

It seems ironic that Masekela is a trumpet player. He has the kind of speaking voice you could lie down and listen to all day.

But there would be no time for that today, because Messrs. Toussaint and Costello were due to take the stage. Bedecked in a yellow blazer, trademark bushy moustache and a smile you could see from Baton Rouge, Allen Toussaint bestrode the stage like a king, then sat down at a Steinway grand piano to demonstrate how he'd come by the regal air.

While effortlessly leading his powerhouse band through a medley of timeless hits, each a stone classic ("Workin' in the Coalmine," "Mother in Law," et al.), Toussaint paused to introduce "Fortune Teller" as a "song I wrote that was made popular by the Rolling Stones." Yeah, no big deal. Just the Rolling Stones.

He then welcomed Elvis Costello—"the man with the biggest heart in show business"—to the stage, and the pair led the band through several more Toussaint gems before debuting the title track from their forthcoming duet LP, "River in Reverse." Costello, normally a somewhat nervy performer, looked to be having the time of his life singing these songs, leading the audience in hand claps and generally deferring to elder statesman Toussaint, who never lost a step of his swagger. It was a joyous, ebullient performance that set the stage for the only thing that could possibly top it.

There had been heavy weather the night before; I hadn't realized how heavy until, just before the headliners' set, festival director Quint Davis told me that if the rain and windstorms hadn't happened precisely when they had— between 8 p.m. Saturday and 8 a.m. Sunday—the Sunday performances would certainly have been cancelled.

I mention this only by way of explaining that Bruce Springsteen and the Seeger Sessions Band's performance actually seemed to command the sun to break through the lingering cloud cover and shine as brightly as possible. This was the first gig for Springsteen's new 17-piece band, which he'd assembled to record an album of songs either written or made popular by the great American musicologist/folk singer Pete Seeger. And if there was any question about the relevancy of singing old folk songs in today's political/musical climate, it was banished after the opening bars of "Oh Mary, Don't You Weep," a rapture of orgiastic brass, stomping drums, guitars, banjo and voices that was pure New Orleans.

From the moment they took the stage, Springsteen's troupe fired on all cylinders, and their bandleader was the most magnetic, urgent, impassioned and compelling frontman imaginable. In a moment tailor-made for an icon, an icon came forward, and his message was as timeless as music itself: "We Shall Overcome."

Unsurprisingly, Springsteen didn't shrink from criticizing the Bush administration, whose "criminal ineptitude" in the aftermath of Katrina made the singer "furious." He didn't stop there. "This is what happens," Springsteen declared, "when political cronyism guts the very agencies that are supposed to serve American citizens in times of trial and hardship." The roar of agreement and approval from the massive audience was thunderous.

He then launched into the most powerful number in a powerful set, the unforgiving "How Can a Poor Man Stand Such Times and Live." Originally written by Blind Alfred Reed about the stock-market crash of 1929, the song now features new verses that directly attack Bush, whom Springsteen called "President Bystander," for not responding to the wreckage of New Orleans with anything like the urgency that was (and still is) called for.

This song was emblematic of not only Springsteen and company's set but also of the entire spirit of Jazz Fest's first weekend—all seemed to be fueled by outrage but girded by a deep and abiding passion for music, and an even stronger conviction that what everyone present needed and wanted most was a joyful noise.

Springsteen and his titanic band (did I mention there were 17 members?) rose to the challenge, summoning not only the ghosts of the city—the mournful closing rendition of "Amazing Grace" inspired many thousands of spectators to a full-throated sing-along—and of the country but also seemingly the power of the sun itself to say New Orleans will rise again. And there and then, if only for an hour, it did.

NAGIN'S BUSINESSMAN SOLUTION

DEDRA JOHNSON, *THE G-BITCH SPOT*

Much of the mayoral runoff buzz, worry, conspiracy theories, etc. hinge on race. A student said to me a few weeks ago, "You know that if Landrieu wins, he'd be the first white mayor in over 20 years?" I said, "And?" But she didn't have anything else to add and her face said that there was nothing else to add. The buzz is that if it weren't New Orleans East and the Ninth Ward that were devastated and still largely empty, as opposed to Lakeview and Uptown, Nagin would be re-elected b/c he is black. That's it. Voting solely on race. The last white mayor N.O. had was Moon Landrieu, a man who consistently opposed segregation. Our black mayors, like our largely black School Board, have presided over the city's long decline with the predictable rise in corruption and minor fortunes made overnight. Is it their fault? Were they on duty during those times? Was it their friends and families who became richer and richer? All yes and no questions. Not all people, white or black or green, are corrupt. And not all are honest. Character does not reside in melanin.

I am repulsed by the focus on race, by the growing buzz or fear that local whites feel it is Their Time To Take The City Back From Those Black People. But what all who follow that line of thought ignore is that this is a Chocolate City, that the bulk of the population yet to return is black, is involved in and the roots of the culture and music and history that makes the city what it is and that made up a huge chunk of the middle class. A Huge Chunk. Not the white folks. Who are deluded about what they are taking back and what the city needs to recover. It is not melanin that is the primary local problem. It is the **economy**. It is STILL the economy. I don't care if Burger King and the hotels are now paying $8-10 an hour–rent for a one-bedroom apartment on an iffy block has skyrocketed to $1000 or more a month. Entergy will raise rates b/c of its bankruptcy and all the repairs still to be done citywide. $10/hour is not enough. It is no improvement. It is no economy

MAY 22, 2006

CONFESS, YA BASTARD!

JACK WARE, *METROBLOGS*

So our boy "Slick-Willie" Jefferson gets caught on tape by the FBI (from multiple angles, mind you) taking what is believed to be $100,000 in a little bribery deal that two other people have already plead guilty to. I will assume for the moment that it was this information which motivated the raid on his house (or office, or where ever the hell they raided—the guy's got property all over the damn place) which turned up $90,000 in cash, hillbillied away in his freezer, wrapped in aluminum foil. Nice.

So today he calls a press conference where he refused to talk about the facts of the case at the advice of his lawyers. Say what you will about lawyers, but when you commit a crime, they're right there in your ear advising you not to tell anyone you did it. So he didn't. But, interestingly, he didn't say he didn't take the bribe either. He abstractly mentioned that he maintains his innocence. There is a difference: One means you didn't do what you're accused of and one means you don't feel what you're accused of was wrong. I'm just saying; there's a difference.

As a general rule, if someone hands you a briefcase with $100,000 in cash to you in the parking lot of a hotel, something illegal is going on. Additionally, if you are storing $90,000 wrapped in aluminum foil in your freezer, it probably came from illegal activity. I'm sure there are one or two very special circumstances where someone would hand you a briefcase with $100,000 in it, you'd take that money home, wrap it up in aluminum foil, and stick it in your freezer; keeping $10,000 out for miscellaneous expenses. I do not, however, think this is one of those times.

I don't know if he's guilty or innocent, but I think he's an asshole. I've thought that since the story came out about him hijacking the National Guard to take him to his house to rescue valuables while people were drowning in their attics and I think that now. I don't even care if he took the money, let's convict him of being an asshole—the legal system can't do it, but the public can.

This is exactly the kind of shit that this city and this state should attack with a kind of wrath held for child molesters to make sure everyone who ever thinks of running for office knows unethical behavior in any manner will not be tolerated while in office. He should be booed and jeered every time anyone sees him in public. Make it impossible for him to even utter whatever "unconstitutional balance of power" bull-shit he and his little flunkies came up with to distract the public and try to get everything declared inadmissible in court. But even if he doesn't end up in jail, he'll still be an asshole to me.

BIPOLAR AND PROUD OF IT (I THINK)

CREE MCCREE, *SMITHMAG*

Today is the first day of hurricane season—which, needless to say, is more fraught than usual this year.

I haven't seen a "Bipolar and Proud of It" bumper sticker yet but I expect to any day, with the highs and lows of today's New Orleans. Sure, Jazz Fest was a spectacular success, a testament to the power of musical healing, as I reported for *High Times*. And just last month, the Aquarium of the Americas reopened to much hoopla, restocked with more than 4,000 marine species temporarily lost to the floods. But they're still finding human bodies—two in the last week alone. That brings the total known death toll to 1,577, a figure memorialized on Memorial Day with 1,577 flowers tossed into the 17th St. Canal.

It's hard not to be jolted by these constant reminders of the precarious thread we're hanging by, especially when the Army Corps of Bunglers holds all the strings as deadlines come and go for fixing the city's breached levees and canals.

Every edition of *The Times-Picayune* reads like the Bipolar News. Jarring juxtapositions also abound on local TV, where a rousing commercial for Abita Beer that was produced pre-K is in heavy rotation as a post-K anthem:

"Celebrate the good things/they're all around in this town," a chorus of voices sings, swelling into the tagline: *"We are Louisiana true."*

Cut to the next spot. "We lost everything," says the bravely smiling blonde sitting on a brand spanking new couch at Gallery Furniture in Houston, which is touting its $79 flat fee for delivering replacement bedroom sets and living room suites to New Orleans.

Life where I live in the unflooded Strip ain't that tough, of course. A roofing crew, conveniently headed by our next-door neighbor, has nearly finished the new House of Boo roof, with the insurance company picking up most (and probably all) of the tab. Our fence is repaired and painted, awaiting my finishing touches of purple and green stripes. And my stepdaughter's husband who works for the state says he can get us a generator tax-free so we can run the fridge, TV, computers and a fan during the next hurricane power outage.

The fan's for my 90-year-old mom, who's not used to the heat. She just moved here from Ohio in December and is living in Malta Park, a senior residence a few blocks away. The plan is to bring her to our house if a Cat 2 strikes, since a "mandatory" Cat 2 evacuation won't actually be enforced, and House of Boo was only grazed by Cat 3 Katrina.

Or at least that was the plan before she fell and broke her wrist and suffered a heart attack at the same time. Now Mom's up in Touro Hospital, wired to heart monitors, her good right hand splinted, unable to do much of anything except listen to classical music on NPR (she refuses to watch TV). She's not terminal, but she's got days, maybe weeks, of recovery ahead. She may ultimately need to go into a full-fledged nursing home, and there's no way we're casting her fate to the vagaries of Louisiana's nursing care system, site of countless post-K horror stories. My sister Jill's coming down this week from Joliet, Illinois—where we'll most likely move Mom when she's strong enough to travel. That means uprooting her yet again just after she got settled, which will be tough on her (and us). But it sure beats drowning in a nursing home.

As for Donald and me, we're still getting that generator. It seems like a wise investment, especially since he'll be on tour in Europe for the entire month of September—the height of hurricane season—leaving me and five (or more) cats to fend for ourselves if the big one hits (again). Assuming, of course, we all make it through June, July and August. (Not to sound all manic-depressive about it.)

And yet, and yet...the spirit of this town is undeniable.

It's why I chose to live here and why I chose to come back.

Case in point: Over Memorial Day weekend, I hit the 33rd annual Greek Festival in Lakeview, site of some of the worst post-K flooding. The ornate Orthodox cathedral was completely restored, the crowds trying gamely to dance to bouzouki bands were bigger than ever, and the spitted spring lamb was divine. Opa!

A little further down the Bayou St. John, hard-hit Mid-City was celebrating its own Boogie on the Bayou. The heavens opened when I arrived, pouring much-needed rain on the grounds and putting the main stage band on hold. I sallied forth with my big umbrella, in search of some musical action, and it didn't take long to find. Mardi Gras Indians were keeping the beat under one canopy crowded with festers, while brass band horns held sway in the tent across the way. Then the sun came out and everybody kept on keeping on, greeting friends in the beer line, scarfing pizza from Slice, and dancing barefoot on the wet grass.

And everywhere, all over town, in random piles of debris, wild sunflowers are blooming. On the eve of hurricane season, that's got to be a good omen, right?

WHO'S RIGHT TO RETURN?

DEDRA JOHNSON, *THE G-BITCH SPOT*

My mother grew up in what were the Magnolia housing projects Uptown. Back then, as in many ways recently, it was a place for poor people with children and elderly people living on pensions. Poor people who worked, older women who planted flowers and tomatoes and scolded children no matter who they belonged to, cooperative communities.

After promising that all have "the right to return," the federal government through HUD is now saying that there will not be enough room for everyone. While multiple condominium complexes go up around the CBD and Lower Garden District, condos that start at $200K, HUD has decided to raze and redevelop 4 housing projects over the next 3 years and to (eventually) redevelop them as "mixed-income" housing. Only 1000 more units will be open by this August, bringing the total of available public housing units to about 2,100, which is 3,046 fewer units than pre-Katrina.* What most focus on in the housing projects is drug crime, teen pregnancy, and welfare dependency. They ignore the elderly who have lived in (and anchored) neighborhoods all their lives and who, even if they wanted to move, couldn't afford to live anywhere else in the city. They ignore the working poor, the single parents.

The most recent "mixed-income" housing in a former housing project area is River Garden. In the year or so that the plans were finalized, each few months, it seemed, the number of units for former St. Thomas residents (the housing project was torn down first, the people scattered throughout the city, then plans were finalized for developing the site) shrank considerably. By the time the present phase was completed, of the 1600 apartment units created, 120 were designated for public housing and only 40 of those units had been occupied before Katrina. Giving public housing land in becoming-pricey parts of town to private developers—this is HUD's idea of "successful" mixed-income housing.

With rents skyrocketing to $1000 or more for rat-traps that face drug deals and nightly gunfire, single mothers are not the only ones having trouble finding a place to live. Condos + razing public housing seems to = an erasure of the poor and middle class. Just b/c Popeye's is paying $10/hour does not mean you can afford a $200,000 house or $1500 a month in rent. Our economy is still largely based in tourism and service, jobs that pay less than or barely living wages in a real estate market fueled by irrational greed and projections. People who live in half a million dollar condos want services—retail workers, restaurant workers, drivers, maids, all those jobs filled by the majority of the folks who lived in the housing projects. If they cannot find a place to live, they cannot return. The right to return should be more than a sound bite.

* Filosa, Gwen. "Four Housing Complexes Will be Demolished." The Times Picayune 15 Jun 2006: A1.

FRANCIE RICH

Ann O'Brien was a much-loved member of the arts community in Abita Springs and the wife of John Preble, creator of the UCM museum and manager/producer for pianist Bobby Lounge.

I have always wanted to write an obituary, but I always thought it would be my own, not that of my friend Ann O'Brien, who died on July 1, 2006, twenty days shy of her 55th birthday. Her sister Betsy O'Brien told me I could make it long.

Ann O'Brien is now playing with my dead dogs, cats, her grandparents, Carmen and Leandre Marechal, and Mary and William O'Brien, her Uncle Rene Marechal, her dear friend Elliot Snellings, other family members, my parents, friends, and total strangers, because that was the kind of person she was and still is.

Ann is survived by her wacky but loving husband, John Preble, and sons, Andrew and William Preble, of Abita Springs. She is also survived by her parents Alyce "the storyteller" and Charlie "God-Loves-You" O'Brien of Covington along with her sisters, Christine Lozes and her husband Bill and their children, Brian and Allison, of Covington, Betsy O'Brien of Washington D.C., brothers Michael O'Brien of Folsom and his children Wesley of New York and Chris of New Orleans, and David O'Brien and his wife Lillian and children Maegan and Sean, of Mandeville.

She is further survived by her mother and father-in-law, Marie-Louise and Warren Preble, her brother-in law Warren Preble and his friend Lillian, Uncle Paul "Brother Elias" Marechal, and Uncles Willam and Edward O'Brien and their families. And oh-mygosh so many friends, more friends than anyone I've ever known, at least 2,649 of them, including myself, Francie Rich, and my husband John Hodge, and others who can't be listed because they didn't pay to have their names listed in this obituary.

Ann O'Brien was born on a really poor share-cropper's farm in Oklahoma...skip that part, I'm saving that for my obituary. Ann graduated from St. Scholastica Academy in Covington and, as long-time SSA teacher Alyce O'Brien remembered her, she was a "pleasant child, with street smarts instead of book smarts." Oh, I'm sorry, she was referring to Cathy Deano, not Ann. Ann studied painting and got her BFA at LSU before becoming the famous jeweler she is today. She was a president of the Louisiana Crafts Council, a member of the Rhino Gallery in New Orleans, the Mississippi Craftsmen's Guild and a host of other organizations. Her work has appeared in national publications and has been exhibited in fine crafts shops around the country.

As Ann perfected her craft she also perfected the craft of helping other artists sell their work. In addition to her own work and helping other artists, she has done extensive volunteer work with children. She also worked as an artist- in-residence in St. Tammany Parish schools and as a tutor at Mercy Family Center in Mandeville. She and her husband, John Preble, founded the UCM Museum in Abita Springs, where Ann loved leading the Push Mow Parade on her bicycle.

She traveled with her grandparents to Europe as a child and made yearly visits to Uncle Paul at the Trappist monastery near Atlanta and to Navarre Beach, Florida. Ann didn't like to be alone and she never was and isn't now.

Ann was diagnosed with pancreatic cancer earlier this year. She never liked going to doctors but ended up caring deeply for her doctors, Drs. Carinder, McCormick, Saux, Suarez, Groves, Seicshnaydre, Ehrensing, Bobrowski, and Torcson. Her hospital room was party central and the place to be. Ann's illness turned out to be an incredible gift to her family and friends. Her room was always full of laughter, love and joy. Personally I'm not one for large group gatherings, but I loved going to see her in the hospital and at her parents' house, where her mother would tell fabulous stories and I met old and new, all wonderful people who have enriched my life.

Whenever Ann called she would say, "Hi, this is Ann O'Brien," as if her thin, shaky voice and caller ID didn't give her away. She didn't like change, so dying is a major step for her. She laughed easily, could talk about anything to anyone and her only fault was that she never talked ugly about anyone. She is the epitome of a gentle soul even when she got mad at John Preble, which to know him is to get mad at him. She was kind and generous and we are still expecting great things from her.

Ann treasured the trees on her property in Abita Springs. She would often give us plants and trees and office supplies for Christmas gifts. Hurricane Katrina took most of her trees in Abita. Maybe she went to be with them. Many of us will think of Ann when we see camellias, azaleas, and trees.

One consolation of dying young is having a large funeral, and anyone who could figure out a way to sell tickets to Ann's would be set up for life. John Hodge had a dream at the moment Ann died. Ann was driving a truck in Mexico then riding a bicycle with flowing skirts. He kept thinking, "doesn't anyone know she is sick?" She fell off her bicycle and everyone "tackled" her with love. When it's your turn to go, be sure to look for Ann if she's not already at the entrance waiting for you.

My only regret is that Ann didn't have a goofy nickname.

ALL THE STORIES WERE HARD

LUCKYDOG, *DAILY KOS*

...Here is where I must depart from a straight timed narrative. 'Cause here is where time breaks down. Where everything breaks down. From Tuesday until Friday morning, the radio, the people, everyone kept saying the same things, over and over. If you went into New Orleans, what you heard was...

"Oh. My. God."

and...

"We gotta get them folks outta there."

and...

"They are not coming."

"They" were the federal government. Regular ol' civilians brought their little flat-bottomed aluminum fishing boats into New Orleans because "We gotta get them folks outta there." A lot of those regular ol' civilians were named Bubba, a lot of them were the folks that some few people here call "rural Southern fucktards." The Coast Guard went to work. The Louisiana Dept. of Wildlife and Fisheries went to work. And the "rural Southern fucktards" went to work, too.

But the Feds...They are not coming.

I don't have to tell you what happened. You saw it on TV if you were not here. They are not coming. Everything broke down. Everything. They are not coming. How could this be happening? They are not coming. Why the fuck? They are not coming. They are not coming. They are not coming. They are not coming. They are not coming.

...and after Forever, on Friday morning, the military was here. They were so here that they were refueling rescue helicopters in-air over Lake Ponchartrain. But not until Friday morning.

After Friday...it seemed to still go on forever, even after the cavalry was coming. How long did it go on? I don't know. I don't know. I was here, still I don't know. And that's all I have to say about that.

And we heard the news on the radio. And we heard the mayor lose it on the radio. And we heard the parish president lose it on the radio. And we said "Yeah you right. Tell it again." And we heard about the Brownies and we heard about the cruise ships and the hospital ship offshore and the crony contracts. And we sucked it up because there was work to be done and they were not coming.

I worked on my parents' house, outside of New Orleans. It took me three days to clear out the first floor. The only people in town were doing the same sorta thing. I cut up downed trees in my parents' yard for something like a week, ten days. People helped each other. One day, I saw a sleek, smallish corporate-looking jet circling overhead. I figured it was Heckuvajob Georgie, and started gesticulating wildly, screaming "FUCKYOUBUSHFUCKYOUFUCKYOU." People who heard me looked at me like I was crazy, I yelled "BUSH!! BUSH!!" and pointed at the jet. They joined in, screaming and yelling "FUCKYOUFUCKYOU" at the jet. Then the jet peeled off, and everyone went back to work.

I filled up the gas tank in my Jeep every chance I could, whenever I saw a gas station open. I drove 40 miles to find a grocery open and stocked up. It was surreal, a grocery store open. People started coming back more and more. Businesses started opening on the outside of New Orleans, power or not. Signs appeared

on the roadside...WE'RE OPEN!!!...We were still here...
we were still here...people drove in from other parts of
the country, with trucks full of generators—and sold
them on the roadside at wholesale prices, no markup.
The Times-Picayune, the local NOLA paper, assembled
its staff in Baton Rouge, at an LSU dormitory. Then
the publisher insisted that the staff come back into the
city and work in the offices. They camped out at each
other's houses.

People came from all over to help. There were
workers from everywhere. They were kind. They
helped. They were citizens, helping citizens who were
in need. They shook your hand, and they worked.
Helping.

The Red Cross started handing out debit cards,
no one knew exactly what the rules were, the rules
changed. People lined up to get cards, everyone was
eligible. A lot of people refused to try to get a card, it
didn't seem right. It didn't seem right...

There were utility workers from all over the country,
working long hot days to get powerlines back up. My
neighbors and I knew—we knew that we should've
been the last to get power. We were getting power
too quickly, even at two weeks after, too quickly, they
should've been in New Orleans...We're out at the end
of the line, New Orleans should've been first. We
knew that the utility companies had written off the
city. Written them off. Still, the utility workers were
busting their asses, living in tent camps, 90 degree days
and nights. It was the decision of the suits. Written off
the city.

Phones came back on. I talked with my parents in
north Louisiana. They wanted to come home. NO! No
power at your house! NO! I couldn't reach my sister.
I talked to one of her friends in Baton Rouge. The
friend started in with "all that shooting and looting,

those people..." NO! UNDERSTAND! You MUST understand! Someone fired a weapon somewhere and it was used as a fucking excuse to not help. NO! That's NOT how it was! NO! UNDERSTAND! They didn't come, they didn't want to come, they could've come, there was no help...the gunfire wasn't enough to keep away those who wanted to help ... UNDERSTAND!

One day, a chainsaw day, a 90-degree-hot, dirty-chainsaw day, a car pulled into the driveway at my parents' house. A frantic middle-aged woman got out, babbling a mile a minute. I finally calmed her down and figured out that she was the niece of my mother's best friend. My parents were her last hope. Her aunt, my mother's best friend lived a couple of blocks from one of the levee breaches. The authorities had no news. Her aunt was not in a shelter. Her last hope was that her aunt was with my parents. Her aunt was not with my parents. I folded my arms around her and told her. She collapsed. Ten days, two weeks, no news, only hope.

The next day, her husband took a boat across the Lake, across what is basically twenty-five miles of open water. Beached the boat on the base of the levee. Hiked to the aunt's house. The floodwater was down by then. They were stopped by the National Guard across the street from the aunt's house—the National Guard refused them access. The guardsmen agreed to go kick down the door and look for them.

The aunt was elderly, in poor health. She had told my mother a month or so before the storm that she felt that Armageddon was coming, the end of the world, the world news was so bad, so bad. She told my mother that she wanted to go in her own home, with her little dog in her arms, that she hoped that it all ended quickly.

The guardsmen found her in her easy chair, with her little dog in her arms. Her house had flooded to the rafters, a couple of blocks from one of the levee breaches. When I told my mother, my mother cried, heart-rending cried, "She knew! She knew! She knew!"

People everywhere would tell each other their stories. And the stories that they had heard. Complete strangers, longtime friends. There was no one-upsmanship. None. None. All the stories were hard. Hard.

My parents came back to their house when the power was back on in their town. Three weeks, maybe, after the storm. They didn't look so well, still they were glad to be back.

Then Hurricane Rita rolled in. The southerly winds pushed the Gulf back into the whole region. My parents evacuated to a high school overnight, were back in their house the day after. My father didn't look so well at all.

Two weeks later, my father had a second stroke. He lingered for a couple of days in the hospital. The hospital was barely functioning, only half of the wards were open. The staff was worn out. They were heroes. Heroes. Worn out heroes. My sister came in from Texas. We held his hand. He passed away. I closed his eyes with my hand, gently, gently. The worn-out heroes contacted the funeral home.

We met with the funeral director. She was trying to explain that yes, it was all pre-paid, the arrangements could be made... but no one had yet been interred in New Orleans, everything was broken down, it might take a couple of weeks to make the arrangements...I explained that it would happen and happen soon... she balked...and I explained, her looking in my eyes, that it would happen and soon...there was a very long pause, eyes on eyes...and she said that she would make it happen. My father was cremated and we interred his ashes where he wanted to rest. The cemetery was desolated, waterline above our heads, all the grass was dead, all the trees were dead, in the bright sunshine of an early morning. I spoke the words he wanted, in a cemetery in a drowned city.

And Thanksgiving came sometime after...and I was thankful that my mother had a mostly intact roof over her head.

And people everywhere would tell each other their stories. And the stories that they had heard. Complete strangers, longtime friends. There was no one-upsmanship. None. None. All the stories were hard. Hard.

SATURDAY, AUGUST 05, 2006

A TERMINAL CONDITION

MARK FOLSE, *WETBANKGUIDE*

Everyone on the plane looks so depressed, my wife said, as we came out into the terminal at Louis Armstrong Airport in New Orleans after our flight back from to Washington, D.C. How could they not be, she asked, coming back to all this?

The B Concourse doesn't look so bad. It's not as if there are debris piles outside of the mostly shuttered shops. Then I think about those shops, notice the emptiness at the far end of the hall. It's one in the afternoon on a weekday, a time when the concourse of any decent-sized airport should be teeming with people, when even in August tourists and business people and even the odd conventioneer should be shouldering their way through the outbound crowd, the shops busy with early drinkers and late souvenir shoppers.

This afternoon it appears as deserted as a terminal at one a.m., half of the shops shuttered. I don't see the faces of excited tourists or determined business travelers. Everyone looks a bit tired, set at the mouth, the look I'd expect to see watching a planeload of National Guardsmen deplaning at Baghdad Airport. They look around quickly as they come off the plane, then heft their bags up and square their shoulders as they set off down the concourse, slightly bent as if walking into a strong wind.

It's not an easy place to come home to lately, the Big Easy. Washington, D.C. is an unfair comparison. The major monuments are as usual scrupulously clean, the stones gleaming in the oppressive heat of a mid-summer heat wave. As a national treasure, these get the full attention even as the government tightens its grip on the funding for the National Park Service. And it's not just the monuments and parks. Washington is a city on the move, construction everywhere and property values skyrocketing, even though it was a place itself near collapse when I left there in the early 1990s, wracked by crime and under a thoroughly corrupt and ineffective government. Would you trade C. Ray Nagin for a crackhead? The vibrancy of DC suggests that there is still hope for New Orleans, in spite of ourselves.

Today, areas of the nation's capitol I wouldn't walk around at night ten years ago are developed and busy. The housing projects of Anacostia in the southeast are gone, replaced by a development much like River Gardens in New Orleans. On the last block I lived on, the flop/drug house with more foot traffic than a 7-11 is nicely redone, a bright brass address plaque on the brickwork. When my daughter needs band-aids for a blister, I begin to notice that our downtown neighborhood is overrun with Rite-Aid and CVS stores. I don't have to go more than a few blocks in any direction to find one. The restaurants are open and busy, the hours long and the menus extensive. It is a stark contrast to the city we left behind just a few years ago.

It is not all perfect. The extensive redevelopment is driving rents through the roof, putting the recovering parts of the city out of the reach of many renters. On the mall, there are vast patches of dirt and dead grass, an unthinkable condition even in midsummer a few years ago. It appears that the vast urban garden that greeted me almost twenty years ago is suffering from the first signs of government neglect. The homeless are as they were then, everywhere you turn.

Still, DC is so clean, so functional compared to NOLA. It is too easy to start to take the debris piles and rutted streets for granted, to expect to drive out into the suburbs for simple necessities, and worry if you'll find the store open, to drive past blocks of shuttered businesses and empty houses only occasionally relieved by signs of recovery. As much as the people of New Orleans put up with before—crime, litter everywhere, dysfunction at every level—they cannot be expected to live this way forever. We want, as one speaker reminds us every meeting of our recovery-planning group, to rejoin the United States.

Our family vacation was not so much an escape from the stress of life in New Orleans as a subtle and constant reminder that we had returned, if only for a few days, to the United States, to the developed first world; that we had escaped for a bit from a place on the edge, a city just barely clinging to the skirts of America, where people long for the days when there was a store on every corner, when things mostly worked, like ex-patriots in a tropical paradise of dysfunction muttering darkly in their Cuba libres that it was never like this back in the States.

I would not be here if I didn't have hope. I know that someday the airport will be the place I remember from the past: the boisterous conventioneers already into their second cocktail, the college kids draped in beads before they reach Bourbon, the aficionados bobbing their heads at the first strains of jazz coming from the airport record store. I can see this entire crowd stumbling out into the subtropical sauna and stopping for a minute, with a distant cast to their eyes and smile on their faces, the look that tells me they have reached the place they dreamed. The renaissance going on in Washington DC tells me this is not a fantasy, but an entirely possible future, because so many have that dream of New Orleans. But today I only see the somnambulant crowd trudging down an eerily silent corridor, returning for another tour of duty.

TUESDAY, AUGUST 29, 2006

OBLIGATORY RECKONING

JASON BRAD BERRY, *AMERICAN ZOMBIE*

I don't really have a lot of sentiment about today's anniversary. I'm not much on reflection but my conscience feels obliged to, so I'll just tell you where m' at.

I am still paying a mortgage on a house I can't live in, I can't tear down, I can't sell, and I can't fix. I am suing my insurance company. I can't get Road Home money to fix my house because I had insurance, but the insurance company has screwed me, so I am essentially penalized for having had insurance. I'm still in the same hole I've been in for the whole year.

My five-year-old son still asks about New Orleans. He still misses it and still considers it his home. Sometimes he cries when he thinks about his friends, namely Thomas, his best friend. He wonders about his house and his room a lot, too.

I have been away from him, my wife and my daughter (she's about to turn two) a lot over the past year. That's my biggest regret and hardship since Katrina did her thing. It's been tough...and still is, but I'm trying to see the bigger picture and tell myself this is temporary and it will end. I hope that's true, and I hope it's sooner than later.

I've traveled a lot this year. I'm in L.A. as I write this. The traveling has been interesting, but at a cost. It's tough traveling so much knowing that you don't really have a "home" to come back to. Sometimes I feel like a ghost just wandering around. I'll catch myself standing in an airport or at a coffee shop in some strange town staring off into space and I just forget where I am or even who I am...kind of like when you get piss drunk and wake up someplace and don't know how you got there, but with no hangover.

I have a lot of bouts of compulsion...and guilt. I feel guilty all the time, mostly about not having a home for my family.

That's about it.

Happy anniversary, fellow New Orleanians.

NEW ORLEANS IS RISING

ALLEN BOUDREAUX, *UNAPOLOGETIC*

It's been a year. I don't know what to tell you. I still cry a lot. Like everyone else here, I witness, live, and struggle with what happened Every. Single. Day. I am forever altered; the thirtieth year of my life can be described, very simply, by the name given to one storm.

• I lost friends and family (but only to other cities).

• I lost my dog (but to a good foster home where she has stayed since, and is happy).

• I lost my vehicle to the flood (but got enough insurance money to lease a new one).

• My grandmother and two of my aunts, and several of my friends, lost their homes and belongings to the flood; I lost a lot of the tangible artifacts of my childhood and the history of my family in that water.

And I was so fortunate.

I'm okay, a year later and I'm okay. But it's still a tentative okay, an "okay-for-now": wobbly and precarious and contingent on factors far beyond my control. To be honest, that's the best I can hope for at the moment, and I'm good with that.

New Orleans is not even okay yet, but it is surviving. New Orleans is still gut-shot, hemorrhaged, disfigured, torn and anemic...and yet very alive. Mending. Healing, slowly, at the same languorous pace at which it has always moved. It will take decades, lifetimes, perhaps—but this city is coming back. It's something you can feel more than you can see; and it will be despite ourselves, despite our immense and embarrassing failings, despite the ridicule and criticism of the rest of the country and despite criminal neglect by the federal government. New Orleans is an irrepressible, elemental force of nature, and one year later *New Orleans is rising*.

Ya'heard me?

JOHN BOUTTE—THE MUSICIAN

INTERVIEW BY STACY PARKER LEMELLE, *THE KATRINA EXPERIENCE*

...I was afraid to leave the city again. I was afraid that if I'd ever leave I wouldn't be able to get back again. I went straight back to work. Somehow we worked it out. We were the first musicians back on the scene.

When we had a gig, it was like church. That was the kind of reaction. People love what we do. They come like a little kid who was afraid to get away from their mom. They always begged me not to [leave New Orleans for outside gigs]. But I got to go, because I got to make money. Some things didn't change. That's the financial situation of musicians in New Orleans.

The first gig I did was at Cafe Brazil on Frenchmen, a club that I first started doing music at. This was in October. It was incredible. It was absolutely incredible. The electricity was still on and off. We were doing it almost acoustically. In this little club. And it was packed. People were amazed that somebody was doing music. It was packed. They were singing along. And musicians—the ones that I knew who were there—I just invited up on stage. We started doing a weekly thing there. Not for any money. I think somebody videoed some of that stuff. I've got some video of that somewhere around. Right after the storm. Very, very, very intense.

It was like church. I got everybody—you know, it's hard to get people to participate, sometimes, to sing along, whatever. When I'd open up, the first thing I'd do is, I'd make everybody stand up and I'd say, now I want you all to do me a favor, I want everybody to scream as loud as you can. Whatever you wanted to do, just scream. It's very therapeutic. People would just get up and aaaaaahhhhhhhh! It was like this enormous roar. Get up and do it again. They'd scream again.

We'd start doing some of the old gospel tunes, New Orleans gospel tunes. It was incredible. "Just a Little While to Stay Here," "Down By the Riverside," "Over the Gloryland," "You Never Walk Alone."

What was the crowd like? The crowd was funky. Everybody was dirty, man. Nobody was dressed up. You never dressed up a lot in New Orleans anyway, but people were dirty. Nobody was like in suits, coats, ties, nothing like that. It was kind of like a lack of a place to wash your behind. It was real funky, but it was real. It was really real. The people who have stayed throughout, they were special. They were people who had bonded together like never before...They really appreciated the fact that we were back and doing the music.

RINGING THE CLOSING BELL ON KATRINA

JOSH NEUFELD, *4-EYES*

As a Hurricane Katrina Red Cross volunteer, I was invited to commemorate Katrina's one-year anniversary by taking part in tomorrow's NASDAQ closing bell ceremony. And it will all be viewable on web-cam! So look for me in a gaggle of NY-area Red Crossers as we mark the hurricane by celebrating the unstoppable storm of hyper-capitalism.

DAY 368: WHY DON'T YOU QUIETLY REBUILD AND GET ON WITH YOUR LIVES?

MAITRI ERWIN, *VATULBLOG*

August 29th has come and gone, and the token visit by Arbusto and camera crews with it. The nation has poured out a little liquor for *L'Isle d'Orleans* and returns to its business. Just like people died the city over last August 31st, the third battle of New Orleans continues today. We still need a rebuilding plan, disaster insurance relief, city sanitation workers, affordable housing and small business impetus. As if affected by the summer heat, the New Orleans Momentum seems to drag its feet on the sticky asphalt, pausing occasionally to grab a cold beverage.

Someone named "jh" commented on my recent Sepia Mutiny post: "I don't hear Mississippi whining. Why can't people just quietly rebuild and get on with their lives? They've gotten ridiculous sums of money to rebuild that city..." While I didn't bother feeding the troll there, I realize the staggering misconceptions people still (want to) have about New Orleans and address them, in the simplest possible terms, in order of receipt.

1. Whino Forever: We are tax-paying Americans who produce a quarter of the nation's domestic oil supply and a fifth of its natural gas—we've earned the right to whine. Therefore, I repeat this one last time to your sensibility-lacking, almost-49-star-flag-waving, supposedly patriotic self:

The New Orleans Katrina experience is a different one altogether. It was an unnatural disaster (levee breaks) and resulting flood that almost destroyed a large portion of the city, while a natural disaster and winds badly thrashed towns like Biloxi and the rest of the MS-AL Gulf Coast. Even residents of those coastal towns admit that our city has it worse than theirs. The story here is that of a broken social contract (and the lack of any accountability); yonder, it is one of rebuilding when and how. Simply put, we have a much more complicated mess here than the other areas you mention.

2. No Money, Mo' Problems: We broke, and can't "quietly rebuild" because our city is bankrupt and needs a cold, hard infusion of cash.

3. Show Me The Money: The entire Gulf Coast affected by Hurricane Katrina and her wake, not just New Orleans, has been allocated $110 billion, of which we have been doled out $44 billion. But wait ... you will see from this post by our City Accountant, Da Po Blog, how the 44 breaks down. Follow closely because there will be a pop quiz later:

- $110 billion is "out the door," but only $44 billion [has reached us].

- "… out of the $44 billion that has gone into some one's hands, 75 percent or $33 billion has gone into the hands of the states and cities affected by the hurricanes."

- "$16 billion [goes to] flood insurance claims, which the federal government has been known to do when reporting how much money they are sending down here."

One year later, that leaves the entire Gulf Coast with $17 billion, which has been spent on immediate help, rentals, trailers, debris removal and health. Independent observers state that Katrina Aid Is Far From Flowing.

4. What's The Plan, Stan? Federal funds for re-building will not be released to us sans a blessed plan. We had a plan, as Mark Folse reminds us: "It was called the Baker Plan, and it would have done the difficult things we are asked to do: clean up not just individual homes but entire neighborhoods; tell some of our friends and neighbors that their areas might not come back. The only real problem with the plan was that you scuttled it and said, no, we won't do that. You said, go back to the drawing board and try again and try to figure out a way to do it that doesn't put the federal government on the hook for all the damage it caused."

Now, we're in process of creating the Grand Unified Plan. (Private to locals: There was another NOCSF meeting this morning, BTW, for which we were sent fancy emails a whole two days ago.) Today's *Times-Picayune* headline blares "N.O. Planning Process Puts Residents On Edge":

...as with the mayor's Bring New Orleans Back Commission, the process could collapse under the weight of an intricate web of interests that must collaborate to produce action, some critics fear. Currently, the lines of authority and accountability remain murky at best. When it comes to crafting the endlessly discussed, all-encompassing "plan" to rebuild New Orleans, it's unclear where the buck will stop.

...The Nagin administration didn't respond to questions about the neighborhood planning process this week.

...[It has only now become widely apparent that] neighborhoods can immediately use their plans in seeking government or private grants not controlled by the state agency.

To get an idea of all the baffles, barriers, hurdles and hoops to contend with in this process, read every sentence of Becky Houtman's last post on the topic of City Planning.

...the [state-level] LRA Fund Committee is holding the purse-strings

A plan is required to release federal relief funding, but little or no funding is given to the creation of a detailed and comprehensive plan.

Also note that rebuilding plans here take place under the specter of the ol' Catch-22: Whom are we rebuilding for? Said differently, if we rebuild, how many will come back? And, what do they come back to if we don't rebuild? Open dialogues, especially important ones, don't happen quietly.

5. Mean Ol' Levees: All of the above is background chatter without federal levees that don't break. The mouse in my pocket and I would "quietly rebuild" with glee if we had the wherewithal, and our entire region wasn't at the mercy of the Army Corps of Engineers for this tremendous engineering task. Even today, Officials Disagree On Readiness Of New Orleans Levees For Storms.

6. The Gettin' Ain't So Good: Many New Orleanians, whether here or displaced, are yet to rebuild a life to get on with. If you were to live in a trailer or with family and friends, were un(der) employed, fighting insurance companies and trying to make life as normal as possible for your family and yourself everyday, you wouldn't consider it "going on." That's simple survival.

Anything else?

It's a pity that, in this age of technology, global business and rapid monetary exchange, Louisiana has to justify itself to the rest of the nation. Yet, we abide.

BROKEN CITY

ANN GLAVIANO, *WHAT THE HELL IS WATER? THIS IS WATER*

I was going to write about the anniversary night but didn't.

I was going to tell you about the Maple Leaf, how it was packed and sweaty, and I waited at the bar for a cup of water, Rebirth was playing and how impossible it is to keep still, sitting or standing, and I'm standing waiting for water, watching the people waiting at the bar and dancing to themselves, watching this girl at the corner dancing and I kept grinning at her, and something in the music changed and suddenly everyone was bouncing, even the bartender as he pours the drinks. And bliss rolling down my back. There aren't words for it. Joy that makes your hair stand on end. Revival-meeting ecstasy, the people are fanning themselves or holding their hands up. They're standing on the walls. I was telling Barrett about it—the whole anniversary thing and whether or not to acknowledge it with some big-deal event—seeing as we're forced every day to acknowledge that it happened—it's not like you can live in this city and not notice it. And that night Breton wanted to see Rebirth, she thought it would be fitting and I agreed—though I was tired and not in the mood for partying. So I didn't drink except the water. And mostly I danced by myself and didn't say much. And I told Barrett that it felt good, like church, like church would be if it were cool and led by a NOLA brass funk band. And what I meant was it felt restorative.

KATRINA KITSCH

EVE TROEH, *TRANSOM.ORG*

Look and leave. That is all I was allowed to do last October—officially—in New Orleans. To be honest, I wasn't sure I even wanted to look. But when I did, the first comforting thing I saw was a refrigerator, sitting on the curb, all duct-taped shut to keep all the liquefied food and maggots inside. But on the outside, it was smooth, white, and shiny, a perfect canvas for somebody—somebody who pulled out a spray can and wrote, "Happy birthday! Free beer inside!" on the front.

The city had started to laugh again, that's what was comforting. I think humor is a good sign after tragedy. I really think it should be one of the recognized stages of grief. There were dozens, hundreds more refrigerators painted with mantras: "Smells like FEMA," "Levee board victim," "Dubya, you forgot your lunch," "Lunch is served, Mr. Brown." Outside a hippie-punk soup kitchen, there was one that said "Electricians not lentils." And my favorite might have been a single word, one I can picture on a teenage girl sparkly T-shirt: "Spoiled." "Spoiled" became the name of the book about the fridges; people loved them.

It wasn't until after Thanksgiving that we had our first semi-public debate over laughing about Katrina. The battleground was Lakeside Mall, and the instigator was the mall's landscape guy, 59-year-old Frank Evans from Gretna, Louisiana. Frank's done the Christmas display at Lakeside Mall for 13 years. Usually he puts up a big model train that runs through a miniature

snow-covered village. Christmas 2005 was supposed
to be a New Orleans theme, with models Frank built
of traditional-style New Orleans style houses. "Then
Katrina hit, so we really made it New Orleans-style,"
Frank said, "with the disaster, and the blue roofs and
the helicopter rescuing people off the rooftops, and
trash, refrigerators."

It was pretty makeshift—the refrigerators were
Ivory soapboxes painted white; blue tarps clung to
tiny rooftops with Popsicle sticks. Little signs with
toothpicks advertised debris removal, and a miniature
pumping station was posted with "Only works in good
weather"—a comment on how no one was around to
pump the floodwater out of the city.

Some people at the mall thought it went too far.
They made Frank take it down. Little did they know,
that's what caused the controversy.

"The mall had to turn the fax machine off; they
had to quit answering the phone," Frank said. "The
lobby was full of the older people who were walking
in the mall, they had been protesting. The day I took
the display down, there was about 50 of them. They
went up to the office and wanted to see the girl who
was in charge of marketing. She wouldn't see them,
she was apparently afraid of them. But, anyway they
made their point."

Frank got to put back Katrina Ridge—that's what he
named it—and the mall was packed with crowds five
people deep to see it. Frank said some people told him
when they drove into New Orleans from hundreds of
miles away, they stopped at the mall first, before going
to go check on their flooded houses, just to get a laugh.

In the end, the mall got thousands of fan mail
letters and only 11 complaints. Frank said he probably
could have sold the whole thing on eBay. But, instead,
Katrina Ridge is going to Louisiana State Museum as

part of their permanent collection on the storm. Frank's piece of homemade kitsch is now a priceless artifact.

There are a lot of people making money off Katrina kitsch—you can buy everything from a diamond-encrusted fleur de lis to a bumper sticker that says "Proud to swim home." Me, I only brought one thing so far—Da Mayor in Your Pocket. It's a keychain that plays six infamous quotes from New Orleans' own C. Ray Nagin: "This is a national disaster!" "Get their asses moving to New Orleans!" "Let's fix the biggest goddamn crisis in the history of this country!" "Excuse my French, everybody in America, but I am pissed." I can't believe I spent $10 on that thing, and I can't believe I'll probably spend another $10 when they make one of him saying "chocolate city." I hope they do, I mean, since New Orleans has bet on Nagin for another go-round, our only consolation may be "Da Mayor, Part 2."

Sometimes all the cheap Katrina merch really bothers me, especially when it's sold like party favorites for folks from out of town. One day when I was working over some serious righteous anger over that, and I went over Bourbon Street hoping to get people to read their tacky Katrina T-shirts: "Mardi Gras: Show your tits, FEMA will send your beads in 8 to 10 weeks."

A sweet, funny, 60-something Pakistani man who works at a T-shirt shop didn't want to be named, but he was more than happy to talk about the shirts.

"It makes a good reasonable business in the French Quarter," he said. "About 50 percent of the business depends on shirts like, "FEMA evacuation plan: Run, motherfucker, run." I read a few, too: "Katrina gave me a blow job I would never forget." Yeah, there you go. "I stayed in New Orleans for Katrina and all I got was this lousy T-shirt, a new Cadillac and a plasma TV"...lovely.

I asked him if anybody has ever said, "Uh, you shouldn't sell those."

"Some people do," he said. "But people do take it as humor ..."

I saw them as worthless, the downside of the First Amendment, but he pointed out, in Pakistan, you can never wear a shirt criticizing a government agency like FEMA. He saw them as a symbol of American freedom.

SEPTEMBER 10, 2006

A KATRINA MEMOIR IN NUMBERS

BILL LOEHFELM, *NOLAFUGEES*

Prologue
> **3:** Katrina's rating on the Saffir-Simpson scale while AC and I watched a zombie movie, August 27
> **5:** Katrina's rating when AC woke me up on August 28
> **1:** how many hours it took us to get on the road
> **19:** the number of hours it took AC and I to reach Atlanta.
> **7:** the number of hours it usually takes to get to Atlanta

Chapter 1—Impact
> **11:** the number of hours after we left New Orleans that Katrina made landfall
> **89.3:** the longitudinal position of Katrina's landfall on the map

89.5: New Orleans' longitudinal position

3: Katrina's rating when she impacted New Orleans

3: the category of hurricane the levee system was supposedly built to withstand

3: the number of levee breaches that allowed water from Lake Pontchartrain to inundate the city

Chapter 2—The Damage

3: the number of houses in St. Bernard parish undamaged by floodwaters

14: the estimated maximum depth, in feet, of the floodwaters after the levee breaches

80: the percentage of the city flooded by the levee breaches

200,000 + : the number of houses in Orleans Parish that got a foot of water or more

15: the number of people I know who lost everything they owned in the flood

Chapter 3—Flashback

1: the number of headlines *The Times-Picayune* ran August 28 about Katrina breaching the levees

1: the number of times Max Mayfield, head of the national weather center, warned Mayor Nagin about possible levee breaches on August 27

6+: The number of times I heard Mayor Nagin's warning about possible levee breaches on the radio while evacuating

1: the number of times President Bush appears on video being warned about possible levee breaches

Chapter 4—Incompetence

1: the number of times the President said on television that "no one could have anticipated the breach of the levees"

2: the number of days before landfall that Louisiana was declared a federal disaster area

1: the number of FEMA officials in New Orleans on August 29

4: how many days after landfall federal assistance arrived in the city

7-10: how many days after landfall the Superdome and the Convention Center were considered evacuated

1500 + : the number of deaths attributed to Katrina in Louisiana

Chapter 5—Competence

1,500,000: the approximate number of people successfully evacuated from southeastern Louisiana ahead of Hurricane Katrina

Chapter 6—Homecoming

44: the number of days AC and I spent in evacuation/exile after the storm

0: the number of other residents on our block when AC and I returned from the storm

5: the number of homes on my block that needed roof repair

4.5: the number of hours AC and I spent salvaging our fridge

6: how many plants from the porch survived sitting in the living room for a month and a half

3: the number of times FEMA called me at my high-and-dry apartment to offer me a trailer

0: the number of my friends who applied for a trailer and got one

2: the number of rejection letters AC and I got from publishers the first day the mail started coming again

2: the number of months after we cleaned it out that AC and I had to drag our fridge to the curb because it died anyway

Chapter 7—Back to Work

3: the number of weeks after I got back that my former employer contacted me to offer me my old job

0: the amount of seconds it took me to tell him I had a much better job already

125: the approximate number of vodka-Red Bulls I make on any given weekend

63: the approximate average IQ of the people for whom I make the aforementioned vodka-Red Bulls

8: the number of out-of-state contractors I've had to reprimand at the bar for calling the mayor a "nigger"

100: percentage of the tips I take from those people anyway

1: the number of times AC offered the mayor and his wife a chocolate dessert after the mayor's infamous Chocolate City comment

0: the number of desserts the mayor and his wife ordered

20: the percentage the mayor typically tips after dinner

Chapter 8—Toward Optimism

1: the number of puppies we adopted after the storm because we felt we didn't have enough to deal with already

65: the current weight, in pounds, of the aforementioned puppy

110: total pounds of dog now sharing our apartment

6: the number of months, to the day, between Evacuation Day and Fat Tuesday

6: the number of months, to the day, between when AC and I evacuated New Orleans and when we got engaged

4: the number of major holidays (Xmas, New Year's, her B-day, Valentine's) I sweated through without proposing because I knew she was looking for it

20 – 30: the number of seconds she spent staring at me like I'd lost my mind after I popped the question

400: the number of years it felt like between when I asked and she said yes

100: the number of Mardi Gras-colored "save the date" refrigerator magnets we received in the mail the other day

75-100: the approximate number of guests we expect to host at our spring wedding in New Orleans

300: the approximate number of years New Orleans has continued to survive after fires, epidemics, wars and hurricanes...and we're still here.

SEPTEMBER 10, 2006

THEY WANT THE MUSIC, BUT... THEY DON'T WANT THE PEOPLE

KALAMU YA SALAAM, *BREATH OF LIFE*

It was Clark High School they went to. And as "urban mythic" as the legend sounds, the truth is even more mythic: they played literally to help pay the rent and keep the lights on. It was not just for fun, it was also for survival.

Back in the Eighties, I produced music. I took Rebirth on the road both nationally and internationally (to France twice). I remember once in New York, some of the band members had been walking up and down Broadway the day before we left and one of them had purchased a cover-your-whole-head gorilla mask. Not only did he decide to wear it to the airport, but he never took it off until we landed in New Orleans and never spoke a word of English the whole time. Of course, this was pre-9/11, but it is only a mild example of uninhibited "Rebirth" behavior.

Yes, there are challenges in traveling with them, but their primal music is worth the disturbances. They keep alive a raucous and vital tradition. I love these cats.

There is an interesting contradiction inherent in Rebirth's hometown popularity. My dear colleague Jayne Cortez has a wonderful poem about Nigeria consisting of two lines repeated over and over: "They want the oil / But they don't want the people." As she repeats the lines, Jayne puts emphasis on different words. You get the point immediately but her recitation is so on point and humorous that you are laughing the whole time even though it's not a funny situation.

In an analogous way, it's the same story when it comes to Rebirth, who regularly play at the Maple Leaf, a club in the University district of Uptown New Orleans whose patrons are largely white collegiates and middle class residents: they want the music but they don't want the people.

There are people who brag about dancing all night to Rebirth and yet for fear of crime and uncomfortableness around large numbers of poor Black people (i.e. more than one maid, one handy man, one gardener and his helper), those New Orleanians would not be caught dead parading through the streets of overwhelmingly Black Central City neighborhoods or even the racially mixed Treme area. Yeah, we want to party to Rebirth in safety, but many of us won't support the return of poor Blacks back into our city. Forgive me if I sound bitter, but it's a classic case of class privilege buttressed by racial fears and antagonisms, even as a self- professed love of Rebirth is worn as a badge of liberalism.

To be fair, I should make clear that there are also a significant number of Black folk who won't roll with Rebirth through impoverished neighborhoods. The fear of what could happen is too much to risk. One could get mugged or shot or murdered. And for anyone, regardless of class or race, those are not unreasonable concerns. The streets of inner city New Orleans are mighty mean during the best of times and are especially mean in this post-Katrina era.

But on the other hand there's no second line like a Rebirth second line. Parading with Rebirth is a unique and exhilarating thrill, sort of like the rush of participating in that perilous Spanish tradition of running down narrow streets just ahead of a herd of thundering cattle, only here you might find yourself dodging bullets rather than bulls.

Implicit in Rebirth's raw lyrics is a celebration of combative street culture. The people laugh and dance, shout and party, but people also get mugged and murdered in this environment. Rebirth's songs are not just entertaining braggadocio, these cats roll with the weapon of their music, stomping through valleys of death singing a defiant song.

This wild music is so full of life precisely because it is joy snatched from the jaws of merciless, oppressive poverty. Yes, it's vulgar. Yes, it's often anti-social. Yes, for sure it's prone toward condoning (if not outright advocating) violence. But it's also some of the strongest music on the planet precisely because it's the sound of those who have come marching through the slaughter, those who some-magic-how have summoned up the strength to laugh, dance and artistically celebrate their own survival against oppressive odds.

THINGS I THOUGHT ABOUT WHILE DRIVING

CLIFTON HARRIS, *CLIFF'S CRIB*

I am a die-hard Saints fan but I have to point out the following: We are going to have a football game Monday and still don't have a public hospital open in the city.

I don't know if I should be excited, sad, or embarrassed.

SEPTEMBER 20, 2006

WHY THE SUPERDOME IS A SACREDOME, NOT A THUNDERDOME

MARK MOSELEY, *YOUR RIGHTHAND THIEF*

A recent T-P Sports article said:

> For [Saints] quarterback Drew Brees and several others it will be their first trip inside the stadium that drew worldwide attention during Katrina.
>
> "I'll be wide-eyed a little bit just looking around and seeing what it's going to feel like for the next 10 years hopefully, the rest of my career," Brees said. "I've only seen it on television.
>
> "If anything, the Superdome was a saving grace for a lot of people; it housed a lot of

people and probably saved a lot of people. For that to have happened —I think several people were killed and there was a suicide, that was horrible. But to think of all the people who were saved, you look at that arena as more than just a football stadium."

While quarterback Drew "Cool" Brees is correct to say that the Superdome is more than just a football stadium, and that it was the refuge of last resort for "a lot" of people (over 25k) during and after Katrina, he did make a factual error which the T-P article failed to correct. YRHT will endeavor to remedy this oversight. However, let me say at the outset that Brees' claim is still probably *far more accurate* than most people's lingering perceptions of the so-called "atrocities" that supposedly occurred in the Superdome during the Katrina aftermath.

First, let's consult the book *Disaster* by Chris Cooper and Robert Block, and see if we can't counter some of these false, lingering perceptions about the "killings" at the Superdome (as well as the Convention Center). From page 223, we begin to learn the real story: that FEMA's deputy coordinating officer estimated there were 200 homicide "bodies" between the Convention Center and the Super Dome. That when FEMA's mortician crew arrived at the Super Dome with refrigerated trucks to collect the bodies, they found precisely NONE in the arena. Overall, the Dome's dead numbered six bodies: a heart attack victim, three natural deaths, a suicide and a drug overdose.

Further:

At the Convention Center, the scene was similar. Despite the lurid tales of wanton violence, the scores of dead that officials insisted were waiting inside, the massive building yielded up just four bodies, only one of which, an apparent knifing victim, seemed to have met with a violent end. There were no dead babies, no adolescent girls with their throats cut, no bullet-riddled bodies at all.

In the entire city, during the anarchy and looting and chaos in catastrophic conditions "hardly any of the victims had died a violent death at the hands of others. City coroner Frank Minyard reckoned there were eight gunshot victims during the storm and its immediate aftermath, and two of those were suspected suicides." (223)

So perhaps someone can please tell Drew Brees that, actually, "several people" weren't killed in the Superdome.

And perhaps someone else can inform the rest of the country that NO ONE WAS KILLED IN THE SUPERDOME DURING THE KATRINA AFTER-MATH!

NO ONE! No killings! Nada. Zero. Bupkis. Zip. Zilch. Squat.

How many Americans know that fact?

Now, I'm not saying it was a picnic in the Dome. Hell no. Tensions were high. Rumors swirled. Some fights broke out, as well as a small fire. There was no running water, there were no working bathrooms, there wasn't enough food or medicine or generators or security. The roof was leaking, it was hotter than Hades, and FEMA wasn't bringing promised supplies. Many New Orleanians who sought refuge in the Dome had just lost family and friends to the floodwaters, not to mention homes and businesses. These are the harsh conditions that 25,000 strangers were dealing with day after day after day. *But it is important to note that people weren't killing one another in the Dome.*

Seriously, try this experiment: Take any major metropolitan area, strip it down to its last 50,000 most desperate citizens, and throw them in dark, stench-ridden, insecure arenas and convention centers during a major catastrophe. Keep them there without enough food, water and meds for several days, and see if you can limit the homicides to under one, total.

Now, when we add five more deaths to the one in the Convention center, we get SIX TOTAL HOMICIDES IN THE CITY OF NEW ORLEANS DURING THE KATRINA AFTERMATH.

SIX. Put that fact in your sugared coffee and stir it, America.

Sure, I wish there were fewer murders, but six is a remarkably low number given the catastrophic conditions. From the media coverage, however, one would have expected *six hundred homicides* city-wide, not six. Everyone remembers the reports about the "atrocities": the raped babies, the slit throats, the mass killings, the shooting at helicopters, the wanton violence and destruction, the bodies stacked up "like cordwood" in the evacuation centers.

But who remembers the corrections?

To his credit, Drew Brees tried to describe the other side of the issue. It's true that people's lives *were* saved in the evacuation centers of last resort. But one can take that point much, much further. The Dome and the Convention Center were places where *humanity didn't unravel during unexpectedly desperate circumstances.* For the most part, these evacuation areas were centers of admirable endurance—perhaps even "superhuman forbearance," as Bob Somerby describes it. And yet, people still associate the Superdome and Convention Center with widespread death and killings, because the traumatic news reports that were seared into our brains during "Katrina week" were wrong, wrong, *wrong!*

New Orleans may never be able to disabuse the rest of the country from the myths and rumors that were reported during the Katrina aftermath. Our tourist-based city's reputation was massively (and unjustly) damaged. Let's revisit one of the main reasons why this happened (the following extended excerpts are again from *Disaster*):

> Rumors [at the Superdome] spread like poison gas. Mayor Nagin and his police chief, Eddie Compass, contributed on this score. For days, the two men had been delivering fanciful descriptions to the press of the Superdome and the city at large. Nagin had spoken of the "animalistic" state of the Superdome's residents, of dead bodies piling up in dark rooms, of killings, rapes and child mortality. Compass let fly with tales of sustained gun battles, assassination attempts, and other accounts of derring-do. At the Superdome on Wednesday night, Compass... [was] in tears. "My guys are getting killed out there," he cried. "A girl, a child died in my arms." (pg 193)

The Convention Center, like the Superdome, would become synonymous with lurid lawbreaking, and again, New Orleans police chief Eddie Compass was stirring the pot. Compass spread unsubstantiated reports that the Convention Center was a hideout for an armed gang that moved among the thousands of evacuees and had commandeered the building's third floor as a vast weapons armory. He said this shadowy force was picking off tourists who ventured too close. He also claimed that he had sent a force of eighty-eight police officers to the building to bring order to the place but that they had been beaten back by a better armed, highly organized thug army. Inside, he (and others) claimed, children were being raped and adults were being executed. Bodies were said to be stacked like cordwood in the building's catering coolers....

> These reports prolonged the suffering at the Convention Center. After getting an earful from Compass, the Louisiana National Guard, in consultation with the city government, withdrew its plan to bring supplies to the building in the middle of the night, deeming the mission too dangerous. (pg 205-206)

> [One] of the enduring mysteries of the fumbling U.S. response has always been why the Pentagon did not move more quickly to quell the unrest in the city shortly after the disaster began. And one of the reasons... was that the federal government believed—largely based on rumors—that it had to plan for a far more complicated military operation, one in which federal soldiers might have to kill American citizens, perhaps in great numbers. Such a prospect added serious political and tactical complications to what otherwise might have been a more straightforward relief effort. [207]

What did the National Guard actually find at the Convention Center, when they finally arrived?

A dispirited crowd that was hungry, thirsty and fully cooperative....

> There were no heavily armed thug forces, no third-floor hideaway. Soldiers searching the crowd said they found a scattering of

> weapons, steak knives mostly, and one rusty
> pistol that didn't appear to be operable. The
> place was secured within a half hour. (pg 211)

Again, I'm not saying everything was fine in the evacuation centers during the Katrina aftermath, but I believe 99 percent of folks were behaving quite admirably under the circumstances. Yet 99 percent of what was initially reported about the violent crime was totally untrue. Out of the 50,000 people in desperate circumstances at the Superdome and the Convention Center, there was ONE homicide during the Katrina aftermath. (Six, total, throughout the city.) There were ten deaths, and most of them were natural. For perspective, consider that about SIXTY people died in Houston's poorly coordinated evacuation from Hurricane Rita.

I'm reminded of Spike Lee's documentary "When the Levees Broke," which includes some tantalizing footage of New Orleanians who attempt to lighten the mood in the Dome by marching through the halls and singing songs. *Now that's what you call a great moment!* The government had failed these people horribly, their city had flooded, there wasn't enough food, water, and medicine... and yet they decide to sing and dance!

Truthdig provides some more detail about this particular episode:

In one of several remarkable scenes from Spike Lee's new four-hour documentary, *When the Levees Broke: A Requiem for New Orleans in Four Acts,* a young man who sat out the flood in the hot and stenching Superdome surprises us with a recollection of grace. During a particularly desperate moment in the sewer—no water, no food, no help in sight—someone took charge. "There was this brother named Radio," he tells us, "...and he started clapping it up, like in a basketball game.... It was a big, big spirit; people just started singing praises."

Our storyteller continues in voiceover as the camera cuts to archived footage from the Superdome—a line of men and women dancing and singing, sweat visible through dirty T-shirts. "It was a proud moment for us. We marched around the dome, and that time I felt back to the Movement, the civil rights movement, when it was real powerful."

In my view, THIS should be everyone's dominant memory of the Superdome during Katrina: New Orleanians marching and singing praises in awful conditions. Despite their government having failed them, these men and women not only kept their composure, *they rejoiced!* They sang and danced and remained faithful amidst tragedy. *That* should have been the hopeful, inspiring story about the Superdome to come out of Katrina. *That* should have been our heroic image, our city's symbol of strength.

New Orleanians are not "savages" nor "Somalians." When everything breaks down we do not rape children and go on mass killing sprees like the media reported; we are not "animalistic" like our mayor said, we do not form "thug armies" in desperate circumstances, we are not anarchists.... But, after Katrina, America was ready to believe the worst about us, as if most New Orleanians were depraved criminals at heart.

The country needs to understand that this is NEW ORLEANS, and that neither hurricane nor flood nor FEMA can stop us from dancing.

Monday Night might be the first time since Mr. Radio "took charge" last year that crowds will be singing and clapping in the Superdome. The Saints will take on the hated Falcons in what is being called the "most anticipated game in franchise history" (T-P), and "the most triumphant moment in the history of American sports" (Big Shot). U2, Green Day and Trombone Shorty , among others, will be performing there. This city of unmatched football loyalty needs its football team more than ever right now, and everyone is very excited about the Saints 2-0 start, and about Reggie Bush, our exciting rookie running back. For the first time ever, the team has sold out every single home game in advance. (Remember that New Orleans is only half-populated.) So, it's hard to describe what this team means to us right now. It is a source of unity and pride, as well as a therapeutic distraction from all the other "real life stressors" that abound here. It's possible that the Dome will never be louder or more energized than it will be Monday Night. I expect the team to surprise the rest of the country and upset the Falcons on national TV. In particular, I hope Brees and Bush perform spectacularly.

However, as we cheer on the Saints, let's remember all those who displayed remarkable patience and forbearance under grueling circumstances a year ago (despite being slandered by government officials who spread wild, unconfirmed rumors about them). No matter what good things happen on the field in the months and years to come, for me, the stalwart spirit of "Saints" like Mr. Radio will always be the highlight of the Sacredome.

JESUS IN CLEATS

DA PO'BOY, *DA PO'BLOG*

And so has Reggie Bush been anointed. The savior of the Saints franchise. The Black-and-Golden One who will liberate Saints fans from their eternal torment. The deliverer of the chosen season-ticket holders to the Promised Dome.

Imagine 70,000 people on one city block, on one special day, all there for one purpose. Imagine over $100 million going into bringing those people together. Imagine a Super Bowl atmosphere, complete with the media frenzy and global interest in what is happening on that day on that block.

Sounds magical, doesn't it?

Now, imagine that the city block the masses have come to is in Gentilly, or Mid-City, or Lakeview, or the 9th Ward, or New Orleans East. Imagine that they are not there to sit in a comfortable seat and watch grown men play a game on artificial grass, but have come together to be part of the action and participate in the rebuilding of that neighborhood. Imagine how much work could get done.

Yeah, I know. I don't believe in magic either.

I will be one of those fans in that number this Monday. I plan on seeing Rebirth at the pre-game show. I will then head home and turn down my TV and turn up my radio. I will yell at the TV (and more strangely, the radio) and lil' po' boy will imitate me, leading to yet another words-we-say-only-around-daddy conversation.

If the Saints win, I will be elated. If the Saints lose, I will still be elated. Okay, I will be deflated first, but elated afterwards that they're at least losing at home again.

But I cannot pretend like this Monday's game is the best thing that has happened in the recovery of New Orleans. I felt the same way about Mardi Gras. People want to make this a symbol that the recovery is going just fine:

> Joe Horn said that the quick repair of the Superdome should give people a sense of hope that the rest of the city can bounce back.
>
> "If you can rebuild a place that's 1.9 million square feet," Horn said, "you should be able to come back here and rebuild a 3,000-square foot house."

I am not so sure that a functioning Superdome is a symbol of a functioning city. If the city were functioning properly, this game would not be such a big deal. It would be expected.

Make a list of all the services a city needs to function. From health care, to police, to firefighters, to electricity, to sewerage and water, to small businesses, to infrastructure upkeep, to housing—none of them are "bouncing back." Limping back, maybe. But no bouncing.

This Monday we will prove to the nation that we can still put on a world class show—even when we haven't yet recovered. But the next day, will anybody be trying to prove to the city's residents that we can put on a world-class recovery? Anybody?

Let me repeat: I will be in that number. I will be distracted for a day by Jesus in cleats ("Cleatus" for short?). But it's only one day, and I am not waiting for a savior to come down from on high to fix New Orleans. I don't believe in Jesus in a Tyvek suit.

People are making money off this game. That's why there is so much attention. The NFL and ESPN want this game to be like a Super Bowl so they can make Super-Bowl-like money off of it. I didn't expect a lot of the real news of the recovery to be told this weekend. The moneymakers want this Monday to be pleasant for all the money spenders. The news need not always be pleasant.

Edward R. Murrow said in 1958:

> We are currently wealthy, fat, comfortable and complacent.We have currently a built-in allergy to unpleasant or disturbing information. Our mass media reflect this. But unless we get up off our fat surpluses and recognize that television in the main is being used to distract, delude, amuse and insulate us, then television and those who finance it, those who look at it and those who work at it, may see a totally different picture too late.

We in New Orleans are not, for the most part, wealthy, fat, comfortable and complacent. We have gotten over our built-in allergy to unpleasant or disturbing information. We had to.

But the rest of the country lives in a pre-Katrina world. They will be sitting on their fat surpluses Monday night distracted, deluded, amused, and insulated from the totally different picture we see down here every day.

I am not saying don't enjoy the Saints or don't go to the game. I know I'll be enjoying the game. I'm just saying that this game will not change my opinion of the recovery.

Only a recovery will change my opinion of the recovery.

NOT FEELING THE HYPE

CLIFTON HARRIS, *CLIFF'S CRIB*

Call me negative.

Call me pessimistic.

Call me the only person in New Orleans that is not excited about the game tonight.

I am all those things.

I am also a realist and unfazed by media-generated inspiration.

I'm just keeping it real.

Honestly, if my friends were not going to be at my house watching, I probably wouldn't watch it. I'm a Saints fan since birth. I don't like the Falcons at all. I hope we win tonight. Everything else about this evening is bullshit. You can get wrapped up in the hoopla all you want. The fact of the matter is that if the same speed and effort put into bringing back Tom Benson's team (who he couldn't wait to move to San Antonio) was put into bringing back even decent surroundings and services for the citizens of the city life here would be so much more encouraging and inspiring than a football game. They were fixing the Superdome before people in New Orleans had hot water and streetlights. I wasn't thinking about the Saints during those cold showers.

I'm definitely happy that the Saints are 2-0 and are playing the Falcons.

I will be even more happy when I actually get a regular telephone and a drug store within a mile of my house in case all the babies and elderly need medicine.

Go Saints!

DAY 393: THE CRADLE OF MUSICAL CULTURE

MAITRI ERWIN, *VATULBLOG*

I lied, for I've made the time to watch the Saints on TV ... in my black tank top with the gold fleur de lis on it. The sniffles began when The Goo Goo Dolls made a passionate case for New Orleans on WDSU, and they grew into all out tears when Irma Thomas sang the national anthem. Through his incessant supply of "you know," Johnny Rzeznik managed to inform viewers that a lot remains to be done here, that New Orleans should be preserved with its spirit because it is the "cradle of musical culture," and that the band will support this city on their website with videos of their visit here.

Holy Mother of Superdome, it hasn't been a minute and a half and the Saints just scored a touchdown. They want it so badly, I can feel the desire through the little television over my computer.

Daaaaaamn, do I want to stay *home* and watch on TV while the city erupts? We are going to remember this game for the rest of our lives.

THE BEST FOOTBALL GAME EVER

POLIMOM

For 30 years, Polimom's been a Saints fan. Even through the paper bag Ain'ts years, the Bobby Hebert disappointment (still can't believe how that went), and the disastrous Bum days, I've defended my team.

I've withstood patronizing laughter from other fans and picked the Saints in every office football pool match (right up to the play-offs, of course)...but I have to tell you: last night was the most emotionally satisfying game ever.

In the stadium that symbolized the pain and trauma of New Orleans, the Saints created a whole host of new memories. It was absolutely awesome! (Particularly that first quarter! Holy cow!!!)

These Saints are unbelievably talented, and last night's commentary about having rebuilt the Dome in a devastated city was bang on: NOLA needs the revenue, and the hope, it brings.

Who dat say they gonna beat dem Saints? Ha! What a blast! My throat's sore today from screaming, and we even let AC stay up a bit late to watch. She created sign after sign for us to hold up to the flat, impersonal T.V. screen...like "We heart the Saints" and "Stomp them! They're dogmeat!" I'm proud to report that she can spell *Geaux* correctly now, too.

Between the razzle dazzle double-reverse and the blocked punt for a touchdown (we went absolutely nuts in my den), last night's game was the stuff of dreams. Wish I coulda been there....

Oh! And for you Houston fans—I probably have an old paper bag or two in a box that I can resurrect for someone to wear this year. Just let me know...

SEPTEMBER 26, 2006

CLIFTON HARRIS, CLIFF'S CRIB

I stand by what I said earlier about the game...
BUT THAT WAS FREAKING SWEEEEEEET!!
SAINTS 23 FALCONS 3
WHO'S YOUR DADDY VICK?

SEPT. 26, 2006

WHO DAT, INDEED

ASHLEY MORRIS

I'm still on the high from the game. I bawled my eyes out, and I still do. I've been a waterworks for the past 3 days, and finally, it's not from the desperate throes of depression.

We are the best fans in sport. We are the loudest stadium in the cosmos. Nobody comes into our house without a beatdown. And U2 and Green Day just rocked the house.

Monday night was beautiful, man.

When I saw all my brothers and sisters (and seesters) in that crowd Monday, I knew we were back. Not just the Saints back in NOLA, back in the dome.

The city was going to come back.

An entire group, 69,503 people (Atlanta got 500 tickets), that you don't have to explain New Orleans to. A group of people that get po-boys, that get second lines, that get Carnival, that get red beans and rice with sausage on a Monday night, that get lagniappe, that get "gimme an amber," that will call you honey and darlin', that know home depot like the back of their hand, that can hang drywall in their sleep, that can recommend the best mask for dust and the best mask for stink-mold, that can tell you where to get your flat fixed, that think both gravy and mayo on a sandwich is a good thing, that party Saturday night and go to church Sunday morning and leave the service in time for kickoff, that go to Vaughn's on Thursday nights, that know the game wasn't rigged, that think we are going to the playoffs, that believe that Buddy D and Vera and Sam Mills were watching from up above and toasting the return of our Saints to their rightful home.

It ain't over until you hug the ushers on your way out of the dome.

It ain't over until you fire up the big ass cuban cigar.

It ain't over until your ears quit ringing (Tuesday at about 3:30 in the afternoon).

This is not a sports blog, this is a New Orleans blog. I care about 2 things: my family and my city, and last weekend I was looking at real estate in the Chicago metro area, because my love for the former makes me consider leaving the latter. It would be so much easier for me to live there. I wouldn't have to worry about school districts or mold or my outrageous power bills or my depression or the cracks in my walls or evacuation routes or day care or doctors moving away or universities closing departments or hospitals shutting down or random bullets.

But then, I wouldn't have to worry about living in a city with a soul, either.

Once again, New Orleans is the only city that ever loved me back. When I was in the dome, I knew why: our people.

I have to go through da East every day. I used to live there as a kid in the '60s. It's toast. It will come back, but it's gonna take a long time.

But it will.

We need to realize that nobody is going to make this happen but us. Nobody really cares about us but us. Sinn Fein.

But we will come back.

We are New Orleans. The Saints are our face to the world. We are champions. Our soul is indomitable.

Who dat, indeed.

SEPTEMBER 27, 2006

THE MARRIOTT IN FOUR ACTS

ANDREA BOLL, *NOLAFUGEES*

Act I. The Biosphere

We call our room the biosphere: a climate controlled environment with giant windows facing Jackson Square and the curve of the Mississippi. There are four of us living here: my best friend, her one-year old daughter, my two-year old daughter and myself. We imagine somebody, somewhere studies us with pity and amusement as we pace the squareness of our lives.

Possibly God or possibly hotel security with nothing to do.

Outside, the calliope music from the Cajun Queen seems too loud and creepy like I could look out and see beheaded children riding a carousel. The music will increase from a half an hour to three because the steamboat is slowly drowning in a poor economy. They hope if they play more music, more tourists might come to New Orleans.

More than once, I've come to understand why they make the windows here unable to open: so people won't kill themselves. Not that it would matter if I did try to jump. I'm on the sixth floor and fifth is the pool deck, so even if I did jump in one of my fits of claustrophobia and frustration, threw the expensive desk chair through the window to escape, I would only break bones, or more likely, land on my feet, no better off than moments before.

It is housecleaning that saves me. At ten am, I live in the Marriott and have been living here for three months. Somewhere on the horizon, in Gentilly, my house is broken and sagging with neglect. I cannot seem to power wash the mold away. The roof I had fixed has a hole. I am not getting married. The rebirth I had imagined when my boss called me in early January to return to New Orleans after Katrina has not been like a phoenix rising eloquently from ash, but seems more like someone clawing to get out of a coffin where she was buried alive. I am sure I will not be able to make it.

But then, I leave. When I come back later in the afternoon, suddenly, there is hope. What once had been a mess is now neat and organized. Housekeeping has once again left me coffee, fluffed the pillows. I want to weep at the white amnesia of clean sheets. Maybe I just got here. Maybe the calliope music is romantic.

Maybe New Orleans isn't as fucked up as it was this morning. Maybe I will be able to teach for another four months without cracking up. Maybe if I wait long enough, someone will come clean my life up, too.

I'll tip them well.

Act II: Upgrade

The fourth month, we are upgraded to a bigger room on the other side of the hotel, the corner room of the 35th floor with two entire walls of windows. We sleep with the curtains open. At night, New Orleans seems like a very small island of light growing slowly.

But, of course, the bigger room and view come at a price: the housekeepers that had once brought us peace and hope do not work in this tower; rather, the ones who hate their job work on our floor. They especially, it seems, hate cleaning our room even though we try to go multiple days without service to give them a break. We bring our dirty towels and bags of trash to their carts. No tip, no matter how large, will sweeten them.

The other price we pay for the upgrade is the elevator. Our tower stands 42 stories high, and the elevator is in the middle of being remodeling to a new system, the cutting edge of elevator innovation in which a person inputs her floor number before she gets into the elevator. There are no buttons to push on the inside. There is no changing your mind mid-ride. Only four or five other hotels in the entire country have this new system of elevators.

So, because it is being upgraded, during conventions and festivals, only two elevators actually work. This means waiting eternities to go up. When I want to go down, the elevators pass my floor with a whoosh over and over. While waiting, I try to imagine what sort of country America would be with no skyscrapers, how might Americans be different if there were only structures as high as they were comfortable climbing. Would we be such bullies...so fat? I try to write haikus about waiting for elevators. Sometimes I curse. Eventually, however, I learn the floors where the two elevators will stop (32 & 27). I never once try to walk the 35 flights.

When the new system actually does work after two months, it baffles most of the tourists and conventioneers. Many of them hop in the elevator at the last second, not realizing they cannot push the button to stop the elevator on their floor. While eventually I do get used to it, I never find it to be more efficient.

Our last week there is the week they finally open the pool that had been closed for "remodeling." Not one time did I ever see anybody working on it. I knew the truth. They did not want to have to pay or care for a pool for FEMA evacuees (eventually evicted in February), the EPA workers, SUNO faculty and students, or Dillard faculty.

"Bye Marriott," my daughter waves as we head off to our new home: a FEMA trailer which is roughly the same size in square feet as the hotel room. The windows are much smaller, the view from them much more depressing, but at least they open.

Act III: Home Sweet Home

In July, after the semester is over and I am out of the Marriott, my parents take us on a trip to Las Vegas where we, of course, stay in a hotel (ironically, it's called the Orleans). When I walk in to the room that is much smaller and dirtier than the Marriott, I am not prepared for the onslaught of anxiety.

"I don't know if I can stay here for four days," I tell my parents as I try to open the windows. And I do, later that day, change our flight to go back to New Orleans in two days instead of four. After the Marriott, hotels hold no enjoyment for me and possibly never will.

From Gentilly, the trailer, my little white beacon of hope and despair, beckons with its small kitchen and windows that can open.

Athena has been busy checking things out: the bounce of the beds, the size of the tub, if there are books in the drawers.

"Mama," she says to me with a panicked voice, "I don't remember living in this house."

"We never lived here, baby," I tell her and laugh. But the comment makes the mother in me start to worry that I have once again caused irreparable damage to my daughter's future well-being and psyche. I wonder if she will grow up always searching in vain for the origin of certain memories and the feelings they evoke, the sounds, smells, and sights that surface in her dreams, as waves of déjà vu, as answers forever on the tip of her tongue. She will search for them in books, in drugs, alcohol, in meditation, in foreign counties, in dancing, in sex, in school, at beaches, in old photographs at her grandparents' houses, in her childhood that doesn't begin until age four. She will search, not knowing she is really just trying to find her way back to the Marriott, to a home that created a small piece of her, a piece she is trying to articulate.

Or, possibly, I tell the mother who worries in me, the opposite will happen. There will be no restless searching for the roots of her subconscious, for a home she only lived in for seven months. Rather, she will find home in every hotel she goes to. Won't that be nice.

Act IV: Happily Ever After

It is early September. Athena and I are driving down Canal Street. She points to the Marriott and yells with delight and desire, "Look it Mama. There's the hotel. Can we go to the hotel? Please mama? We haven't gone for a long time."

"No," I say.

"I miss the hotel," she tells me and pouts. "I want to live there again."

I ask her what sorts of things does she miss.

"Living in the hotel," she says. "You know, the hotel."

I know though. I know what she misses: the elevator rides, the big tub, the Cartoon Network, the mirrors where she could see her whole body, the giant chandeliers of twinkling light, the echo of her fancy shoes made running along the lobby's marble floors, the employees who knew her name, giving her candy and dollar bills, and how, when we looked out the window, we could imagine we lived as queens in a castle, high above our not so magical kingdom.

"When are we going to live there again?" she asks. "Tomorrow?"

"We're not," I say and try to explain it in a way I think she would understand. "It was something special. Just for a little while."

"Why?" she asks. "Why for a just a little while?"

I consider making it a story with a happy ending: that the only reason we ever got to (or had to) live at the Marriott was because once upon a time, a strong hurricane became a disaster (the shadow of which you will grow up under) in the form of a flood that broke New Orleans with water, destroying our house as well as the place where Mama worked. But then something miraculous happened, I would tell her. Once the water was drained, New Orleans was not drowned, but alive. Not only that, she wanted us back; so New Orleans used her magic to make mama's school ask her to return. Then, because New Orleans knew we had no home, she gave Mama's work the idea to offer housing in the Marriott. Everybody thought it was a splendid idea. There we lived happily ever after...

But of course, that is how we got to the Marriott, not necessarily why we will never live there again. Athena would still want an answer. But I know the answer she will not understand, that mama, no matter how successful, will never be able to afford living in a Marriott suite in the French Quarter for seven months. That, and because I have to believe this was our one get-out-of-disaster-free-card. The next time we, and the rest of New Orleans, are on our own.

OCTOBER 3RD, 2006

WARREN EASTON MARCHES AGAIN

BART EVERSON, *B.ROX*

Yesterday, as I was cooking dinner, I heard the beat of drums outside our house. I recognized that sound immediately and knew what it meant: Warren Easton marches again!

It's probably the coolest thing about living on my block. The high school marching band comes down our street almost every school day. Or rather, they did, before the city was flooded. It's been over a year since they passed by our house.

I came out to take a look. Other neighbors filtered out of their homes to check it out.

They were standing at parade rest, and the instructors were scolding them to stop talking and pay attention. This got me to thinking about the fact that their program is probably starting over essentially from scratch. When they passed by our house on the Thursday before Katrina, they were playing songs. Now they seem to be working on fundamentals. I didn't even hear a horn. Will they be ready in time for Mardi Gras?

I bet they will.

OCTOBER 4, 2006

WHERE I GOT THEM SHOES: DESIRE AREA EDITION

SWAMPISH THOUGHTS

So far, my weekly treks haven't exactly been uplifting experiences. The luck of the draw has sent me to or through some of the worst-suffering neighborhoods in the city. Now, that either says something about the extent of the damage and the lack of progress or it says something about my luck. The former is definitely true, but I'm staying away from casinos just in case.

For the most part, Desire lacked even the smiles and waves I had seen from FEMA trailer residents in the St. Bernard area. It even lacked the FEMA trailers. But then, at the end of a block, I happened upon a cluster of six houses, all either repaired or undergoing repairs, four of them with FEMA trailers in the yard. I stopped to chat with one of the residents, who was waxing his pristine red pickup. "Oh, we're coming back," he assured me. And he ticked off the names of each of his neighbors who was back, pointing out that nearly every house on his block had already been gutted. "They're just waiting on the money, you know.

It's slow, but they're coming. By this time next year, I think we'll all be back."

There were three houses on the block too damaged to be repaired. Those, he assured me, would be torn down and rebuilt.

Beside the row of repaired houses across the street was one still abandoned. On the plywood that still covered the front window, someone had spray painted, beside and partially covering the black search-team markings: "Do Not Bulldos Mr. Presiden." Apparently they ran out of space, but we get the message.

I headed up Almonaster to look for a seafood restaurant I'd found in the open restaurant listings. On the way, I passed a makeshift RV campground that had taken over a wide, curved section of the neutral ground. Three battered Winnebagos sat beside two truck campers, the kind usually attached over the bed of trucks, but here resting on cinder blocks. The campers were a rough looking bunch—mountain man beards and beer guts, relaxing in lawn chairs around a hibachi pit—and I figured they were a group of the storm chasers who've been amassing here, laborers and roustabouts who came looking for work from employers in need who may not ask too many questions.

The restaurant, "St. Roch Kitchen #2" (which, I assume, is owned by the same Vietnamese family that ran the seafood market and Creole/Asian plate lunch restaurant in the historic St. Roch Market near my house—either that or somebody is courting a lawsuit), was closed. Toddlers played inside while their older brothers mopped up and put the food away. I took a few turns around the Gentilly edge of the neighborhood but could find neither food nor drink at 7 p.m. So, glumly, I headed home.

Down on St. Claude, I decided to lift my spirits by enjoying one of the undeniable benefits Katrina's wake has brought us: the taco trucks. If you live in the Southwest, you're already privy to the wonders of the taco truck, but they are a new emergence on the culinary scene of New Orleans, arriving with the waves of Hispanic workers who are doing the lion's share of the gutting and roofing and sheetrocking around town. These rolling restaurants, portable taquerias in delivery trucks, have set up shop on the parking lots of gas stations and building material suppliers. Like a spicy version of the ice cream man. My nearest truck is Taqueria Las Cazuelas. I was mentally practicing to order in Spanish until the grandmotherly proprietor greeted me with "How are you tonight?"

Watching her prepare my tacos, I was struck by the care she showed: lime wedges cut on the spot, shredded lettuce artfully arranged, sauce and salt containers set in counterbalance to the two lime wedges, the plate carefully wrapped in aluminum foil. It was the antithesis of the distracted, rushed, slightly annoyed manner of the typical fast-food worker. The tacos were first rate, and the sauce—an edgy burn around the lips lent character and nuance by cilantro and tomatoes chopped infinitely fine—is calling me back as I write this.

O Madonna of the Cazeulas, our Lady of the Double Tortilla

Wield your saute pan of mercy and dispense the balm of your chopped cilantro

Fortify your faithful that they may vanquish the night of the blue roof

And intercede for us with your Patron, who has granted us your vision

as a sign of our renewal

Amen

WHY DON'T WE KNOW WHAT WILL HAPPEN?

MATT MCBRIDE, *FIX THE PUMPS*

....I placed a Freedom of Information Act (FOIA) request to the Corps for the Water Control Plan as soon as I learned of its existence, on August 11, 2006. They never acknowledged the request, despite the unambiguous language of FOIA and their own regulations, which direct that a substantial response be made within 20 days. Unfortunately, for some reason the Corps has decided to fight that request, and six others I have made since April 30th for various documents, in federal court. I believe the trial is scheduled for some time in March. Why they wouldn't release to the citizens of New Orleans and Jefferson Parish their complete plans for those citizens' homes, businesses, and livelihoods is beyond me, and seems to be in direct contradiction to their expressed wishes to somehow communicate openly and honestly with those citizens. After all, in their "12 Actions for Change," (this link may be broken, so try this to see the Actions for Change) released on August 24, 2006, the Corps had these two items under "Communication":

> Communication: Effective and transparent communication with the public, and within the Corps, about risk and reliability.
> 9) Effectively communicate risk.
> 10) Establish public involvement risk reduction strategies.

In light of the fact that the water in the London Avenue Canal can obviously get pretty close to or above four feet without much effort, we have a right to know what will happen in that eventuality. That would be "transparent," "effectively communicating risk," and involving the public. Fighting the release of documents which would achieve those goals does not fall within those "Actions for Change."

In sum, there is real risk to the people living and working in the areas along the London Avenue canal, as well as those draining into the canal. There is not—and there won't be—adequate pumping capacity to evacuate rainfall if the floodgates drop. And even before the gates drop, it seems likely that pumps will be turned off to safeguard the canal walls and levees as the canal level rises close to 4 feet. And part of that risk is because the Corps is not effectively, transparently communicating with the public.

So while much of the press attention has focused on the 17th Street canal, I believe the real story is on the London Avenue canal. Hard questions need to be asked of the Corps on this issue, and documents—specifically the Water Control Plan— backing up their answers must be released.

And just in case you'd like to ask those questions, here's some email addresses below...

THE BLUES COME HOME

HARRY SHEARER, *HUFFINGTON POST*

A day and a half—in the middle of a tour flogging a book and movie, that's all the schedule allowed me in the Crescent City. So, if these impressions strike locals as off base, you have my excuse in advance.

Nonetheless, conversations and news stories lead one to an overall impression: there's a different mood in the city now. Existential questions are being asked about its future by thoughtful people who a few months ago might have just assumed the place had one.

For one thing, there's this: the major writer of commercial insurance in New Orleans is pulling out. That's bad, but this is worse, a quote from the state's insurance commissioner Jim Donelon: "They cited the state of the rebuilding of our levee system as the primary reason for their decision."

He adds: "I have lived in the New Orleans metropolitan area for 61 years, and I can personally vouch for the fact that the levee system is better and stronger than it ever has been, and is getting stronger as every day goes by."

Well, okay, but maybe the insurance company is the canary in the coal mine, warning us that—can this be possible?— the Corps of Engineers, the agency rebuilding the levee "system," is not to be trusted. We know the Administration will ignore this cue, as they've ignored the entirety of the tragedy, but maybe Speaker Pelosi could spare a moment, and a committee, to look into the Corps and its work.

The occasion for my return was a benefit screening of "For Your Consideration," an evening at Canal Place Cinemas organized by New Orleans magazine and friends, and it proved once again that nobody knows how to throw a party like New Orleanians.

A guy stood up at the end of the Q&A session and embarrassed me in front of my fellow cast members by saying overly nice stuff about these posts, but the fact is, it's easy for me to continue loving New Orleans, since I get to leave and come back. The true heroics are shown by the people who are there every day, working against increasingly enormous odds to bring the city back.

Which gets me back to those conversations. They were mainly with media people, but the questions and the concerns seemed deeper and more profound than the ones I've heard on previous stays. There seems to be a cumulative impact of the national neglect, of the glacial pace of the so-called "Road Home" program—

> BATON ROUGE, La. (AP)—Only 28 homeowners have received checks so far from Louisiana's $7.5 billion hurricane housing aid program, but the private contractor running it assured Gov. Kathleen Blanco on Wednesday that it is dramatically picking up the pace. ICF International Inc. officials said they will tell 10,000 homeowners by the end of the month what grants they are eligible to receive from the Road Home program.
>
> More than 77,000 people have applied since the program kicked off in August, but fewer than 5,000 awards have been calculated, only about 2,500 letters have been sent out

notifying people of the grants they can receive and only 28 people have received their grants, according to Road Home officials.

—and of the crushing lack of local leadership. The local community groups are still working their butts off to craft plans for their neighborhoods' future (go to www.fono.org for links to them). An outfit called AmericaSpeaks organized a large local meeting (and several out-of-town satellite meetings) on Saturday to gain local input into the next "real" "unified" New Orleans plan.

But...but...the Quarter is quieter than it normally is in the run-up to Christmas, and store owners told my wife that the fall—anticipated through the long, slow summer for the resumption of convention business— did not jumpstart tourism. USA Today's front-page conflation of street crime and domestic violence to craft a weirdly frightening portrait of the city certainly won't help that project.

And yet, 30,000 Realtors came to town, had their convention, and I at least saw no reports of crime "taking hold" of them.

Maybe what we need, we Americans, is a large-scale public debate on whether or not we're going to rebuild New Orleans. If we decide not, then folks down there will know, as they seem to already, that they're on their own (a recent poll says 30% of current residents contemplate leaving within two years). If we decide yes, then Speaker Pelosi and whoever leads the Republicans while the President leads the Iraq retreat will have a mandate.

And yet, for all the existential angst that gripped at least a few of my friends, a major film is shooting right up the street from me, the restaurants are full and turning out the usual splendid fare, musicians are staying and playing, and so, though I didn't have time for my usual tour of the devastated areas, my personal experience was one of a warm, welcoming city just yearning to be whole again. But then, I had to—and was free to—leave.

UPDATE: I neglected to mention that two couples at the Thursday night screening were folks who had moved to New Orleans after the flooding.
There are believers still.

DECEMBER 06, 2006

THE VERY FIRST SAINTS GAME

MOMINEM, *TINCANTRAILERTRASH*

I had planned a post prior to the Saints game. Unfortunately, I was not able to be in that number. I will probably post it before the next home game.

Last Thursday while I was in Atlanta I got a call from my sister. My Dad had been taken to the hospital. I started figuring out how to get from Atlanta to East Texas. I was a little disappointed to be missing the Saints game.

Whenever I think of the Saints, both the song and the team, I usually think of my Dad. My Dad came late to New Orleans. He moved here in 1965 to help build the Union Carbide plant in Taft. I was just starting high school. We got here just in time for Hurricane Betsy. Almost all of our furniture was destroyed when the storage warehouse flooded. Welcome to the coast.

My first Saints game was the very first Saints game. We attended almost all of the home games while I lived in New Orleans. I spent many Sunday afternoons in the end zone of old Tulane Stadium with my brother and my Dad. When I left for college I continued to follow the Saints. Going to LSU, I came home frequently and still attended many games, until the rest of the family moved to Puerto Rico the next year. After I graduated we moved away for a while but I still followed the Saints, of course She is a much bigger fan than I am. When we moved back to New Orleans for good a few years later She and I started going to the games again, this time with her father. He was another "plank owner," having held his tickets since the beginning. We eventually took over two of his seats.

Before I could finish my travel arrangements, my sister called back. My Dad was gone. Suddenly, unexpectedly.

When he lived here my Dad loved to go to Preservation Hall. He loved tradition, all sorts of traditions. He recognized the value of them. He also recognized the value of passing tradition to the next generation. He often took families with children to Preservation Hall early in the evening to sit on the floor and listen to the music.

The family gathered from around the country. Lately we only seem to gather at times like this.

What started as a sad occasion became a remembrance of a life well-lived, a man and his family.

We played the Saints game at the end of his service.

DARKNESS CONTINUES

MOMINEM, *TINCANTRAILERTRASH*

Darkness at The Trailer continues unabated. We are still without electricity in our Emergency Living Unit.

I'm staying in the Kenner Kondo, but I go back to The Trailer and the house every few days.

Yesterday I made a visit. Work on the house next door is progressing nicely. More good news. Down the block construction has started on one of the cleared lots. They haven't done much but they have started. Further down the block another house has its yard all torn up, with big piles of sand in the yard. They seem to be getting ready to complete the work.

Entergy has now been out three times. They identified the problem. The conductors from the manhole to the meter are shorted out. Entergy sort of knows where the short is: It's under our house or our driveway. Entergy thinks it's because the conductors were submerged for however long they were underwater or because of flood-related settlement. Entergy also says its our responsibility to provide a 2 1/2" conduit from their manhole to our meter cabinet. That was a month ago.

We also called FEMA. They said they would send someone out to put up a pole and a meter. The said they would call us back. That was three or four weeks ago. Someone dug a hole next to the manhole and drove a very stout red metal spike in the ground. That was a couple of weeks ago. No call yet.

Not much progress on my part but the neighborhood is starting to show signs of recovery.

LETTER FROM THE PEOPLE OF NEW ORLEANS TO OUR FRIENDS AND ALLIES

We, the undersigned, represent a wide range of grassroots New Orleans organizers, activists, artists, educators, media makers, health care providers and other community members concerned about the fate of our city. This letter is directed to all those around the world concerned about the fate of New Orleans and the Gulf Coast, but is especially intended for US-based nonprofit organizations, foundations, and other institutions with resources and finances that have been, or could be, directed towards the Gulf Coast.

In the days after the storm, there were promises of support from the federal government and an array of nongovernmental organizations, such as progressive and liberal foundations and nonprofits. Small and large organizations have done fundraising on our behalf, promising to deliver resources and support to the people of New Orleans.

Many organizations and individuals have supported New Orleans-led efforts with time, resources, and advocacy on our behalf, and for this we are very grateful. These folks followed through on their commitments and offered support in a way that was respectful, responsible, and timely.

However, we are writing this letter to tell you that, aside from these very important exceptions, the support we need has not arrived, or has been seriously limited, or has been based upon conditions that become an enormous burden for us.

We remain in crisis, understaffed, underfunded and in many cases in desperate need of help. From the perspective of the poorest and least powerful, it appears that the work of national allies on their behalf has either not happened or if it has happened it has been a failure.

In the days after August 29, 2005 the world watched as our city was devastated. This destruction was not caused by Hurricane Katrina, but by failures of local, state and national government, and institutional structures of racism and corruption. The disaster high-lighted already-existing problems such as neglect, privatization and deindustrialization.

As New Orleanians, we have seen tragedy first hand. We have lost friends and seen our community devastated. More than 15 months later, we have seen few improvements. Our education, health care and criminal justice systems remain in crisis, and more than 60 percent of the former population of our city remains displaced. Among those that remain, depression and other mental health issues have skyrocketed.

While many nationwide speak of "Katrina Fatigue," we are still living the disaster. We remain committed to our homes and communities. And we still need support.

In 15 months we have hosted visits by countless representatives from an encyclopedic list of prom-inent organizations and foundations. We have given hundreds of tours of affected areas, and we have assisted in the writing of scores of reports and assessments. We have participated in or assisted in organizing panels and workshops and conferences. We have supplied housing and food and hospitality to hundreds of supporters promising to return with funding and resources, to donate staff and equipment and more. It seems hundreds of millions of dollars have been raised in our name, often using our words, or our stories.

However, just as the government's promises of assistance, such as the "Road Home" program, remain largely out of reach of most New Orleanians, we have also seen very little money and support from liberal and progressive sources.

Instead of prioritizing efforts led by people who are from the communities most affected, we have seen millions of dollars that was advertised as dedicated towards Gulf Coast residents either remain unspent, or shuttled to well-placed outsiders with at best a cursory knowledge of the realities faced by people here. Instead of reflecting local needs and priorities, many projects funded reflect outside perceptions of what our priorities should be. We have seen attempts to dictate to us what we should do, instead of a real desire to listen and build together.

We are at an historic moment. The disaster on the Gulf Coast, and especially in New Orleans, has highlighted issues of national and international relevance. Questions of race, class, gender, education, health care, food access, policing, housing, privatization, mental health and much more are on vivid display.

The South has been traditionally underfunded and exploited by institutions, including corporations, the labor movement, foundations, and the federal government. We have faced the legacy of centuries of institutional racism and oppression, with little outside support. And yet, against massive odds, grassroots movements in the south have organized and won inspiring victories with international relevance.

In New Orleans, despite personal loss and family tragedies, people are fighting for the future of the city they love. Many are working with little to no funding or support.

We are writing this open letter to you to tell you that it's not too late. The struggle is still ongoing.

Evacuees are organizing in trailer parks, health care providers are opening clinics, former public housing residents are fighting to keep their homes from being demolished, artists and media makers are documenting the struggle, educators and lawyers are joining with high school students to fight for better schools.

We ask you, as concerned friends and allies nationwide, as funders and organizations, to look critically at your practices. Has your organization raised money on New Orleans' behalf? Did that money go towards New Orleans-based projects, initiated and directed by those most affected? Have you listened directly to the needs of those in the Gulf and been responsive to them? Have you adjusted your practices and strategies to the organizing realities on the ground?

We ask you to seize this opportunity, and join and support the grassroots movements. If the people of New Orleans can succeed against incredible odds to save their city and their community, it is a victory for oppressed people everywhere. If the people of New Orleans lose, it is a loss for movements everywhere. Struggling together, we can win together.

Signed,

Jordan Flaherty
Cherice Harrison-Nelson, Director and Curator, Mardi Gras Indian Hall of Fame
Royce Osborn, writer/producer
Greta Gladney, 4th generation Lower 9th Ward resident
Corlita Mahr, Media Justice Advocate
Judy Watts, President/CEO, Agenda for Children
Robert "Kool Black" Horton, Critical Resistance
Jennifer Turner, Community Book Center
Mayaba Liebenthal, INCITE Women of Color Against Violence, Critical Resistance

Norris Henderson, Codirector Safe Streets/Strong Communities

Ursula Price, Outreach and Investigation Coordinator, Safe Streets/Strong Communities

Evelyn Lynn, Managing Director, Safe Streets/Strong Communities

Shana Griffin, INCITE! Women of Color Against Violence

Min. J. Kojo Livingston, Founder Liberation Zone/ Destiny One Ministries

Shana Sassoon, New Orleans Network Neighborhood Housing Services of New Orleans

Althea Francois, Safe Streets/Strong Communities

Malcolm Suber, People's Hurricane Relief Fund

Saket Soni, New Orleans Worker's Justice Project

Nick Slie, I-10, Witness Project, Co-Artistic Director Mondo Bizarro

Catherine Jones, Organizer and cofounder, Latino Health Outreach Project

Jennifer Whitney, coordinator, Latino Health Outreach Project

S. Mandisa Moore, INCITE! New Orleans

Aesha Rasheed, Project Manager, New Orleans Network

Dix deLaneuville, Educator

Rebecca Snedeker, Filmmaker

Catherine A. Galpin, RN, FACES and Children's Hospital

Grace Bauer, Families and Friends of Louisiana's Incarcerated Children

Xochitl Bervera, Families and Friends of Louisiana's Incarcerated Children

Bess Carrick, Producer/Director

John Clark, Professor of Philosophy, Loyola University

Diana Dunn, The People's Institute, European Dissent

Courtney Egan, Artist

Lou Furman, Turning Point Partners

Ariana Hall, Director, CubaNOLA Collective

Gwendolyn Midlo Hall, Historian, writer and lecturer, New Orleans and Mississippi Pine Belt

Susan Hamovitch, Filmmaker/Teacher, NYC/New Orleans

Russell Henderson, Lecturer, Dillard University and Organizer, Rebuilding Louisana Coalition

Ms. Deon Haywood, Events Coordinator, Women With A Vision Inc.

Rachel Herzing, Critical Resistance, Oakland

Rev. Doug Highfield, Universal Life Church, Cherokee, AL

Joyce Marie Jackson, Ph.D., Cultural Researcher, LSU Dept. of Geography & Anthropology, and Co-founder of Cultural Crossroads, Inc., Baton Rouge

Elizabeth K Jeffers, Teacher

Dana Kaplan, Juvenile Justice Project of Louisiana

Vi Landry, freelance journalist, New Orleans/New York

Bridget Lehane, European Dissent and The People's Institute for Survival and Beyond

Karen-kaia Livers, Alliance for Community Theaters, Inc.

Rachel E. Luft, Assistant Professor of Sociology, Department of Sociology, University of New Orleans

Damekia Morgan, Families and Friends of Louisiana 's Incarcerated Children

Ukali Mwendo, (Hazardous Materials Specialist, NOFD), President, Provisional Government - Republic of New Afrika / New Orleans LA (former resident of the Lafitte Housing Development)

Thea Patterson, Women's Health and Justice Initiative

J. Nash Porter, Documentary Photographer and Co-founder of Cultural Crossroads, Inc., Baton Rouge

Gloria Powers, Arts Project Manager

Bill Quigley, Loyola Professor of Law

Linda Santi, Neighborhood Housing Services of New Orleans

Tony Sferlazza, Director of Plenty International NOLA

Heidi Lee Sinclair, MD, MPH, Baton Rouge Children's Health Project

Justin Stein, Neighborhood Relations Coordinator and Community Mediator, Common Ground Health Clinic

Audrey Stewart, Loyola Law Clinic

Tracie L. Washington, Esq., Director, Louisiana Justice Institute

Scott Weinstein, Former codirector of the Common Ground Health Clinic

Melissa Wells, New Orleans,

Jerald L. White, Bottletree Productions

Morgan Williams, Student Hurricane Network, Co-founder

Gina Womack, Families and Friends of Louisiana 's Incarcerated Children

2007

BLUE NOTES

ADRIENNE LAMB, *AFTER KATRINA*

I've been trying to get back here all week to finish "key notes." The handwritten draft's been in plain sight, right there, on top of the closed laptop. I had the time, despite a busy week of work and a guest for New Year's. I had the time, but not the inclination. I wanted to write about music last week, but my plans were hijacked. Yet again, crime has elbowed its way into the headlines.

Last Thursday, at 5:30pm, the 25-year-old snare drummer for the Hot 8 Brass Band was shot in the back of the head, in his car, as he drove his family home. His wife and stepchildren were with him and he steered the vehicle another four blocks before he collapsed. He died about an hour later.

And the cause of this? The beef? It's wasn't with Dinerral Shavers. The 17 year-old murderer (streetname: "Head") had his sights on Dinerral's 15 year-old stepson, an "Uptowner" amongst the "Govs." He spotted the boy in the neighborhood and chased after the car, gun-a-blazing. Just a little turf war. "West Side Story" meets the Wild Wild West. A blend of flashy gunplay and tragic endings.

Although it's not really an ending. No one expects this to be the last one. Indeed, there have been at least 3-4 murders since then. We've rung in the new year with three, bringing the 2006 tally to 161—the lowest number in 30 years, but when adjusted to our current population, it's exceptionally high (*shame, shame, Warren Riley, for fudging the data like that*).

I'm just so bewildered. I don't see this getting better and I don't see anyone with any ideas. More patrols, sure, though we don't have the police force for that and to be honest, I doubt it would make much of a difference. The problems are deep and endemic and I don't hear anyone talking about it like that. This is a sign of how desperate people are becoming down here: the risks they're taking, the edge they're on. High anxiety and depression, general uncertainty, unsteady income, and a lack of basic security (often, a home) makes us all very touchy people. People are setting off over things they might've shrugged at a year and a half ago. After losing so much, people are looking for things to claim, for something to hold onto, for respect, and for protection. Some turn to God. Others get a gun.

New Orleans is full of hustlers these days. Grifters, drifters, workers and goldminers from all over the country. Yes, it's always attracted these sorts. The culture is set up for it, encourages it. Piecework is easy to get; jobs lead to jobs; and you can make a lot of money in a short span of time. Especially now. The construction boom will continue for years and we currently have 40,000 construction workers in and around the area. Local bars are doing great business and cottage industries have cropped up to service these hard-working men, often single or at least away from their families. Both prostitution and the drug trade are flourishing, adding more hustlers to the mix.

We're all hustlers to an extent, in that we all possess some ability to negotiate and barter our way through life. Some people are more fluent. And some people are amoral. The two together makes a con man, and the losses are often monetary. But amoral and incompetent is more dangerous and senseless, leading to losses like Dinerral Shavers.

He will be honored, I assume, with a Jazz funeral. No doubt it will be well attended. In addition to family and friends, there will be fans and curious onlookers. A Jazz funeral is a distinct part of the culture here, combining faith, grief, remembrance, music, parading, and partying into a joyful, soulful send-off for the dearly departed. The procession begins at the church, after the service, as a horse-drawn carriage carries the body to its final resting place at the cemetery. Behind, a brass band plays a dirge and mourners follow along. When the body is released and thus the soul as well, it is time to celebrate. The music turns raucous and the dancing is amazing. I've never seen feet move so fast.

A few years ago, I drifted along with the second line for Papa Joe's Jazz funeral. He had owned and operated a bar in Treme, a corner institution called "Joe's Cozy Corner," known alternatively and equally well for its open Sunday night jams and the school supplies and breakfasts passed onto the neighborhood children.

His funeral procession traveled from St. Augustine Church to his bar, where the casket rested for a few rounds before continuing on to the cemetery. Attendees and onlookers merged at this point. It's a street party now and everyone is dancing, tipping large at the bar, and smiling—because the rain that plagued us at the church has eased and the sun is shining.

It's going to be hard to turn from dirge to dance for Dinerral's funeral.

Music soon. Take this early closing as a moment of silence for each of the 161 people murdered last year in Orleans Parish.

MARCH FOR SURVIVAL SPEECH

BART EVERSON, *B.ROX*

I'm speaking at today's march for five minutes, a task for which I feel utterly inadequate. I've been trying to collect my thoughts. Here's what I'm planning to say:

Helen Hill was a close personal friend of mine, and her murder affected me deeply. Helen's funeral took place yesterday in South Carolina, and today we're marching in New Orleans. But make no mistake: We're not marching just for Helen Hill. We're marching for Dick Shavers. We're marching for Jealina Brown. We're marching for Steve Blair and Corey Hayes and Eddy Saint Fleur and Monier Gindy. We're marching for Don Morgan and Larry Glover and Mike Frey. We're marching for Preston Turner, a 15-year-old child who was gunned down in broad daylight on the street corner near my house in Mid-City, back in 2004. And does anybody remember that day in June of 2004 where nine people were killed by guns in just over 24 hours?

This is not a new problem. It's not a Katrina problem. Katrina just provided a momentary interruption. This wave of violent crime has been on the rise for years and it had left us feeling sad and scared and very, very angry. I'm still sad, but they tell me you learn to cope with that. I'm still scared but anyone who's lived in New Orleans for a while knows you learn to cope with that too. But the anger sticks around. And that's why we're here. Fear keeps you in your house, but anger drives you out into the streets.

But there's another feeling that doesn't get talked about as much and that's shame. I think we all feel a sense of shame—or we should—because this murderous, violent society is our society.

Fueling our anger is the perception that our leaders do not share our fear and our sense of shame. And so today I want to say shame on you, Mayor Nagin, Superintendent Riley, District Attorney Jordan. You've really let us down. You have failed us. The criminal justice system and the government are broken. And I want to communicate to you the level of outrage that my friends and neighbors are feeling, because we don't think you get it. Families that have lived in New Orleans for over 300 years are talking about leaving. People displaced by the flood are saying they are afraid to come back. That is the level of hopelessness and despair. They'd like you to step up and just do your jobs—but they don't think you can. They'd like you to step down and resign—but they're afraid you'd be replaced with equally incompetent people. Many of my neighbors believe that we need to see the federal government step in and literally take over New Orleans, or at least the criminal justice system. The feeling seems to be that even FEMA couldn't screw up any worse than we have. At first I thought that was a joke. But it seems more possible every day, and there's nothing funny about that.

Leaders, you need to do something that many of us think you can't do. You need to be honest. You need to admit that what you're doing isn't working, and plan a return to true community policing. I've got an article here from six years ago that praises New Orleans as a model for how to reduce violent crime. Between 1994 and 1999 the murder rate here went down 65%. The credit goes to something called community policing, decentralizing personnel into neighborhoods, with increased responsibilities and accountability for district commanders. Of course to do community policing we will need more police, and that means better pay, so that a cop can get assigned to just one or two zones and really get to know that neighborhood, and neighbors can know them. Let's get back to that.

But we also need to think of creative solutions outside traditional law enforcement strategies. We desperately need to experiment with some kind of decriminalization, to eliminate the black market for drugs. Some will say that's too radical, but we say there's nothing too radical when the stakes are this high.

Of course we want action, not rhetoric. Above all we want results. We must have a higher felony conviction rate. The national average is 57%. Our current rate is 7%. We must see a reduction in crime, and especially violent crime, and that is the bottom line. But how will we know whether or not this is being achieved? That is why we must have full, independently audited disclosure of crime statistics.

We know that law enforcement alone can't solve these problems. We need long-term solutions too. We must have better schools. We must have an economy beyond tourism. We must pay workers a living wage. We must fight racism and classism. It will take all of us. It will take community involvement. Well, look around. The community IS involved. And we will stay involved. To our political class: You're on notice. We will be watching.

REAL LEADERSHIP

ASHLEY MORRIS

Earlier this week, I asked what it would take to get you to leave New Orleans.

I read Mr. Cl10's reply: "I hate to say it, but if the Saints left, that would factor into my thinking," and I thought, wow, but it's just a sports team.

No, it isn't.

The more I thought about it, the more I thought that he was right.

The only leadership we've seen in this city in the past 2 years has come from Sean Payton and the Saints. The only leadership.

The only thing we've really had to give us any hope in the past year has been the New Orleans Saints.

Today, going to a barber shop in da East, going to Casamento's for lunch, at a daiquiri shop on Chef Menteur, going to da quatah, dropping off some donations at Common Ground and submitting my daughter 's application to pre-K (that's Kindergarten, not the other thing), I ran into people that were just brimming with excitement.

Why?

The Saints.

I've learned that despite the citizens' best efforts, the only optimism we have in this city is due to the Saints.

If they were to leave, it would be tragic, it would be painful, it might be fatal for the city of New Orleans.

There's no leadership here. When Nagin and Riley made the announcement of their toothless plan, council people Stacy Head and Shelley Midura were standing behind him.

Silent.

Thus, tacitly agreeing that this was a good idea.

Oliver Thomas made a good old preachy announcement, full of nice sound bites like "check your thug card at the city line."

Pathetic.

Where are the ideas, where are the plans? We're the Baghdad on the Mississippi, except they're rebuilding Baghdad.

Where's the leadership?

We desperately need it from our elected and appointed officials.

Can someone please explain to me why we need to crack down on littering? Is this the best use of police time? Will this lower the murder rate?

Can someone tell me how having hundreds of officers involved in checkpoints is going to catch murderers? How many of those murderers were driving cars? How many were out exactly between the hours of 2 and 6? Well, what do I know. It seems to me that nothing is being done to change things...only to shut us up.

That ain't gonna happen.

If things don't change, expect a bigger march next time.

But thank God we're getting leadership from people like Michael Lewis, aka Beerman.

"The city believes," Lewis says, with feeling, "because we believe."

We get it from Deuce McAllister.

We get it from Fred McAfee.

We get it from Sean Payton.

The last Saint game of the regular season was used to rest the regulars. Fred McAfee scored a touchdown, after being cut at the beginning of the year, then resigned, then cut, then resigned 2 days before the game.

This week, Fred McAfee was put on the injured reserve list.

The way the IR works in the NFL is that a trip to the IR list means you're done for the year. You still get paid, you're still part of the team.

Coach Payton did not cut FreddieMac, rather, he put him on the IR.

So Fred is still part of the team, and will still get a ring if we play in Miami.

We all know that FreddieMac isn't hurt. He may have played his last game, but he's still a Saint, he's still getting paid, and he'll still get a ring.

Coach Payton is a class act. Coach Payton is a leader.

Perhaps Mr. Nagin, Mr. Riley, and Mr. Jordan could learn something from Mr. Payton.

Perhaps not.

They haven't learned anything yet.

Does Nagin's bodyguard look like he's gonna go all Danziger on Bart at any second or what?

Maybe they got the message on Thursday. They learned that we didn't number a couple a hundred bloggers and friends of Helen and Dinerral. They learned there were thousands of us.

Thousands.

Oh, and the idea that people showed up because a white woman got shot is wrong. They were there because of everybody.

They were there because of Steve Blair, Monier Gindy, Corey Hayes, Eddy Saint Fleur, Don Morgan, Jealina Brown, Larry Glover and Cheryl Nitzky.

They were there because of Etienne Nachampassak and his mom.

They were there because they've had enough of this lack of leadership...

So for now, I'm going to enjoy the biggest event ever to happen in the Superdome. I'm going to be part of the loudest crowd of people ever assembled in an American Football arena. We will not just not allow them to hear the snap count, they won't be able to hear the plays in the huddle. We will deafen them, we will crush them, we will break them.

Then, we will celebrate. We will show that country to our north, as well as Canada, how to pass a good time.

Then we'll wait for Seattle to come down, and do it all again next week...

It's sad here, it's desperate. But tomorrow, between 7 and 10 pm, we will see the best examples of leadership New Orleans has to offer.

At this point, the only example.

The Saints are Coming. Thank God.

JANUARY 24, 2007

DEFINE TRAGEDY

GREG PETERS, *SUSPECT DEVICE*

Mayor Nagin and Police Chief Riley visited a class in a local elementary school yesterday and the teacher suggested that they participate in the day's vocabulary lesson. "Today's word is tragedy, " said the mayor.

"Can anyone give an example of a tragedy?" asked the police chief.

One child raised her hand. "If a drug dealer was trying to shoot another drug dealer and hit my sister instead," the child offered.

"No," said the police chief, "that would be an accident. Anyone else?"

"How about if everyone quit visiting the city, my daddy lost his job and couldn't provide for me?" another child ventured.

"No," said the mayor, "although that would be a great loss. One more answer from Johnny in the back."

"Well," said Johnny, "if the mayor and police chief were shoved off the viewing platform during a Mardi Gras parade and killed when a float ran them over, THAT would be a tragedy!"

"Now that's correct," agreed the mayor and police chief.

"And can you tell us why?"

"Because," said Johnny, "it sure as hell wouldn't be a great loss, and I doubt very seriously if it would be an accident."

JAN. 31, 2007

WHY COME?

CLIFTON HARRIS, *CLIFF'S CRIB*

Look, I know "Why Come" is improper English but it was "Why Come Wednesday" on 102.9 here in the city. Since LBJ and Kelder are the last local morning show since Q93 dissed C.J. Morgan and replaced him with Steve Harvey, I felt like using the term as a tribute. I don't want any of you English teachers sending emails trying to correct me. That includes my sister who has never used slang in her life.

Why did my coworker bring her own cake to celebrate her last day today?

Is it wrong for me to want my money back for the cake and gift we were going to surprise her ass with?

Why do I feel like the only black guy in New Orleans that doesn't own a pistol?

Why do sometimes I feel the need to go and get one sometimes?

I have been reading the Unified New Orleans Plan and I like it. I think it's pretty well done and covers everything. But why do I not have any confidence in leadership here getting it done?

Why are the policeman accused of a capitol offense going back to work? What if they are guilty? They don't let regular people that get accused of murder go back to work when they are arrested for capital murder. Warren Riley should have left them on leave until this thing was over.

Am I the only one that thinks it's cheesy that women have personal web pages with pictures of their children right next to a picture of themselves in a thong? That don't match.

What the hell are Tyra Banks and Serena Williams doing defending those thick bodies to the mainstream media when they think the Olsen Twins are sexy and they weighs 20lbs combined? You guys need to start hanging out in the hood again.

How long will it be before a disc jockey on a black radio stations snaps and admits he or she is tired of playing the same three songs all day long? They can't like that "Irreplaceable" that much.

Will my blackness make me vote for Barack Obama for president even though I am not sure he is going to do a good job?

CRAWFISH BOIL SALAD

CHEF CHRIS DEBARR

This is one of the 'Yat-iest dishes I've ever created, and I can't believe I was the person who made it happen. I like to say, "It's everything you love about a crawfish boil reconfigured into a salad." We warm up spicy LA crawfish tails, artichoke slices, and early in the season corn is blended with the first two elements. When corn is super fresh at the end of crawfish season, I'll change the corn to pickled corn to set off texture and temperatures to different degrees. Before, we've boiled potatoes in spicy crab boil, and we leave 'em to steep until needed. Typically we use little red "creamer" potatoes, but the other night we had to substitute Yukon Golds, which worked just fine. For the pick-up, we drop a cut crab boiled potato into our little duck fat fryer, you know, to warm it up real nice. We put a sturdy field green, like mâche or arugula, in the center of the plate. You could downscale and use romaine or even iceberg lettuce, but I especially like the buttery flavor of mâche. It surprised me how well the little green leaves of mâche stood up to the onslaught of warmed crawfish and vegetables, but it's quite sturdy. Then we sprinkle salt over the duck fat fried, crab boiled potatoes, and finish the plate with roasted garlic aioli. The aioli, as every French person knows, goes very well with the potatoes, and that merges our Louisiana heritage w/ the ancient French roots of our cuisine.

I like a crawfish boil's extras as much as the fiery crustaceans: the boiled potatoes and wheels of corn-on-the-cob. I especially love those Creole-Italian flourishes to a good boil with several entire heads of garlic picking up the heat of the boil and getting so soft. The first guys that put artichokes in a boil were my kind of cook. It's a serious 2-for-1 deal getting artichokes, which are as messy as crawfish to enjoy so bust out the reams of newspaper on the picnic table and let's get after it!!

I first made this dish up at Christian's, right around Jazzfest, April '05. We sold an ever-living ton of 'em. Right now at The Delachaise, we don't really deal in tons, but the salad is selling pretty dang good with nothing but clean plates coming back.

As far as I know, I was the first cook to call it a "Crawfish Boil" salad. Sure, there have been lots of crawfish salads made in and around Louisiana for a long time. But I swear I had never seen or heard of a dish that encapsulated all the elements of our favorite Bayou State pastime into a salad before I made it up. I woulda believed that some little seafood, neighborhood joint woulda had this on their menu, but I've been to several of these places around New Orleans and never saw it.

Of course, my better half gets all liquored up at Commander 's Palace in May '05, and starts blabbing about this very dish to my good friend, Danny Trace (then a sous chef at CP, now Exec. Chef at the very fine Café Adelaide). Next week, CP has their own version on the menu, and it's something Danny still does at Adelaide. That's fine w/ me because honestly there is no such thing as an original idea in cooking. I do not believe cooks should entertain the idea of legal trademarks on their recipes. It rubs me the wrong way. I have confidence in my abilities, and if somebody else likes what I do, can they steal it? What's to steal? It's all food, using techniques that are exchanged across generations, and ultimately it comes down to the nuances of flavor. I make my food according to my tastes, another chef pursues the very same ingredients with a very different outcome. I'm happy to make the contribution to Louisiana foodways, if the whole city starts to make "Crawfish Boil" Salads, I'll be proud as hell. Do I deserve to make a million dollars from it? I guess if I was Al Copeland I could, but being a suit ain't my strong suit.

So I give it two weeks before somebody who reads this post trademarks this dish. If it gets on an Applebee's menu, I'll want to learn to shoot a sawed-off; nonetheless, I'm excited to put this dish on The Delachaise menu tomorrow. I'm curious whether the sales will still be as hot as now once it's an official member of the menu. We'll see. Meanwhile, I reserve my rights to have as much fun as possible, and if I ever figure how to make money at it, I'll be sure to let you all know.

MARCH 5, 2007

CONGRESSIONAL TESTIMONY

MICHAEL HOMAN

I fly in to D.C. Tuesday night, and Wednesday at 9:30 AM I'll testify before the Senate Judiciary Committee.

As I understand it, the senate is once again looking into repealing theMcCarran-Ferguson Act which gave the insurance industry a federal antitrust status. The thinking at the time was that the states would regulate the industry. Some states do a good job of this, like California, and others, like my state of Louisiana, well, not so good.

What seems to have turned the tide against the insurance industry's powerful lobby is that some key Republican senators, led by Trent Lott, are now in favor of repealing the anti-trust status. I'm told they need 60 votes for this to move forward without the chance for a filibuster. I think that Trent Lott and myself will be the only ones at the hearing who had their homes severely damaged by Katrina. That means, at least in my megalomaniacal mind, that I'll be speaking on behalf of thousands of people who were screwed by the greed of the insurance industry, and millions more who will be screwed by their insurance companies after future disasters unless something drastic is done to change the industry.

Here is the testimony that I will be presenting:

Testimony of Dr. Michael M. Homan, Homeowner, New Orleans, LA
Before the Senate Judiciary Committee
March 7, 2007

...We were very happy living in New Orleans. We were employed with jobs that we loved, working to make New Orleans a better place, and at the same time we were building up equity in our beautiful 100-year-old home. However, our dreams were literally blown and washed away on August 29th of 2005, or to be more accurate, our dreams have died a slow death over the past 18 months because of Allstate Insurance. My wife, two children and I currently live in a FEMA trailer in the front yard of our collapsing home, as we continue to battle with Allstate over our insurance claim.

We insured everything we had with Allstate. This included homeowners, flood, and automobile insurance. They cashed every check we gave them. We slept well every night thinking that we were adequately insured with the self-designated "Good Hands" people.

But we weren't in good hands.

On August 29, 2005, Hurricane Katrina ravaged New Orleans and our beautiful home. I was inside my house during the storm and it was like being on a large boat rocking back and forth from the wind gusts. The winds of hurricane Katrina racked our two-story house so that now it leans severely. The house next door to ours is also racked in the same direction.

Then later that night, after the levees failed, flood waters covered the first three feet of our house and this water remained for more than 10 days, damaging the foundation and piers and causing our house to lean even more. Right now as I speak, our home is in danger of falling onto our neighbor's house. We have been told by several experts not to gut the house, as it would likely fall over, because the plaster and lathe is helping to support it.

We filed our claim for wind and flood with Allstate the day after Katrina. We expected things to move along quickly, but we were wrong. We called Allstate every day for several months, and wrote them frequently, but we rarely received answers. They played a shell game with us, providing us with 10 different agents through this ordeal, and it took nine months to get a wind adjustor to even visit our house.

The third flood adjuster we had was the first person representing Allstate to visit us at our house. He arrived in October of 2005. He noticed, as do all people, that our house was recently racked, and he ordered an engineer from Allstate to assess whether it was racked from wind or flood. We knew it was wind, but didn't care either way, just as long as we received the funds to fix our home. But then we waited and waited, and the engineers never showed up.

We were told that everything hinged on that report, and we were told to be patient. The Allstate representatives all told us that the engineers would say it was racked from the flooding and we would be able to fix our home that way.

Several months passed, and we were running out of savings. We had to pay for our rent on top of our mortgage. We were insured so that Allstate would pay us "Additional Living Expenses" should our house be destroyed or be in an unlivable state like ours was; but Allstate said they wouldn't pay "Additional Living Expenses" until they received the engineer's report. In addition, FEMA would not give us rental assistance because we had "Additional Living Expenses" coverage with our insurance company. We clearly would have been better off if we had had no insurance, and we had never purchased a home.

Because of our financial situation, my family was forced to move into our structurally unsound home and spend nine months living in the upstairs portion that wasn't flooded. We had to live there through a cold winter without heat.

Finally in February of 2006, after 6 months of phone calls and letters, two men from Haag Engineering arrived at our home. They spent 15 minutes in our house taking pictures, and then they left. We didn't hear anything until May 2006, when we received a letter from Allstate saying they were denying our claim for structural damage because of the Haag Engineer's report. I read the cover letter and report several times in disbelief, as we were left with a $150,000 mortgage for a property that before Katrina was worth $215,000, but now in its damaged state is worth about $30,000. We thought about declaring bankruptcy, but we didn't want to live with bad credit.

Fortunately for us, the Haag Engineer's report was full of mistakes. They called our house the Wilson house, and they included pictures in their report that weren't of our home. Their report actually claimed that the winds of Hurricane Katrina were not strong enough to rack a house, and at the end they even seemed to question whether or not our house flooded, even though the flood line is still visible nearly 3 feet above our floors and we have pictures of our house being under water.

My story is not unique. I've heard from dozens of other people in the same situation as us, where the insurance company hires an engineering firm to write the report they desire, and then they deny the claim. Thus the insurance company won't be liable since they relied on a so-called "expert" witness. Haag Engineering has a long history of doing this work for the insurance industry, as I later learned.

Now Allstate is doing all they can to leave the region and cancel their existing policies. We qualify for funds to raise our house three additional feet so that the floors are just above where the floodwaters rested. But to do that, our house would have to be five feet off the ground, and Allstate would cancel our policy because they now won't insure any house more than four feet off the ground. Personally I would love to never write a check again to Allstate. All I want is for my home to be repaired and to have good insurance that my family can depend on.

My wife and I have kept an extensive journal documenting every phone conversation, unreturned calls and letters, and interactions we have had with Allstate Insurance. We filed a complaint with the Louisiana Insurance Commissioner James Donelon, and we have filed suit against Allstate in federal court. All we want is for Allstate to fix our house so that it is in the condition it was before Katrina. That's what our insurance policy says and that is what Allstate must abide by.

We believe that our situation exemplifies the immoral and unethical way which Allstate and other insurance companies are acting towards the citizens of the Gulf Coast. We are fighting back and have the truth and extensive documentation on our side. I am confident that in the end through the court system justice will prevail. But Allstate is counting on many people to give up from fatigue and frustration and to not fight back.

In conclusion, I want you to know that there are many people like me, who were responsible, careful and civic-minded, and who had insurance. But when the worst disaster in this country's history struck and severely damaged our insured home, Allstate purposefully waited eight months, and then told us that our insurance was basically worthless because of a fraudulent report. They need to be held accountable and they need to be forced to live up to their end of the contract.

Allstate, like other insurance companies in the Gulf Coast, is at times acting unethically, immorally, unjustly, and their actions are in violation of the laws of this great country. Thank you for your time and attention, and I hope that this committee will take action with people like my family in mind. Thank you.

THE PIE MEN

DAN BAUM, *NEW ORLEANS JOURNAL*

Hubig's pies cost eighty-nine cents apiece, and can be found at almost every cash register in southeast Louisiana. New Orleanians adore these packaged, deep-fried pies, endlessly debating the merits of the lemon filling versus the apple, or whether the pies should be eaten microwaved or cold. Some locals even dress up as Hubig's pies for Mardi Gras.

During our first two months here, Margaret and I ignored the Hubig's pie. We wrote off its popularity as the irrationality of hometown allegiance; we never understood Atlantans' affection for the Varsity hot-dog stand, or Cincinnati's love of Skyline chili, either. We assumed that Hubig's pies were made in some vast, soulless factory from the cheapest imaginable ingredients. The building on Dauphine Street that we rode our bikes past every day, the one with a big neon sign, was, we figured, a distribution point, a downtown office, or a cute condo complex that retained the old insignia.

Gradually, it dawned on us that this was the actual factory, and we grew intrigued. Commerce has been largely banished from American residential areas, and industry almost completely. It's the rare American factory worker who can walk to work.

Otto Ramsey, one of the owners, gave us a tour of the cement-block bakery, which Simon Hubig opened in 1927. (The company is owned by the son and the nephew of the men who bought into the company in the nineteen-forties and fifties.) Hubig's cooks all its fillings, mostly from actual produce—evaporated apples, fresh-frozen strawberries and cherries, whole raw sweet potatoes in the fall—and buys locally as much as it can. (Much to Ramsey's regret, Hubig's makes do with canned peaches and pineapples.) The company now uses liquid corn sugar in addition to cane, but otherwise its recipes haven't changed. Hubig's dough is made with ninety-nine-per-cent animal fat. "We've got the trans fats down to 0.65 per cent," Ramsey said proudly.

A single, clankety machine turns out all the pies— between seventy-five and seventy-eight a minute. A wizened man hand-loaded balls of dough into a hopper. A long sheet emerged onto a conveyor underneath, and the machine folded these around dollops of filling and then cut and pressed them into pies. Lined up in echelons of ten, the pies entered a fryer for four minutes before passing under a curtain of icing.

After cooling on a towering multi-level carrousel, they slid down a ramp, and a worker fed them onto a belt.

"Time from fill to bag, two hours," Ramsey said. The wrappers are stamped with a date one week hence, at which point they are retrieved from stores and destroyed.

Ramsey has invested more than the family fortune in these high-calorie snacks. He started telling us about the cold- storage company that had warehoused the ingredients before Katrina, and had done so for generations; overwhelmed with sadness, he had to stop. "I'm sorry," he muttered, as he struggled to collect himself. When we asked later how his employees had gotten back to work after the storm, his voice caught again and tears ran down from under his glasses. "I don't know how they did it," he said quietly. "Some of them had lost everything. Yet when we needed them they were here."

Ramsey lightened the mood by giving us a Hubig's lemon pie from the carrousel; it was still warm. We told several locals about this, and their eyes grew wide with envy.

After the tour, Ramsey's son Andrew came down from the upstairs office to meet us. Andrew is a burly young man who attended the New Orleans Police Academy so he could volunteer as a reserve cop. (The night before, he said, he'd arrested a man wanted for beating his wife.) Seven Hubig's vans—nearly half the fleet—were lost in the flood, Andrew said. One van, which had arrived a week before Katrina and hadn't been paid for yet, ended up five miles away in St. Bernard Parish, overturned and caked in mud.

Hubig's has been buying vans from the same dealer for the past twenty-five years, Andrew explained. "I called him up when we were getting ready to reopen and had to say, 'Not only can't we pay you for the brand-new van you just delivered to us but we need two more and can't pay for those, either.'" He stopped, an odd smile frozen on his face, trying not to burst into tears. "And you know what he said?" He paused again, lip quivering. "He said, 'What color?'"

THE BALM OF SAWDUST

CHEF CHRIS DEBARR

We had a most excellent St. Joseph's Day! The heart of our day was found in St. Bernard Parish, where we celebrated the feast in a rebuilding home in Arabi. The strength and devotion of the people who gave the altar in their home, where we ate in an unfinished room covered in fresh drywall, where the hostess of the altar carried on despite the recent death of her husband of 47 years, where the beauty of the red gravy surpasses any tomato sauce to be found in any restaurant, the hospitality and blessings offered by such people to us, strangers allowed to walk into their world on the basis of love and devotion, is the richest gift I can ever receive. It just doesn't get any better than that. Especially nowadays when so much has been shattered in Louisiana and the Gulf Coast, it has been a constant source of strength how so many people from all walks of life have given their time and energy to come down here and fix stuff up, and how proud I am of the local people who've had to rebuild their lives despite incredible mountains of frustration. The simple act of sharing food and memories, which is the calling card of St. Joseph's Altars, is still profoundly moving to me, particularly the home altars. I know I'm a heathen when it comes down to what I call the hmmmana hmmmana—the church rituals, but a deeply felt prayer is an honest thing capable of changing the worlds, both interior private realms and hostile reality. I'm spiritual, not religious, and I'm probably a voyeuristic food tourist at some level when it comes to the altars, but I do feel a kinship with the intimacy of the cooking for the masses because that's my waking, working world. The purity and sense of purpose behind the altars recharges my batteries. The generosity and joy presented in the beautiful displays and copious quantity of food reminds me that truly good food is more spiritually nourishing than it is about calories and food costs. It's a fantastic holiday, easily my very favorite day of the year. I know that since finding out about St. Joseph's Altars that slowly I am turning out to be more grounded in my faith. It's not Catholicism, but I do have a catholic sense of spirituality—it doesn't matter to me if it's Shinto or Buddhism or evangelical Christians who have come down to New Orleans to help us rebuild—if it gives you peace in your heart and propels you to give a damn about your fellow beings, then that's alright with me. If your religion tells you to scheme against somebody who has a different viewpoint, then you're a hater and your religion is utter crap, the worst plague of stupidity on the planet.

We're all here to give it our very best, to do whatever we can to celebrate life, love, and joy. I really don't have time for anything else because if I'm not totally focused on doing my best, I won't be in place to truly "be there" when the good things in life come rolling along. I embrace St. Joseph because he was humble; he worked to protect his unprecedented blessings as we should all work to protect our unprecedented blessings.

We're here! We gotta roll HARD every day to keep it going in the right directions, ya heard me! It's taken me a lifetime of work to get to where I don't screw up something as simple as a crème brûlée, so I'll just keep on "sawing" so I can finally learn to do even better stuff. I guess that's some kinda religion, but whatever it is it does make a big difference in my life. Thanks, St. Joseph, for leading by example, for answering prayers, for teaching us how to make a better world.

EVER-AFTER-KATRINA

ELIZABETH MCCRACKEN, *GOURMET.COM*

Novelist Elizabeth McCracken was a writer-in-residence at the Newcomb Institute in 2007. She traveled with her husband, Edward Carey, and with Gourmet *correspondent Ann Patchett.*

APRIL 2, 2007

On our first full day in town, we went on a "devastation tour" with Crystal Kile, one of my hosts at the Newcomb. Even at a distance, safe again in Saratoga Springs, New York, I'm struggling for adjectives to describe what we saw. I can describe myself after the tour—awestruck, astonished, appalled—but the actual ruin is harder. No photograph can capture it, neither still nor moving: Everyone knows that ghosts don't show up on film...

We saw the yellow shotgun house in the Marigny where the filmmaker Helen Hill lived with her husband, Paul Gailiunas, and their son, Francis, where on January 9 she was shot and killed—only one of the 32 murders in New Orleans so far this year. We drove through neighborhoods where the only evidence of damage on the houses was the protoplasmic high-water mark at three or four or six feet high (which means that anything left in the houses below that line was ruined). This was a few weeks after Mardi Gras, and the trees on the main streets were all chandeliered with cheap beads. We drove through Gentilly, St. Bernard Parish, and into the Lower Ninth Ward, whose houses (some occupied but plenty abandoned) bore the same tattoo, a spray-painted international orange X with the date searched, the number of occupants, the number of bodies found.

Crystal doesn't think they're done finding bodies. The Lower Ninth is a murdered neighborhood, houses washed out by the failure of the levee on the Industrial Canal. Some have been gutted, and some seem to sit where the water picked them up and left them. Nearby Chalmette, hit nearly as hard, is salted with white FEMA trailers, but in the Lower Ninth we passed by block after block of houses whose occupants seemed gone, dead, or moved away for good—though there was one woman standing on the porch of what seemed like a miraculously renovated house, four chairs on the lawn and a moving van parked out front. I'm still thinking about her. What is her life going to be like?

And then we went back Uptown, where we were staying, and it was as though in the previous hours we had traveled not a city but a continent, from Eastern European slums to glittering clean Scandinavian cities. We needed groceries and finished the day at the vast, very busy Whole Foods on Magazine Street, where the perfect cut flowers and stacks of produce seemed awful and disorienting.

We were glad to have gone on the tour—there's a terrible adjective, glad, but it's all I've got—for a reason I hadn't expected: We ended up having a great time in New Orleans.

The magnolia trees were in bloom, for Pete's sake. We stayed in someone's converted carriage house near Magazine Street, where we wandered and ate fried oysters at Casamento's and bowls of gumbo at a place called **Ignatius**. We browsed **Octavia Books**, one of the nicest independent bookstores I've ever been in. Shopkeepers asked us where we were from and said, wistfully, that they needed more of us. We went with friends to a neighborhood joint called Cafe Atchafalaya, which was so good that when my friend Ann's plane was delayed a few days later, I called up to see whether they were still serving. This is one of the many minor ways that New Orleans has changed: It's harder to eat out late.

"What time is it?" the guy said.

"Not sure," I said. "Nine-thirty? If we showed up now, would you give us dinner?"

"Oh," he drawled, "I 'magine so." And he did, and it was great.

It's a funny thing, having fun in New Orleans these days, especially because New Orleanians will ask you, worriedly, whether you're having fun. You feel guilty for having a good time, all things considered, and then you assure yourself that it's your DUTY to have a good time, for New Orleans' sake. Though it seemed frivolous to get a pedicure, Ann and I did.

APRIL 3, 2007

It doesn't take much to get New Orleanians to talk about Katrina and ever-after-Katrina—what they lost, what they worry about, the people they know who lost everything, the people they know who lost nothing except their homeowners insurance and therefore are nearly guaranteed to lose everything sometime in the future, the incompetence of government at every level, the uncertainty of the crime and the unrepaired levees. Someone explained it to me: New Orleanians aren't suffering from post-traumatic stress disorder, they're suffering from current, ongoing traumatic stress disorder.

People who'd heard I was going to New Orleans had said, "I hear there are a lot of parts of the city that weren't affected by the flooding." That's what I'd thought, too. Once you're there you can see how impossible it is, the idea that any part of the city wasn't affected.

The city feels, above all, melancholy. I just kept thinking about all those empty houses—the little ones in the Lower Ninth, the larger ones in Lakeview, the colossal ones with for-sale signs uptown. Where did all those people go? It feels presumptuous to type this, but it's hard for even a visitor not to miss those people. The streets are full of longing.

But let me end with one of the best nights. My husband and I and my old friend Tom went to a bar called **Mimi's in the Marigny**. We went upstairs and ate tapas and listened to Gypsy jazz and watched a bunch of preposterously drunk young women dance. They danced every dance they'd ever learned, weird ballet turns from elementary school and out-of-sync hip-hop moves cribbed from videos and parodic tangos with each other that they clearly meant to be sexy but seemed, frankly, Three Stooges-flavored. An older man who looked a lot like one of my Jewish great-uncles sat down in a chair a little bit away from the rest of the band. He opened a small case, looked in, and closed it. The drunk girls kept almost accidentally sitting on his lap. Finally, he removed a cornet from the case and played in with the band—he wasn't a random audience member after all!—but the drunk girls didn't care, they just kept spinning within inches of the bell of his horn until he was moved into the bosom of the band for his own protection. The drunk girls began to bump and grind with one another, looking over their shoulders at the boys they'd come with.

Then, in one of those moments of barroom beauty, two relatively sober women in their late 30s or early 40s—an actual romantic couple—got up to dance in their smart black suits and showed us all what sexy was. Once or twice, a drunk girl unsteadily boogied into their orbit but got bucked away by pure authenticity. I'd been feeling both young and old all night, happy to be in a raucous bar, remembering the days when I might have been one of those drunk girls—not that I would have danced with that much menace, but I remember being intoxicated with lots of things, working very hard to look as though I didn't have a care in the world. That night in New Orleans, I was driving, and so I was hopped up only on very nice tapas. The triumph of the black-suited women did me a lot of good.

At the end of the night, my husband went up to the cornet player to shake his hand.

"Hey!" the cornet player said to another band member. "Didn't he look exactly like Mad Bottom?" Mad Bottom turned out to be another New Orleans cornet player. "I swear," said this cornet player to my delighted English husband, "you could be Mad Bottom's twin!" So there you go. New Orleans is still the place where you find out that you have a doppelganger and feel lucky—but somehow unsurprised to learn— that his name is Mad Bottom.

GOD WILLING AND THE MF-ING LEVEES DON'T BREAK

CHEF CHRIS DEBARR

We went to a favorite destination, Grand Isle, to celebrate the Big Daddy's 40th Birthday. Readers of PZB's blog already have a good series of snapshots describing the festivities, so take my word to vouch for all her commentary and photography—we passed a good time chilling on the Izzle! I wanted to focus on something briefly mentioned by PZB, the sudden swooping appearance of four Magnificent Frigate-birds on the back bay of Grand Isle on PZB's actual b-day, late in the day as the sun began to set. As you might have come to expect from me, there's always some back story to add layers of meaning and memory before I can go on telling the story. So....

We first saw these incredible birds with the fascinating name hovering over the main road in Port Fourchon. Magnificent Frigatebirds are sea birds capable of seemingly effortless soaring flight. They rarely spend any time over land, preferring the oceanic perspective on life. These large birds are seen from time to time in coastal settings, typically in small groups, always capable of dizzying heights. They have a unique sillhouette, with deep V wings, that makes them easily identifiable once you get used to seeing them. Hmmm, "get used to seeing" a Magnificent Frigatebird...well, for me, these birds remain a special treat to see, and I believe you'll see why catching sight of them remains a genuine thrill.

On this trip, we enjoyed so many great birding moments, from seeing fuzzy little babies on the back lanes on the island to finally seeing our first two Roseate Spoonbills down there post-K.

Still, the moment that seemed to make the world seem right involved the truly Magnificent Ones.

There were many awful moments surrounding Hurricane Katrina. It's a catalogue of memories I don't find it helpful to think about. Despite all of my personal problems relating to the hurricane, and ultimately because of the subsequent horrific levee failure that ruined my city, I feel that all my suffering was small potatoes compared to what others have endured. In some ways, I have even been supremely lucky: with my new job as chef at The Delachaise I have prospered creatively. We were lucky to get back into New Orleans early at an affordable rent. My love for PZB has grown deeper, and we have stuck through this stressful period of our lives with better appreciation of each other. Still, there's no doubt my world has been blasted to smithereens by the failed levees: we lost more than enough to drive us over the edge many times, and the sheer persistence it takes to deal with all the facets of our uprooted life has worked my last nerve so often. It's an ongoing struggle to defend my right to continue living in New Orleans, but it's a struggle that gives me serious, dig-down-deep unwavering commitment to doing the best I can with what I can handle. Have I felt a soul-searing rage most days, as I contemplate the never-ending carousel of pain and injustice that hinders the rebuilding of New Orleans? Absolutely yes. Am I proud to be here? 100%. I find that when the stakes are life and death, which we have dealt with throughout this entire ordeal, the mind insists on clarity, zooms ahead to defend my inalienable rights to live my particular life on my particular terms cooking and loving here in New Orleans. I have a richer soul now because being here matters. There has been a reward to all this pointless fucked-up suffering.

Would I wish that all this terrible ordeal never happened? Frankly, what I wish doesn't matter one tiny bit. Of course, I want my fellow citizens throughout the Gulf Coast to have not had to endure this, but I more importantly want to be in that number who will rise above this monstrous challenge.

Kick ass and take names, especially the names of those who give us false promises.

I bring that general screed of anguish up because my most telling, defining moment on the whole horrible hurricane mess involves a sighting of Magnificent Frigatebirds.

When we evacuated, late in the day the last day before that old world vanished, we were stuck on I-10 East, a little beyond the old Six Flags. The sun was well on the way toward setting. Suddenly, a wave of Magnificent Frigatebirds appeared overhead. It was a large flock of them, all sorts of ages, and the leaders of the flock were keeping their charges together in their forced migration from the horrible foreboding hurricane. As an omen, it couldn't get any worse. These strong birds could find no way around this huge storm, and they knew they couldn't survive it at sea. They were flying from the direction of the Gulf of Mexico toward the west—across Lake Pontchartrain and points beyond. Clearly they knew where I was stuck in traffic, New Orleans East, was way too dangerous for them to stay. I was only headed north about an hour—as the bird flies—and I was not going to be particularly safe, either—although we made it through unscathed through amazing good fortune that none of the 12 trees that broke on the property where we stayed hit the house.

Despite the omen of impending doom these birds signaled, it was amazing and beautiful to watch them. So many, so much magnificence. The obvious communication among the hierarchy to keep their flock rolling away from danger was another signal available to my mind. They were taking care of each other in a time of crisis. It was only our second time to see the frigatebirds, and it was a marvelous spectacle, beautiful and scary and so fragile in the face of certain destruction.

We've seen the frigatebirds all three times we'd been back down to Grand Isle since then, including a brief glimpse of them this trip soaring over Port Fourchon again. So let's freeze the moment we're examining: turning it like a precious specimen of memory in my hands so it can be properly saved for future strength, here on the leading edge of summer before we earnestly begin to worry about the onset of another hurricane season with shaky levees. It's Poppy's birthday, symbolic enough already. We've taken a little trek to the back bay of Grand Isle to see how a favorite bird-watching place has fared since the storm. There was a nice boardwalk there before crossing over a big ditch leading to the unpopulated (by humans anyway) marsh. The storms have buckled the boardwalk to splinters, but that's okay—we wander apiece and spy a new lifetime bird—a young Orchard oriole, still vividly yellow with his "soul patch" of black marking under his chin—only the males have this marking which makes it a done deal to ID him. He stands across a different little ditch perched on high grass, somewhat defiantly watching us watch him. We move on, see some other birds: red winged blackbirds also standing sentinel, a cagey green heron, and a hopping water thrush exploring the ditch for a last meal. The sun is setting, setting just like it was when we were stuck on I-10 just past Six Flags and the flock of frigatebirds ignited my fears... and my observation that we gotta care for each other when we face tough times, and don't we always face tough times?

Behind me is Barataria Bay, which used to be a patchwork of marsh, wetlands, and rough tides. Now Barataria Bay is a super highway of environmental destruction; basically the Gulf of Mexico doesn't stop until it hits the little town of Lafitte, only a 30-minute drive from New Orleans. The federal gov't has written off rebuilding the levees in neighboring Plaquemines Parish, the little thread of land accompanying the mighty Mississippi River as it empties into the Gulf, and the mouth of the river is not a long boat ride from Grand Isle. Entire communities have vanished into the saltwater maw of Barataria Bay. It's happened gradually these last 40 years, but where I stand in that moment, along a little island with 50 plus miles of water behind me, it is truly the Last Island of Louisiana.

At that moment, during a sun setting in more ways than I might want to acknowledge, four Magnificent Frigatebirds are headed over this little spit of land. They're flying low for Frigatebirds, even a near-sighted doofus like me can see them clearly. I'm entranced, I point at them. Poppy is 10 feet behind me, but I know she's enjoying seeing them just as much. Then the unexpected happens. The birds see us, alter their course, dropping a little lower and changing direction just enough to go directly over our heads. The moment slows down; the birds are checking us out, too. My spirit feels like saying, "Hey, long time no see. How you been making out since the storm? OK? That's good. Yeah, we're gettin' by, gettin' better. Hey nice to see you, too. Take care. Thanks for stopping by for this birthday celebration."

I hope they understood my sincere happiness. It's always nice to be recognized when you're in a place you truly love. We'll be back there again, God willing and the mf-ing levees don't break.

Take this memory of mine and use it to see why it matters, why people should want Louisiana to be saved. Maybe it can now be a memory for you to share, you reading these words in your place and deciding to pass it on—tell somebody today that Louisiana matters and convince them of that inalienable fact. If you can fit it in, use the word "magnificent" referring to all of us down here who just want to keep doing what we do best, because we mean to keep bringin' it every day. Worth remembering? I hope so....

MAY 31, 2007

TWO MYTHICAL CREATURES APPEAR ON THE SAME DAY

JASON BRAD BERRY, *AMERICAN ZOMBIE*

In an eerie, supernatural coincidence....two elusive creatures made public appearances on the same day. The Loch Ness Monster, aka. Nessie, was captured on videotape taking a swim in the murky waters of Loch Ness, Scotland.

Unbelievably, on the same day, the enigmatic and rarely spotted Mayor of New Orleans, C. Ray Nagin, popped up at the National D-Day Museum in the city's Central Business District.

While Nessie seemed to gain credibility with her appearance, C. Ray cast further doubt on his existence by reciting an extended diatribe of pure shiite while repeatedly professing, "It's not me...It's not me...It's not me."

Scotland now believes in the Loch Ness Monster....
New Orleans still doesn't believe in their mayor.

JUNE 17, 2007

DECLARATION OF SECESSION

NOLA FUGEES

II. A First Draft: THE UNANIMOUS DECLARATION
OF THE FUGEES OF NOLA

When in the Course of events, human and otherwise,
it becomes necessary for one people to break the
political chains which have bound them to another,
and to assume among the powers of the earth, the
separate and equal place to which the Laws of Nature
entitle them, a half-hearted respect to the opinions of
the rest of the world requires that they should declare
the causes which impel them to the separation. We
hold these truths to be as self-evident as the sun on
Ash Wednesday morning, that New Orleans was
not created equal, that it is endowed by Nature with
certain obvious cultural advantages, that among these
are a Laissez-Faire disposition, an Innate Ability to
create universally unrivaled Music and Cuisine, and
the Resilience of cockroaches.

—That to secure these advantages, Governments
are instituted among Men, Women, In-Betweens,
Crossovers, and the Gender Agnostic, deriving their
just powers from the consent of the governed.

—That whenever any Form of Government pimps
to these ends, it is the Right of the People to alter or

to abolish it, and to institute new Government, laying its foundation on such principles and organizing its powers in such form, as to them shall seem most likely to secure their Natural advantages. A Laissez-Faire disposition, indeed, will ensure that Governments long established will not be changed because it is too strenuous, too time-consuming, and for the most part, unimportant; and accordingly, all experience has shown, that people, especially New Orleanians, are more disposed to suffer, while evils are sufferable, than to right themselves by abolishing the conventions to which they are accustomed. But when a long, Mega-Krewe parade of abuses and encroachments, pursuing invariably the same Object evinces a design to reduce them under absolute Cultural Despotism, it is their right, it is their duty, to cast off such Government like a cheap whore or parasitic boyfriend, and to provide new Guards for themselves.

—Such has been the patient suffering of New Orleans; and such is now the necessity which constrains it to change its former System of Government. The history of America is a history of repeated injuries and usurpations, all having in direct Object the establishment of an absolute Tyranny over this city. To prove this, let a few Facts be submitted to a can't-care-less world.

She has plundered our natural resources and ravaged our coasts and wetlands. She has cut off our trade with many of our natural allies, such as Cuba and Venezuela, because they refuse to kowtow to Her every geopolitical whim. She has forced our state legislature into changing the legal age for purchasing and consuming alcohol from 18 to 21 by means of extortion, threatening to withhold millions in funds for infrastructure improvements and maintenance if Her demands were not met, thereby denying those old enough to fight in Her wars the liberty to buy and drink a beer. She has promoted the development of some artificial up-start, desert town in Nevada as Her place of whoring, gambling, and general debauchery when we already had plenty of brothels, gambling houses, and opportunities for debauchery here, authentically. She has endeavored to bring on the inhabitants of our frontiers, Her merciless and savage commercial chain and franchise establishments, which are characterized by their cheap products, long checkout lines, and poor customer service, and whose known rule of warfare is an undistinguished destruction of all mom-and-pop entities. She has allowed Her National Football League to hold its Superbowl in our backyard for the single purpose of flaunting in our faces the fact that our team has not played, and will probably never play, in such a game, engendering in us the sort of hopeless angst from which an adolescent male suffers when not allowed to mingle with, or even go anywhere near, his older sister's hot slumber party friends who lounge around in skivvies one room away. She has tried with all Her power and in all of Her Puritanical Self-Righteousness to convince us that an exposed female breast is somehow bad or dirty. She has for years dumped her trash, sewerage, toxic waste, and various other refuses into the Mississippi River with the full knowledge that it all would eventually pass through our city and, in many cases, enter our water supply. She has invaded us as part of a "civil" war with which we wanted to have nothing to do and, after we let Her "win," put us under the charge of that silverware-stealing asshole from New Hampshire, Benjamin "Spoons" Butler. She has continuously sent us Her Carpetbaggers and rarely accepted ours. She has irrevocably fucked up the Claiborne Avenue neutral ground, our historic promenade, parade grounds, meeting place, and locus of culture, by placing Her silly little Eisenhower Interstate System above it. She has won a World War largely with boats made in New Orleans and only given us in return a big propaganda vehicle, the National D-Day Museum, devoted mainly to revising Her early- and mid-20th century history and assisting present-day Americans in getting themselves off to fantasies of how great their empire is. She has covered up the vast, nefarious conspiracy of Her agencies, officials, and operatives who saw to the elimination Her 35th president and pinned it all instead on an easily-duped New Orleanian, who'd failed at nearly everything else he did in life. She has stolen Jazz from us and designated it as Her sole indigenous art form. She has mandated the rendering of Her national anthem in our territory though it has little if any Soul and no Bounce whatsoever. She has offered on the menus of Her restaurants ill-prepared, bland dishes and, after crowning such dishes with a half-inch of black pepper, called them "New Orleans Style." She has continuously misrepresented our dialect in films and made-for-TV movies, portraying our speech to sound like that of either twangy Texans or run-of-the-mill, Bible-Belt crackers. She has continuously misused our words "Cajun" and "Creole," mistaking them as interchangeable. She has continuously misused our word "lagniappe" and consistently mispronounced it "lag-nap," as if it were the sleep one needs after flying on a jet across numerous time zones. She has come to our city and worn Mardi Gras beads when it was not Carnival season and believed that wearing such beads gave Her complete license to act like a barbaric imbecile. She has visited our taverns and saloons and thought it okay to impatiently elbow Her way to the bar without ever, seriously or not, requesting pardon. She has bought our booze and thought it okay to continuously remark how inexpensive it is and yet not leave tips. She has danced with our brothers and sisters, groped them, and thought it okay to say that She was "going to the restroom" before leaving the establishment to find other brothers and sisters of ours to molest and desert. She has hurled on our floors and pissed on our streets and thought it okay to leave and return to whichever pristine place from which She came without ever cleaning up a god-damned thing. In almost every stage of these Oppressions, Transgressions, Impositions, and Nuisances We have Petitioned for Redress in the humblest terms of which we are capable: Our repeated Petitions have been answered only by repeated injury. A Prince whose character is thus marked by every act which may define a Pimp is unfit to be the ruler of a free people.

Nor have We been wanting in attentions to our American brethren. We have warned them of attempts by their Puritanical Representatives to extend Jurisdiction over us. We have reminded them of the circumstances of our settlement and of our way of life here. We have appealed to their instinctual leanings toward liberty, and we have conjured them by the ties of our common kindred to disavow these Oppressions, Transgressions, Impositions and Nuisances, which would inevitably fuck up our connections and correspondence. Those bastards have ignored us too. We must, therefore, acquiesce in the necessity, which denounces our Separation, and hold them, as we hold the rest of the fools on this planet, Enemies in War, in Peace Friends.

We, therefore, in General Congress, Assembled, appealing to the Supreme Judge of the world for the rectitude of our intentions, do, in the Name, and by the Authority of the relatively good People of New Orleans, as solemnly as we can, publish and declare, That New Orleans is, and of Right ought to be Free and Independent; that it is Absolved from all Allegiance to America, and that all political connection between it and that Bitch, is and ought to be totally dissolved; and that as a Free and Independent Nation, it has full Power to levy War, conclude Peace, contract Alliances, establish Commerce, determine its own Holidays, identify its own Heroes, and to do all other Acts and Things which it Damn Well Pleases. And for the support of this Declaration, with a quasi-firm reliance on the protection of divine Providence, whatever that is, we mutually pledge to each other our Lives, our Fortunes and lack thereof, and our somewhat-less-than-sacred Honor.

JUNE 25 2007

THE LONG AND WINDING ROAD WHERE?

CHEF CHRIS DEBARR

We are embarking on a lost cause, something I question if we even have a snowball's chance in July here in New Orleans of ever reaching. We are trying to finish The Road Home, the federal program administered by the State of Louisiana to give money, in the form of grants, back to homeowners who suffered definite financial losses from the destruction of their property in either Hurricane Katrina or Rita, or as what has devastated my city of New Orleans, recompense for the shameful failure of the levee system designed by the US Army Corps of Engineers that flooded the city and killed over 1,000 people.

Poppy and I had about 7 feet of water in our old house. It crumbled the foundation, ruined the entire

electrical outlets, killed everything in our garden—
even a bird of paradise plant that was over 50 years
old, and caused severe structural damage to the
building. Luckily (and I mean this sincerely) we also
had significant roof damages, which caused even more
structural damage to the house, but it also meant we
had the right to collect something on our homeowner's
insurance policy, too.

We finally were paid off on both insurance
policies: the flood policy was settled quickly, but the
homeowner's from Allstate lingered. At one point they
cancelled a check right from underneath us, which
caused us a delay in paying off our old mortgage. That
significant problem also delayed us from bidding on
another house we wanted, and that delay sent PZB
into a spiral of doom that we almost couldn't get past.
It was hairy, frightening, and utterly infuriating to the
point of rage. We finally received the last check from
Allstate on May 31, 2007.

We hired a public adjuster, who was expensive
but efficient. Public adjusters have the sole ability to
negotiate your settlement with your insurance co.
before you enter the battle in the courts with lawyers.
As a result, we are somewhat ahead of many Gulf Coast
citizens: we have been paid something, whereas many
people are still either waiting for further insurance
settlements or waiting for their day in court. If you live
somewhere normal, you might think that life is picking
up down here, and in certain ways, you'd be right to
think so. However, insurance companies have put the
region, particularly south Louisiana, in an economic
stranglehold. If people truly understood the scope of
what's happened to Louisiana, the rest of the nation
should be terrified of future national disasters.

People are systematically being kicked out of
insurance policies for every reason these companies can

dream up. Live near a national forest? Better get a new "fireproof" roof at your own cost of $20,000 plus, or we're dropping you. Oh, you need to upgrade your insurance policy because your house has gone up in value? That sounds like a new policy to us, never mind that you've been writing Allstate a check every month for 18 years, so when you do finally have to make a homeowner 's claim, we can drop you because, well, because we can always drop new policies if your state declares a local emergency, and it's so convenient we tricked, ahem, you selected a new affiliate in our company for that reasonable upgrade, ahem, new policy. Tough luck, that new policy that, incidentally, you paid us more to get.

If Americans truly understood the savage risks they will be subjected to if a national disaster occurs in their hometown, maybe they'd put down the remote control and give a crap about what's going down in New Orleans. You're next, buddy. The insurance companies are perfecting their scam now on us down here, and honestly, we're too dazed, worried, and beaten down to galvanize much of a protest, but I hope you're taking notes where you live because they're gonna own you, too. They already own your politicians. They already have it figured out so that you have no chance but to deal with them on their terms.

I really like how they can kick the living shit out of New Orleans, then use our Sugar Bowl in our Superdome to sponsor the biggest college football game the city can host. Allstate's Sugar Bowl. Yeah, you gotta bleed before we pay you, but we got so much money we can blow it on sponsoring millions of dollars to cover over the fact we're killing your city ... softly. So the Sugar Bowl is gonna host the college football National Championship this season, and Allstate will be the lead sponsor. It's disgusting.

DEMOLITION

KAREN GADBOIS, *SQUANDERED HERITAGE/THE LENS*

According to the latest FEMA list the following properties are going to be demolished. To see all the houses click here [*links to Flickr photo set*].

These houses are all cleaned out and very sturdy. This demolition would take out the entire block and leave a gaping hole in the Neighborhood.

SHOW US THE LISTS

KAREN GADBOIS, *SQUANDERED HERITAGE/THE LENS*

I spent Friday researching these houses on the previous post and asking how is it that they could be on a FEMA list for demolition. Logic tells you that the owner wants them demolished, that there must be some scheme or "plan."

Today, Sunday, I decided to drive to all the properties that this very large family owns, to try and see what the houses had to say. All in all, there were a remarkable number of unremarkable properties. They were all unoccupied but clean and for the most part secured.

I did notice one remarkable structure that DOES NOT belong to the Macaluso family.

After I took a look at that very clear example of blight, I worked my way back to Leonidas.

There in the hot sun was one, solitary man unloading plywood from his truck. I knew that he must be one of the owners but I was a little anxious about confronting him about the ominous status of his property. I took a deep breath and did just that. After a minute or two of dodging the issue I finally blurted out, "What are these houses doing on the FEMA Demo list?" To which he replied, "You tell me!"

We then had a nice conversation in which he told me that the City had never held his adjudication hearing. They have never notified him of their intent to demolish and that he has made repeated calls to City Hall and received *no call back*. He also told me that his Grandfather had built these houses and that they are sturdy and well-built. He is right about that.

What we are facing here is a new landslide of demolitions, those initiated by the City, and afterwards a potential landslide of shared remorse. I have discovered a number of unwanted demolitions and I have only begun to scratch the surface of the recent City Imminent Danger list and the FEMA list for overlap.

Many of the properties fall within the Housing Conservation District Review Committee.

The HCDRC process is flawed. The meetings are held in a back room at City Hall in the Safety and Permits Department without any public recording device for the record. In addition, little to no public notification is given. There is a set criteria for allowing demolition and that criteria is seldom mentioned or met. Even though it's a Housing Conservation Committee, the Chair of the Committee, Nelson Savior, refers to it as a "Demolition Committee." Robert's Rules of Order are as alien as an actual alien. The criteria for protocols for these meetings are outlined in the Municipal Code at Article 1: Sec. 26-1 through 10. You can search the municipal code online at Pick your State. It was down today but is usually very reliable.

The fabric of our City was horribly damaged by the storm, now the arrogance and indifference on the part of a *few* cocky city employees could cause yet another storm of unnecessary demolitions, leaving wide swaths of vacant lots, trash, and distrust and despair on the part of owners and nearby residents trying to rebuild.

This City needs to think about where we stand in this process regarding transparency and accountability for our citizens. The Executive Branch, ultimately, Mayor Nagin and City Hall, has been dodging the Citizens on these issues. It is time to stop, listen, and work with us, not against us by stonewalling us. Show us the Lists, explain to us how you create these lists. Show us the criteria for the assessments of these properties, NOTIFY the owners per the legal process required. Show us what you will do *for* Neighborhoods and show us meaningful leadership. We may not expect absolute solutions such as this demolition-or-nothing proposition. We need a closer relationship on the ground to find solutions that make real sense.

Right now, the failure of City Government is chasing us away, how much longer can we hold on?

HELEN HILL AND ME

PHIL DYESS-NUGENT, *THE HIGH HAT*

I met Helen late in the summer of 1992, after she moved to New Orleans to kill a year off from college. I was working for the New Orleans Film Festival, running interference for Dean Paschal, a doctor who had joined the board of directors on a lark, been horrified at how little thought and hard work was being put into the section devoted to undistributed and short films, and started spending the bulk of his free time (and going into his own pocket) to shore things up out of a sense that somebody ought to do it.

To have something to show, we used to put ads in the trades soliciting submissions; send us a videotape of your masterpiece, throw in fifteen bucks to cover the cost of sending it back plus general aggravation, and we will run it past our deluxe screening committee and include the keepers in our festival. The deluxe screening committee consisted of people I knew who'd watch anything on a Sunday afternoon if there was beer in the fridge. (One of the most prized members once asked me if I'd ever thought about putting more ads in more trades, upping the submission fee, not sending the tapes back, and pocketing the money. When you think about it, he said, you *could* do this and not bother to hold a festival. I'll confess that I did think about it.)

Helen was introduced to me at a screening by someone, who explained that she had a film she'd done at school that she'd like to submit, and that she would also be invaluable for any volunteer work I had that needed doing. Going on their body language and how comfortable they seemed together, I assumed that this person must have known Helen for most of her life and probably owed her life to her based on a timely organ donation. I later found out that they'd known each other for about an hour. That should have been my first clue.

At the time, Helen seemed to be with Elijah, another Harvard alum who had metallic blue hair and more quiet gravity than I thought Louisiana's atmosphere could support. They both did a hitch together on the screening committee; one night the more cruel and drunken among us were having a good time guffawing at some turgid nightmare that some regional Tarkovsky had been trusting enough to send, and I still remember the guilty shiver that went up my spine when Elijah gently suggested that watching it all the way to the end seemed "kind of sadistic." Much throat-clearing and sitting up straight and a muffled insistence from Dean and myself that, no, no, it's kind of ... interesting, just so that we wouldn't have to admit that we were sitting there at two in the morning letting this thing unspool just so that we could continue to make fun of it. We felt so guilty that we let it into the festival, so the filmmaker owes Elijah one.

It was a month or two before Helen's friend Paul showed up, taking his own year off before finishing his medical studies, waved goodbye to Elijah, and moved in with Helen. I'm not sure that I'd actually bought into the idea of soul mates before I saw the two of them together. The first time could be a little unsettling. It was as if God had made the first one and said, "Hey, let's re-use this mold just once before we break it. Make the second one a different gender, though. Who knows, maybe something'll happen." They didn't look alike, precisely, though they were both bantamweights, built to the same scale, as if to provide for maximum convenience when hugging. I knew them for a couple of months before they noticed that they were in love, and they were definitely the last people to notice it. That's the time I'd really love to live through again. Part of the fun of it was just seeing the expressions on people's faces when Helen and Paul would patiently explain, once again, that no, they were just friends. You could see people wondering if they should break the news to them or if that would amount to spoiling it.

The major difference I can think of between Helen and Paul is that I can visualize Paul not smiling. I know there were times when I saw Helen not smiling, but those times are hazy in the memory and seem kind of irrelevant, like the memory of having seen Fred Astaire not dancing. She was simply the best person I've ever known, and I knew Paul, and Dean, and my maternal grandmother, any of whom would normally amount to fierce competition in that particular sweepstakes. (They'd have made a heck of a superhero team, if I could picture my grandmother in spandex.)

They were politically active, socially concerned, creative and playful, and, in perhaps their most astounding feat of generosity and kindness, they were exceedingly tolerant of me. That was a lucky break for me, because I needed them in my life, badly, and I imagine that there were times when my lazy slacker's attitude and fondness for lapsing into despair must have been personally offensive to them at times. They never let on, though. I always knew how to talk myself out of things; that's part of what made me the perfect New Orleans smart bum. They were incapable of seeing some unhappiness on the TV news without snapping to attention and trying to find out what *they* could do about it.

At the New York memorial gathering for Helen, with more people than I could count crammed into a home that must have seemed pretty roomy under most circumstances, I heard one of Helen's friends, Jenny Davidson, say that "Helen *chose* to be good!" She said it in a hard-edged way that made it sound as if it were a challenge; that may just have been Jenny trying to hold herself together when she wanted to cry, but Helen's goodness *was* a challenge, and the observation that it was a choice is one that needs to be made. It was one that I was willfully blind to for a long time. I thought that Helen and Paul were wonderful people from the time that I first spoke with them, but I also thought that they, you know, didn't know the score, that they were missing something. That's how attached I was at the time to my own moodiness and how badly I wanted to believe that there was a higher wisdom in not trying. (Sometimes when we were out together, it must have looked as if Herman Melville's Bartleby had been adopted by Up with People.) I was actually able to persuade myself that people might be graduating from Harvard without knowing the score.

Of course Helen knew that cynicism would be easier and, sometimes, seem more emotionally and intellectually satisfying than keeping her chin up and hoping for the best while trying to make it a reality, one reversible little bit at a time. She even knew that, to some people, her goodness made her look silly, even ridiculous. Whoever killed her probably thinks that she died for being a chump. Helen didn't care. She wasn't dumb or innocent or unhip; she was simply too strong to let the world bend her into something different from the person she preferred to be. I suspect that there must have times when that was very hard for her, and that she suffered for being the person so many of us loved her for being. I'm not sure I really want to know. But if she was ever vain enough to imagine that there were hundreds of people who would have thought the world a much worse place if she'd been any different—well, I hope she was vain enough to think that, because it was the truth.

I got fired from a bookstore the day after St. Patrick's Day, in 2001. My boss had always been a moody freak, with something unreadable nagging at her under the surface. I had a new girlfriend at the time; we had met online and she had flown in to stay with me for a week, and my boss, knowing that, had volunteered to me that maybe I'd like to take a couple of days off to enjoy the visit. I said sure. The first day I came back to work— work I needed now, since I'd run through what money I had pretty fast showing my girlfriend the town, which is something my boss must have expected—I was at my desk for about an hour when my boss came down from her upstairs apartment, blearingly informed me that, "as we both know," things "just aren't working out between us" and so I was terminated, immediately. I'd been there for five years and she had "fired" me maybe three or four times before, always as abruptly and never for any stated reason more solid than that, but somehow it was clear that this time, she meant it to take.

I still don't know what the problem was supposed to be, but I went back upstairs to my apartment, told my girlfriend that I'd lost my job and my home, she mentioned that she wouldn't mind having a roommate, and six months later I was living in the Bronx. Now, five years later, I'm still here and my ex-girlfriend is living in Kosovo. If my ex-boss had not fired me, I'd almost certainly have never left New Orleans—which means, among other things, that I probably would have been squatting in the Superdome after Katrina hit. So, as crazy and unpleasant as my ex-boss was, I owe her one. Or two.

The person who was probably most upset about my leaving New Orleans was Helen. She and Paul spent a lot of time driving me around to prospective new apartments, checking out whatever options might be left to me in the city, long after I'd already made the move to New York in my head. Once that was clear, they spent a lot of time helping me move my stuff into storage and setting me up for the move. After returning to school in 1994, Helen and Paul had moved around a lot but they kept in constant contact and often talked about moving back to New Orleans for good, and it finally happened—in January of 2001, just a couple of months before I got my walking papers.

Helen was actually peeved that I was leaving just when we were neighbors again, and kept urging me to visit them in their new family home, but the last couple of times I saw them, the last time being just before Christmas in 2005, it was when they were in New York. The closest I came to ever visiting the place where they were planning to raise their son was when they e-mailed me some video they'd taken of what was left of the house after Katrina had trashed it. When I spoke to them in the immediate aftermath of Katrina, Paul kept saying that he wasn't sure they'd be moving back to the city, but apparently Helen was deeply committed to the idea. It makes perfect sense. They had a kid and needed to get on with rebuilding their lives together, but I suspect that all that mattered to Helen was that there would never be a time when the city needed them more. How could they spurn it at a time like this? People there needed a doctor who, like Paul, was willing to help people, with or without insurance, for little or no money, and Helen had to do whatever she could do to help. If nothing else, as a filmmaker and an artist she could record something of what was left of the city at a historic moment in its history. So Helen nudged Paul, and she organized a sort of letter-writing campaign, asking all their New Orleans friends to deluge Paul with postcards, begging him to come back.

"And thank God it was her that did that," a friend was telling me after the funeral. "Because can you imagine how Paul would feel now if she *hadn't* had to drag him back here kicking and screaming? Because you know that if he had any grounds at all for telling himself that this was in any way his fault, he'd jump at it; any of us would. But that was the place where she wanted to be."

Helen's murder set off shock waves throughout New Orleans, and not just among the people who knew her, though she knew plenty of people, all of who wanted to raise holy hell about it. Hers was the seventh murder in the city before the new year was a week old, and it came on the heels of a preposterous statement from the city fathers to the effect that the city's crime rate was way down. This was based on figures they had arrived at that failed to take into account the fact that the city's post-Katrina population was about half what it had been before the hurricane. Thousands of people took to the streets in a march to demand that something be done, despite warnings from the NOPD warning that they were ill-equipped to protect the marchers and that if the local Capones objected to being marched against and decided to open fire from the rooftops, the marchers would just have to fend for themselves. The police were publicly imploring people to come forward with information regarding violent criminals, explaining that one reason crime was out of control was that nobody wanted to be a witness; if they really wanted to encourage the giving of eyewitness information, publicly declaring their inability to protect people on public streets in broad daylight can hardly be called a genius move.

The fact that Helen was white, educated, definitely not involved in the drug trade, and gunned down in her own home all made it harder for people to ignore the crime or tell themselves that it had no bearing on their lives. But you had to know who Helen Hill was and what her life was about to perceive its full awfulness. In its maimed state, New Orleans could have used a platoon of Helen Hills; it was lucky to have one. The fact that it lost her in the way it did was one of those rare, too-perfect-in-the-wrong-way events that can make a devoted realist conclude that there is indeed a God, and He's a sick fuck.

New Orleans had always been a violent city, and about a month before Katrina, news stories began appearing pointing out that the crime rate, which had declined in the late 1990s after a major shake-up of the police department, was inching back up towards the levels it hit in 1994, when New Orleans was the homicide capitol of the United States. That was around the time that federal agents, running an undercover sting operation on corrupt cops, hired one policeman to hire other cops to keep an eye on a warehouse where the feds claimed to be storing a huge load of cocaine. The feds supplied their man with a cell phone that was recording his conversations, which is how they wound up with a tape of the master criminal literally directing a young crackhead of his acquaintance to commit a hit on a woman who had filed a brutality complaint against him. (The feds would later claim that they felt they'd only scratched the surface on corruption in the department but decided to shut the investigation down early after picking up word that the New Orleans cops were discussing whether to murder the "dealers" who were employing them and steal their coke.)

Even after things settled down after that, there would still be one ripe tabloid news horror show once a year or so; another bad cop would murder everyone she saw in a family-owned restaurant—including her police partner, who was moonlighting there as a security guard—just to rob the till, or some lunatic would abduct a woman as she was leaving her workplace and make her drive him across the state line to murder her. But at least those jokers always got caught, though that sometimes seemed to have less to do with anything the cops did than with the fact that the city had some of the stupidest criminals on record.

(One of my neighbors in an apartment building where I used to live once decided to stroll in through my back door and steal my TV set while I was at work. The next day, a friend who he was allowing to sleep on his floor, and who had helped him carry the set up the stairs to his room, ratted him out to the cops, who found him sitting there watching the TV when they knocked on his door. Then the guy who he'd been putting up asked my landlord if he could take over the lease.)

And every once in a great while a tourist would get hurt—which, given the importance of tourism to the city, was actually worse in New Orleans than killing a cop. But mostly, the real crime stayed in the projects and the Ninth Ward. It was black on black crime, predators casually making life worse for the poor and disenfranchised, and gangsters killing each other in drug warfare. It was an uneasy, unpleasant vibe at the back of the city's consciousness, but nothing that led the local news or made the middle class or the better-off look over their shoulder at dusk. But Katrina has emptied out the areas where the poor used to cluster, and the few people still there have less now than they had before. There's no one there to rob, so increasingly desperate people who never dreamed they'd have to find a way of supporting themselves that didn't involve taking something from someone who couldn't fight back are being forced to venture out into unfamiliar areas, where their actions get noticed.

New Orleans is a place that's gone through a lot of nicknames. When I was a kid, the most popular one was "the city that care forgot," which I misunderstood for years; I thought it meant that it was a city rampant with blatant disregard for the important things, which seemed a peculiar claim around which to build a promotional campaign. What was shocking about the Bush administration's response, or rather its initial lack of any response, to Katrina was the discovery that the president and the people around him *didn't* care, and this was a scary and horrifying thing to learn about the people who were supposed to be running the country.

There was plenty of evidence of that already, but people seemed willing to give them the benefit of the doubt on things like Iraq, maybe because that does seem complicated and remote. But when a major American city is washed away and the people there are left begging for help, and the president takes no notice of it for three days and then is convinced that he should at least interrupt his vacation long enough to pretend to be concerned for the TV cameras only after his nervous advisors convince him to watch a few minutes of TV news clips so he can have some small sense of what the rest of the country has been goggling at in horror for seventy-two hours, well, no amount of making me-sad faces on TV can really repair the damage, especially when your idea of showing that you're on top of the situation is to say that nobody knew that levees can fail.

This is not to let the local muck-a-mucks off the hook; there's no doubt that they, unlike the president, care about New Orleans and its people. But as major players in a city that for decades has reserved its highest offices for those who pander the most aggressively and whose corruption seems the most entertaining, it should come as no surprise that they don't know how to do anything about their concerns. The mayor, Ray Nagin, had no idea what to do in the face of Katrina and has now given ample evidence of having no idea what to do in its aftermath. In between they held an election, and maybe the worst thing one can realistically fault Nagin for is that he ran for a second term, and won. Based on what he's done since re-election, it seems likely that he wanted the second term mainly because he didn't want to be remembered as the guy who lost his job over Katrina. Instead, he'll be remembered as the guy who had a pretty good idea that he was in over his head and chose to stay there instead of making way for someone who might have had a clue.

In the wake of the march against violence, I've heard a few people say that maybe Helen's death will help inspire people to save the city. I'd like to believe there's something to that, but the truth is that I can't imagine where New Orleans goes from here, and I'm not sure that there really is a New Orleans anymore. When the story was fresh, a lot of promises got made— promises of money and other forms of assistance from the federal government—and they haven't been followed through on, and they won't be. People were genuinely upset about it in the fall of 2005, and now they've moved on; you can tear your hair out about that if it makes you feel better, but it seems a lot to ask that people stay upset about it forever, when it doesn't impact their lives directly and every day brings new things to get upset about.

People who do care about such things are getting used to the idea that the city's population is going to remain at about half of what it was. Some kind of rebuilding will occur, but the thing is that what made New Orleans what it uniquely was—a place where people low on money and ambition could live comfortably and happily, savoring a regional culture that was all its own, and coexisting with other people of different ethnic backgrounds and income status in an interlocking assortment of checkerboard neighborhoods—wasn't something that was planned and wasn't anything that anyone *would* have planned. It just evolved over the course of a century or more, and it's never going to come back, any more than all the hundreds of people who've been scattered across the country and who are now back to living paycheck to paycheck at their new jobs are going to come back. Either New Orleans will be resuscitated under the deliberate work of the new city planners, becoming something a little closer to Jim Bob Moffett's dreams, or it'll remain a broken wreck. Either way it won't be what it was. My city is gone.

TWO YEARS LATER...

ROBERT X. FOGARTY, *POST-KATRINA NEW ORLEANS*

Dear Family and Friends,

It's midnight in Katrina's garden of ups and downs. Yes, two years ago Michelle Mohammed, like so many other New Orleanians, watched her city drown.

She lived in Portland, Oregon for over a year after the storm. In October, 2005, she flew from the Northwest to see the home she'd owned for 11 years for the first time.

"There's nothing else you can do when you see that, I broke down and cried."

I work with Michelle. I went to the University of Oregon so we had a connection from the first day. Over time Michelle and I grew closer. She has a 23-year-old daughter and a 19-year-old son.

One day Michelle said to some coworkers, "Look ladies, that's Robert, that's my son!" We joked about it. A black woman with a white son. We joked about going to restaurants and telling the waiter.

And then something real happened. On my 24th birthday, Michelle showered me with gifts. Like only a parent gives kind of gifts. A new shirt, a tie, a pair of pants, and a bottle of cologne.

"I wanted my son to look sharp on his birthday," she says. Later that week, a friend and I spoke of the gesture. What started out as fun had become something much more for the both us.

"Robert, you know she's really adopted you. You're her son, she tells us that when you're not around."

Mohammed's house took eight feet of water. Her

husband still lives in Portland. The 21-year-veteran of the New Orleans Public Schools was without home or career because of Katrina.

She's shown me that people overcome obstacles and do it with grace.

"It's been a struggle."

It's close to 1 a.m. She walks me back to my car. "I love you," she says.

"I love you, too."

"You know I pray for you, Michael and Aryanna every night. It's the only way I can go to sleep," she says.

I drove home. And slept well.

Best,
Robert

AUGUST 11, 2007

CITY OF NEW ORLEANS IMMINENT DANGER LIST

LAUREEN LENTZ, *THE LENS NOLA*

Laureen Lentz: This week the mass media and local media have helped us illuminate this issue of unsolicited demolitions:

Dangerblond has posted the WSJ Front Page Story Here: *Wall Street Journal.*

It must be said that local freelance radio reporter, Eve Troeh, captured this story first, way back in March of this year for a piece I know many of my friends caught on NPR.

The Times-Picayune did a front-page feature, and we thank them for the thorough job they did on this complex issue.

One FUNDAMENTAL role of the press and journalism is to expose serious problems so that the general populace affected by an issue can take the proper action as well as force the checks and balances needed to keep our Government in line with the law. In this case, to police the expenditure of public money. The press has been an enormous help in doing this for our citizens in New Orleans confronted with accidental demolition. Our City employees have been left by our Mayor to fend for themselves. They are understaffed and many have gone beyond the call of duty to help the citizens who have contacted us and we thank them from the bottom of our hearts.

Right now, concrete information is what Citizens of New Orleans really need. It's not glamorous, but it is hard to come by from the City itself. We hope to make public information actually public! Thanks to the bloggers and geeks who have been assisting us to get files and posts up while we beat ourselves to death on the ground. We cannot rebuild successfully without teamwork and solidarity.

Editor B. at *b.rox.com* posted Karen's official stipple on his site and he has been a very big help getting these documents on a server so you can access them at your leisure wherever you are in the diaspora.

Ashley Morris, a local blogger, created a very sexy and useful online map of the scope of the Imminent Danger List. Thanks, Ashley.

The current Imminent Danger Demolition List from the City of New Orleans contains about 1700 properties. If you did not see the public notice in the newspaper, the list is linked here.

As we can see from these two homes, some houses may be on the list erroneously. We have included a link to instructions on how to get your house removed from the list.

IF you need urgent assistance, please leave a comment. We can email you back and get your personal information and give you a hand in working with the City Agency to get your home removed from this list.

The City of New Orleans Imminent Danger List

How to Appeal the Demolition of Your Home

On the City's Website:
http://www.cityofno.com/portals/portal2/resources/

UPDATE: This week we attended the City Council Meeting all day as part of our/Stacy Head and Cynthia Hedge-Morrell's effort to revise the original *Imminent Threat Ordinance* which was designed to allow the Army Corps to continue to work AFTER the emergency status of the City was lifted so they could demolish homes they had deemed Imminent Danger.

In March/April, the City of New Orleans created their own list of properties deemed Imminent Threat to Health/Safety/Danger, which we see is being sloppily managed but exploits the original provision of the ordinance.

The City is using this ordinance to circumvent the due process of notification. Thus, it is time to update the ordinance to address this new application. The staff at Squandered Heritage is advocating for this revision. Due process of notification of homeowners is necessary because many homes on the current

Imminent Threat lists created by the City do not meet the same criteria originally understood under the creation of the ordinance.

Furthermore, no one at the City level is currently assuming ownership of the job of helping homeowners on the list, which is about 1700 people. One person needs to manage this process so that homeowners get the proper attention regarding their disposition on the list. We are pressing for reinspection of the list so that the burden of providing costly and inconsistent documentation for getting a home removed from the list does not lie on the homeowner. It is obvious that this list was mashed together from the seclusion of someone's desk at City Hall in order to meet the FEMA deadline for City reimbursement of federal funds. Our photos show that reinspection of these properties is needed as they are using public funds to excise demolition privileges some two years after the event. The files/evaluations must be current/ accurate to justify the use of public funds.

In an effort to meet a deadline for the Feds, the actual status of the property was not updated. We urge you to request a copy of your property's file from the City to reveal this gap in the evaluations. Norris Butler can provide you with access to your file so that you may see how it was evaluated: 658-4300.

As of Aug. 7, 2007, Squandered Heritage Has *731 Photographs* Of Properties on The Imminent Danger List: (actually we have more but we are releasing them slowly).

BANH MI AND EAST BILOXI

FRANCIS LAM, *GOURMET.COM*

The story I want to tell you is hopelessly inadequate, because the story of East Biloxi cannot be contained in a sandwich shop. My inclination is to tell stories through food, but sometimes I have to be honest with myself and say that the food can't tell enough of the truth of the story.

Still, for a while, after Hurricane Katrina destroyed 8 out of every 10 homes in this Mississippi community of 12,000 people, to come here meant that you would most likely eat a banh mi from Le Bakery, a Vietnamese-run bakery and sandwich shop, the de facto commissary of the relief effort.

When I first arrived here, a full 6 months after the storm, Le Bakery was one of maybe four places you could get something to eat. The others were the hospital cafeteria, the gas station market, and, if you could find the run-down St. Andrews apartments and knock on #4 before three o'clock, Doña Lucy would pack you up a lunch, just like she did for the newly arrived Mexican day laborers working for contractors who had a nasty habit of stiffing their pay and firing them when they got hurt on the job.

Driving around, I saw scenes that could make me think that the storm happened just the day before, but the place was already looking way more normal than it had.

Thousands of volunteers worked goddamned hard to make it so, and some continue to this day. College kids on spring break, recent grads, tradespeople,

people with problems back home, people without somewhere to call "back home," kind people, secular people, religious people, caffeinated people, drunk people, angry people, beautiful people—they all came to work, some to gut houses and kill mold, some to talk to locals and make them feel like the world didn't forget them, some to settle in and find their calling. And, like I said, they all ate these sandwiches.

Through my month and a half in this neighborhood, these people filed into Le Bakery every day, the ovens cranking hard toasting bread and warming up lemongrass pork and sausages. They would come in their mold-proof Tyvek suits, or if they were big important foundation donors, in their three-piece suits.

Sue, the owner, greeted everyone standing in front of her cardboard sign: "Katrina made us a po' boy and a po' girl." Her cheer and good food served to give people a moment of normalcy in a place that seemed to lack it, a reminder that East Biloxi is not just a disaster zone, it was never just a disaster zone.

Once, while ordering my daily sandwich, I started talking to her, telling her about my work there. She smiled, as usual, and thanked me for coming down here. But then she said, "I wish you could have seen it here before the storm."

She meant nothing untoward by it, but suddenly I felt...I don't know, like I didn't belong. Like I was here to take advantage of this disaster, that this terrible thing that happened to other people was an opportunity for me to do something I could be proud of.

Just then a team of volunteers came in, dusty from work. They ordered their lunches. If the story stopped here, it might be perfect. There would be this little shop, cranking out these sandwiches, feeding the noble volunteers who would go back out there and fix this neighborhood right back up. And through the drama and the struggle and the glory of coming together in common cause, there would be this little bakery in the background, fueling it all. The story would be beautiful and wrapped up neatly, which would be nice because it was a great moment, an exciting time and place to be, and Le Bakery is great shop, run by great people, and it sells great sandwiches.

But this is what I mean by inadequacy. It would be nice for the story to end there, but it can't. Sue's comment reminded me that those dusty, sweaty lunchtime rushes can't tell the story of this place before the storm. They can't tell the story of where the place is now, after all the house gutting is done, when the neighborhood has to settle in to the long, bleak, unsexy work of permanent rebuilding. A few more places for food have re- or newly-opened since, and, two years on, the throngs of volunteers have diminished to a few bands here and there. The work is still going on, in some ways better—more professionally, more far-reaching than ever— but lunchtime at Le Bakery can be pretty slow now, a couple of orders here and there, some people coming by just to pick up some loaves of bread to make their own sandwiches.

WILLIE TEE IS DYING

STEVE ALLEN

*New Orleans funk and soul legend Wilson "Willie Tee"
Turbinton, pianist and producer of the Wild Magnolias
1973 debut recording, died on September 11, 2007. Many of
his early recordings were sampled by artists from across the
musical spectrum, from Lil' Wayne to Alex Chilton. New
Orleans saxophonist Steve Allen posted the following as a
comment to Turbinton's obituary written by Keith Spera for*
The Times-Picayune.

Last night around half time of the Saints season
opener I left the house and went to Touro Infirmary
on Prytania Street. When I got there the guards at the
desk told me visiting hours were over at 8:30. It was
about 9:30. I persisted and they wanted to know if the
patient was near death and if the hospital had called
me. Yes, near death in the oncology ward, that's cancer,
and no, no call. I told them I was his sax player, that he
was Willie Tee, Teasin' You, Wild Magnolia producer,
many other "comebacks" and reinventions, a name
that it would have been impossible for even a jaded
New Orleans security guard not to have known. The
officer went in the back and came out and asked what
Willie Tee's real name is, which is Wilson Turbinton.
He let me go up to the room.

This month's Offbeat magazine has an obituary for
Earl Turbinton, Willie's brother, in it. Since Katrina,
Earl had been in a long-term medical facility, first in
Memphis and lately in Baton Rouge, because he'd
had a couple of strokes and lung cancer, apparently,

according to the obituary. Willie and he had an album several years back called "Brothers for Life," and now it looks like they will become brothers in death as well. Earl passed away and his service was four short weekends ago.

Willie visited his brother daily in Baton Rouge. They were very close, in every way, bearing a very pronounced resemblance to each other, working together on-and-off for their entire careers, even starting a music academy for young people years back, which evolved into NOCCA, The New Orleans Center For Creative Arts High School. It was something Willie never mentioned to me, having happened many years before we met.

When we were together there was only time to talk about music, the music we were working on in the right-now frame of reference. Improvisational ensemble music, as free and spontaneous as possible at all times, anything goes, and as little structure as possible. That was what playing with Willie Tee was for me. Just follow him, anywhere, 20-minute medleys, change keys, change feels, pick up different horns, constantly searching for new keyboard sounds, writing new grooves on the bandstand...the most challenging and fun musical experience I've had maybe ever. And we communicated so instantly and the flow just laid itself out in front of us so easily, it was like driving a Cadillac through the sky.

And now that ride is over? Willie looked small in the hospital bed. He was knocked out on pain medication, heavy stuff that Hospice can supply, which is the point at which a patient gets no treatment for their disease, just to be made comfortable until the end. I know about this intimately. Juanetz and Jack, my mom and dad, both died within 3 months of each other. They were old and very sick, and ready to leave this world. Willie Tee, however, is 63. It would seem he has plenty more to give. He was invited to be an Artist in Residence at Princeton for a year after Katrina. Handy, since his home near City Park had been destroyed by the storm. Princeton did well by its students, having the street genius around to exude musical knowledge in its purest most direct form, no academic filter composed of concepts, theory, reflection and words words words, just the pure spark of creativity. Let the academics sort it out and theorize it in the past tense, if that's all they can do. Creation happens in the eternal now, and that's the only place it happens. You see the difference, yes?

Willie said, Pray to the Lord for me. On this subject I must watch my step not to hurt the feelings of my fellow humans who need every bit of hope and comfort they can get. There is a God, and God is all-powerful, and miracles do happen, things that can't be explained in conventional physics.

Sometimes the Big Guy seems interested in what we're going through, other times not so much. And I know from our perspective, living in this world, there could very well be a great deal we can't and couldn't understand, even if we could see what's on the other side. So it's probably best not to come off cynically on this subject. Yet I find it hard to keep some thoughts to myself. Will it change anything, no. Am I registering a complaint, absolutely. Willie Tee just deserves some free and easy time right now. He should be sitting at the piano somewhere singing, not lying in the gown breathing through plastic tubing. That should be later, much later. Why now? Why is the spark being extinguished so suddenly and abruptly? I don't mean to challenge your faith, but can you explain that?

I went by the Hospital again yesterday afternoon and there was a handwritten sign on Willie Tee's room that said NO VISITORS. I had just seen Paul, the owner of Sweet Lorraine's, where we had played so many great sets, and he hadn't gotten in either, but he had spoken to Marilyn, Mrs. Turbinton, and she said they were making arrangements to move Willie to a Hospice off of St. Charles somewhere nearby. Marilyn didn't even come out of the room to talk to me. The nurse said she was upset.

And today, September 11th, while I was setting up my studio at my house, the radio announcer on WWOZ said they wished to extend their love and sympathy to the Turbinton family, and that Willie Tee had gone to join the Ancestors.

I'm happy for him that he didn't have to just lay there in the hospital bed and suffer. He didn't say much to me the night I visited him there. Just "I feel terrible, I'm dyin', pray to the Lord for me, and I've been thinkin'." I told him when you get there, tell 'em we're not too happy about this. Well, he's there now. I have to say, I feel like there is a "there" there. It is and always will be the BIG MYSTERY to us on this side, but I feel feelings and hear voices that come from there, my parents in dreams, mainly, and now Willie Tee, too, I'm sure will visit me. I'll sure be glad to see him and I hope he sends me some inspired sounds from time to time. In fact, I know he will.

ACKNOWLEDGMENTS

This project was my attempt at an honest recollection of the post-Katrina experience. Many of the memories shared here felt truer and more trustworthy than even my own. I am deeply grateful to everyone who agreed to let us print their personal memories in these pages, in spite of the fact that the process of resurfacing them was sometimes a painful one.

Thanks first and foremost to GK Darby and Abram Himelstein at UNO Press for believing that this anthology was a good idea in the first place, and for being so patient while I tried to finish it.

Several of the bloggers included here contributed ideas and inspiration well beyond their individual excerpts, in particular Rob Walker, Mark Moseley, Bart Everson, Allen Boudreaux, David Olivier, Karen Gadbois and Maitri Erwin, all of whose guidance greatly informed this book.

There's a long list of people who were willing to dig back through defunct websites and email archives, reach out to long-lost contacts, or otherwise go out of their way to steer me toward promising leads. I am especially grateful to Lolis Elie, Sam Jaspar, Larry Smith, Eileen Loh, Anne Gisleson, Jarret Lofstead, Bebe Ryan, Jordan Blanton, Sarah Griffin Thibodeaux,

Ed Skoog, and Katy Reckdahl for providing invaluable help with the early research.

There are dozens of others who pointed me in the direction of bloggers I'd either forgotten about or hadn't been previously aware of—Rebecca Snedeker, Alli DeJong, Ian McNulty, Todd Price, Pableaux Johnson, Sue and Mario Ceravolo, Sara Roahen, Valerie McGinley, Joel Dinerstein, Ann Yoachim among them—and this collection is much richer for it.

Thanks to all my colleagues at the University of Mississippi's Meek School of Journalism for providing professional support and personal encouragement, especially Dean Will Norton, Assistant Dean Charlie Mitchell, Alysia Steele, Vanessa Gregory and Deb Wenger, who is the only person I know who gives good advice 110 percent of the time.

There were plenty of times while researching this anthology where I very nearly got stuck in the sedimentary layer of late 2005. Christine Schomer, Theresa Starkey, Dawn MacKeen, Chris Schulz, Carol Mockbee, Sara Camp Arnold, Sara Wood, Nancy and Sean Callahan, and the entire Evans clan—your expressions of interest and encouragement always came at exactly the right time.

For years now, my husband Corbin Evans has lovingly fed me great advice and even better food, and I've often pretended to ignore the former while indulging in too much of the latter. The truth is that I've benefited from both in equal measure.

I am incredibly grateful for my parents, Don and Carmel Joyce, who continue to demonstrate every day the power in keeping a collective memory.

CONTRIBUTORS

STEVE ALLEN is a New Orleans saxophone player and songwriter. He has scored countless compositions for film and television and performed with Leon Redbone, Iopsy Chapman, Leigh "Little Queenie" Harris, Rita Coolidge, Allen Toussaint, Willie Tee Turbinton and scores of others. http://www.steveallenthesaxplayer.com.

BLAKE BAILEY graduated from Tulane and taught gifted children at a magnet school for seven years before moving away from New Orleans. In the summer of 2005, he and his family moved back to New Orleans and lived there for just over two months before fleeing Hurricane Katrina, an experience he wrote about in a series of articles for *Slate*. Bailey is the author of, among other titles, *A Tragic Honesty: The Life and Work of Richard Yates*, which was a finalist for the 2003 National Book Critics Circle Award; the biography, *Cheever: A Life*, which won the 2009 National Book Critics Circle Award; and a memoir, *The Splendid Things We Planned*, which was published by W. W. Norton in March 2014.

DAN BAUM is the author of *Nine Lives: Death and Life in New Orleans*. While living in New Orleans to research *Nine Lives*, Dan wrote a daily online column, the *New Orleans Journal*, for *The New Yorker*. He has been a staff writer for *The New Yorker*, as well as a reporter for *The Wall Street Journal*, *The Asian Wall Street Journal*, and *The Atlanta Journal-Constitution*. His most recent book is *Gun Guys: A Road Trip*. You can find him at http://www.danbaum.com.

JASON BRAD BERRY has been providing original, independent, investigative reporting since 2006 on corruption issues that affect New Orleans and the state of Louisiana at his *American Zombie* blog (http://www.theamericanzombie.com). Covering everyone from government officials to the power players who pull the strings behind the scenes, AZ has fearlessly dug up the story after story, shedding light on the corruption, dirty politics, and backroom deals among power players who have enriched themselves at the expense of the public.

ANDREA BOLL lives in New Orleans where she teaches literature and writing to young people. You can read more of her Katrina adventures in *Year Zero: A Year of Reporting from Post-Katrina New Orleans* and *The Soul is Bulletproof: Reports from Reconstruction New Orleans.* Her novel, *The Parade Goes On Without You*, was published by NOLAFugees Press in 2009.

ALLEN BOUDREAUX is a native New Orleanian, raised in Lakeview and Metairie and currently residing in Algiers Point with his wife and one-year-old daughter. He's only lived elsewhere twice—four years of college in Memphis and a month in Florida after Katrina. A lawyer by training, Allen works in marketing and graphic design and moonlights as roller derby referee. It has been a long time since he's written a blog post, but he'll get back to it, someday...

JOHN BOUTTE is a beloved jazz vocalist who grew up in New Orleans' Seventh Ward, where most of his Creole family still lives and sings.

SCOTT BROOM is a multimedia and television journalist at WUSA9, the CBS affiliate in Washington D.C. He's been a broadcaster since 1981 and was the subject of an exhibit at the Newseum in Washington D.C. highlighting dramatic technology changes in the news business. In a career thats included stops everywhere from Duluth, MN to Baltimore, Broom has covered everything from epic natural disasters, to politics, the environment, corruption, and crime of all stripes.

MICHAEL BROWN served as the first director of the Federal Emergency Management Agency (FEMA). He was appointed in January 2003 by President George W. Bush and resigned following his controversial handling of Hurricane Katrina in September 2005. Brown currently hosts a radio talk show on 630 KHOW in Denver, Colorado.

ANDY CARVIN recently joined First Look Media as one of its senior editors. He was formerly senior strategist at NPR's social media desk, where he pioneered the use of Twitter and Facebook for news reporting—most notably during the Arab Spring, during which he used social media to become a virtually embedded reporter among revolutionary groups. Follow him on Twitter at @acarvin.

TARA JILL CICCARONE lives, writes, and sometimes waits tables in New Orleans. She is the captain of Guise of Fawkes, a Mardi Gras krewe that honors whistle-blowers and political prisoners. Her collection of Post-Katrina short stories can be found at postcardsofthehanging.wordpress. com and in piles on her bedroom floor.

DEBORAH "BIG RED" COTTON: is an author, blogger, publisher and videographer who has been chronicling the city's cultural and political scene since 2005. She is the author of *Notes From New Orleans: Spicy, colorful tales of Politics, People, Food, Drink, Men, Music and Life in Post-breaches New Orleans*. She has written columns for national and local publications such as AOL, B.E.T., EURweb, Nola. com and the *Gambit*. Her Big Red Cotton Youtube channel boasts 1.6 million plus views, hosting the largest catalogue of second lines and brass bands videos on the internet. Follow her at @DebCotton.

JOSHUA COUSIN, AKA "Book," is a New Orleans native & blogger with a passion for Technology & The Arts. Thanks in part to his *Note from the Book* blog, he and his work have been featured in films & books & magazines. In the year following Katrina, he assisted with hurricane relief, managing a technology center for a "Tech For All - Houston" community development project. He currently resides in the Seventh Ward with his family and their favorite dog, Cheddar.

CLAYTON CUBITT is an award-winning photographer, filmmaker and writer whose art and music videos have been viewed more than 50 million times. Raised in New Orleans he is now based in NYC.

MICHAEL "T MAYHEART" DARDAR was born in the Houma Indian settlement below Golden Meadow, Louisiana. He served for sixteen years on the United Houma Nation Tribal Council. Currently he works with Bayou Healers, a community-based group advocating for the needs of coastal Indigenous communities in south Louisiana. His latest book is *Istrouma; A Houma Manifesto*.

CHEF CHRIS DEBARR cooks soul food with a roaming circus of his own imagination. He is currently traipsing about between Portland, Oregon and the Spice Islands, but New Orleans will always be his home.

DR. SCOTT E. DELACROIX, JR. is a native of New Orleans and currently lives and works in the metropolitan area. He is the Director of Urologic Oncology at Louisiana State University School of Medicine.

PHIL DYESS-NUGENT was born in Louisiana and lived in New Orleans for many years. He has written for *Nerve, HiLoBrow, The A.V. Club*, and the *New Orleans Times-Picayune*, and was a regular contributor to the defunct music magazine *Global Rhythm*. He now lives in Texas.

MAITRI ERWIN is a geoscientist, writer and maker. Maitri is advisor to Project Gutenberg, the oldest publisher of free electronic books, and publisher of *Back Of Town*, a blog-community dedicated to the New Orleans-based HBO television series Treme. Between August 2005 and March 2009, Maitri's *VatulBlog* actively chronicled the aftermath of Hurricane Katrina, The Federal Flood and the recovery of the city of New Orleans, and has been used as an example of disaster communication during a time of rapidly-evolving media. Maitri's blog posts from the first post-Katrina year have also been published in *A Howling In The Wires: An Anthology of Writing from Post-Diluvian New Orleans*. She currently lives in Houston with her husband Derick and an attic full of costumes and beads. Visit vatul.net.

BART EVERSON is a media artist and community activist who lives in New Orleans. He earned the soubriquet "Editor B" as coproducer of the long-running underground television series, *ROX*. His first fictional work has just been published the spring 2015 issue of *Red Rock Review*, and he will have an essay in the forthcoming anthology, Fin*ding the Masculine in Goddess' Spiral* (Immanion Press). More at BartEverson.com.

JORDAN FLAHERTY is an award-winning journalist, author, and TV news producer whose work has appeared in *The New York Times, The Washington Post*, and *The Village Voice*, among many other publications. He has appeared as an actor in HBO's television series *Treme*, playing himself in a storyline about resistance to the demolition of New

Orleans public housing. Jordan was the first journalist to bring the case of the Jena Six to a national audience, and he has so far been the only journalist identified as a subject of the New York City Police Department's spying programs. He is the author of the book *Floodlines: Community and Resistance From Katrina to the Jena Six*.

ROBERT X. FOGARTY is the founder of *Dear World* (dearworld.me), which began when he asked residents of New Orleans to write a "love note to their City." *Dear World*'s work now includes portraits, videos and stories of survivors of the Boston marathon bombing and Syrian refugees as well as recognizable people like Nobel Peace Prize winner Muhammad Yunus, Susan Sarandon and Drew Brees. He has been featured on the *Today Show*, CNN, PBS and in *The Washington Post*, *The New York Times* and *Inc. magazine*. He's also the cofounder of Evacuteer.org and a graduate of the University of Oregon's School of Journalism and Communication.

MARK FOLSE is coeditor of *The Katrina Anthology: A Howling in the Wires*, by Gallatin & Toulouse Press, and the author of *The Wet Bank Guide* blog.

SARA FORD is a software engineer at Microsoft. During her 10 years at Microsoft, she's worked on a variety of products, including Office for iPad, Outlook.com, and Visual Studio. Sara is a Distinguished Fellow in the Department of Engineering at Mississippi State where she double-majored in Computer Science and Mathematics. She's finishing a Masters degree in Human Factors at San Jose State, where she coded a Kinect application for the Kinesiology department to study motor learning. When not in front of a computer, Sara enjoys cycling, critiquing the cuisine at "New Orleans" restaurants on the West Coast, and overcoming the challenges of becoming a stand-up comic. Her lifelong dream is to become a 97-year old weight lifter so she can be featured on the local news.

ARIANA FRENCH is the current Director of Digital Technology at the American Museum of Natural History in New York. She lived in New Orleans from 2001-2007 and misses it dearly. Ariana holds a Master of Arts degree from Tulane University and lives in Manhattan.

KAREN GADBOIS cofounded *The Lens*. She now covers New Orleans government issues and writes about land use for *Squandered Heritage*. For her work with television reporter Lee Zurik exposing widespread misuse of city recovery funds—which led to guilty pleas in federal court —Gadbois won some of the highest honors in journalism, including a Peabody Award, an Alfred I. duPont-Columbia Award and a gold medal from Investigative Reporters and Editors.

CRAIG GIESECKE spent 32 years in broadcast journalism, starting with various radio/TV stations throughout the South, then moving to UPI in 1986 and to The Associated Press from 1990-2004. He founded a specialty food company and moved to New Orleans in late 2004, losing his Mid-City business to Hurricane Katrina in 2005. After the storm, he worked briefly at Dick & Jenny's before founding his own restaurant (J'anita's) on Magazine St. in late 2007. He and his wife Kim left New Orleans in late 2013. He is now a chef in Escondido, CA.

TROY GILBERT is a native New Orleanian and a freelance maritime and boating journalist as well as a cookbook author. He started his blog, *GulfSails*, only about a week before the landfall of Hurricane Katrina. Troy remained in the city for the storm and the aftermath and his blog became a very personal accounting of his experiences that was read by millions of people worldwide. Today Troy has returned to his rebuilt home in Lakeview and when not traveling to Europe or the Caribbean to cover competitive sailing, he can be found on his back porch typing or out enjoying the restaurants of New Orleans.

ANN GLAVIANO is a born-and-raised New Orleanian. From 2004 to 2014 she maintained a Typepad blog of personal writings with the eventual title *What the hell is water*, after David Foster Wallace. When Katrina hit and the levees broke, she was twenty-one years old and a fresh graduate of Louisiana State University. She went on to attend the MFA creative writing program at Ohio State and, upon receiving her degree in 2013, immediately returned home, where she runs an all-vinyl dance party called HEATWAVE! and a DIY contemporary dance and music project called Known Mass. She has recently been published in *Prairie Schooner*, *The Atlas Review*, and the New Orleans alt-monthly *Antigravity*.

BROOKS HAMAKER is a writer, brewmaster and barstool philosopher who still makes whiskey because he still knows how. Follow him on Twitter at @Hadacol.

CLIFTON HARRIS (http://cliffscrib.blogspot.com) is a native New Orleanian who loves writing, being a dad, Saints football and making people laugh. He was the winner of the Ashley Morris Award at the Rising Tide 5 blogging conference.

DR. GREGORY HENDERSON is a native New Orleanian and the Vice Chairman of Outreach, Pathology and Laboratory Medicine at Mt. Sinai. A recognized leader in applying digital pathology technology to serve populations in developing countries, he has practiced medicine in

Wilmington, N.C., Puget Sound, and New Orleans, where he worked in the pathology department at Ochsner Clinic from 2005-2007.

ABRAM SHALOM HIMELSTEIN is the cofounder of the Neighborhood Story Project, and has written for the *Houston Chronicle* and the *Daily Racing Form*. He is the author of *What the Hell am I Doing Here: The 100 T-shirt Project* and coauthor, with Jamie Schweser, of *Tales of a Punk Rock Nothing.*

MICHAEL HOMAN is a Professor of Theology at Xavier University of Louisiana. His scholarship focuses on the Old Testament in its historical, linguistic, and archaeological context. His many publications include *The Bible for Dummies* (Wiley) and a forthcoming book, inspired by Katrina and its aftermath, about the origins of social justice. He and his family are proud to live in Mid-City New Orleans.

DEDRA JOHNSON has blogged as G Bitch at *The G Bitch Spot* since 2005. In 2011, G Bitch won the Ashley Morris Award for blogging about New Orleans public school reform. She is a native of New Orleans and the author of *Sandrine's Letter to Tomorrow* [lg, 2007].

CATHERINE JONES is a native New Orleanian and a physician at University Hospital. She teaches at Tulane University.

CYNTHIA JOYCE has been a writer, editor, and web producer for more than 20 years and has contributed to several regional and national publications, including *The Washington Post*, *Newsday*, *NPR.org*, *Entertainment Weekly*, and *MSNBC.com*, where she was a senior producer; *Nola.com*, where she worked briefly as a producer post-Katrina; and *Salon*, where she was arts and entertainment editor. She lives in Oxford, Mississippi and teaches journalism at the University of Mississippi.

WILLIAM JOYCE is an Academy Award®-winning filmmaker with worldwide recognition as an author, illustrator and pioneer in the animation industry. Joyce has written or illustrated nearly 50 books including *The New York Times* bestseller, *The Fantastic Flying Books of Mr. Morris Lessmore.* He and his team at Moonbot Studios in Shreveport, LA have been honored the Webby, Cannes Lions, Emmy and Clio Awards.

MICHAEL KELLER is an award-winning writer and editor who has reported on science, technology, the environment and international affairs. He was part of a team that won a 2006 Pulitzer Prize for coverage of Hurricane Katrina's impact on South Mississippi. His work has appeared online and in newspapers, magazines and books. He is also the author of an Eisner Award-nominated graphic novel adaptation of Charles Darwin's *On the Origin of Species.*

PETER KING is one of the most authoritative and respected sports writers in America. He has covered the National Football League for nearly three decades, most of it as the lead NFL writer for *Sports Illustrated* and *SI.com.* His weekly Monday Morning Quarterback column on *SI.com* (http://mmqb.si.com) attracts millions of readers. Follow him at @ SI_PeterKing.

KIERSTA KURTZ-BURKE is a rehab specialist at the LSU health Sciences Center. She worked at Charity Hospital for 10 years and spent five days there during Hurricane Katrina caring for patients as they awaited rescue. She lives in Mid-City with her husband, Dr. Justin Lundgren, and their two children.

FRANCIS LAM is Editor-at-Large at Clarkson Potter and a columnist for *The New York Times Magazine*. His writing on food and culture has been nominated for three James Beard awards and five IACP awards, winning three. In past lives, he was a judge on *Top Chef Masters*, Features Editor at *Gilt Taste*, senior writer at *Salon.com*, a contributing editor at *Gourmet* magazine (RIP), and his work has appeared in the 2006-2014 editions of *Best Food Writing*. He believes that, in professional football, that would count as a dynasty; in ancient China, not so much. Lam resides in New York City and tweets at @francis_lam.

ADRIENNE LAMB is a poet, playwright and essayist and is currently writing her first long-form work, *The Healy Gene for Misery*. She lived in New Orleans for eight years over a 10 year period (spanning pre- and post-Katrina) and currently resides on Long Island, NY. Follow her on twitter, @TheAtomicGal, where she retweets more than tweets, and read more writing at adriennelamb.com.

KELLY LANDRIEU is a native New Orleanian who has inhabited a wide variety of positions within the food industry, with brief forays into tech, urban planning and general merry-making. Currently she works with food and artisan producers of all stripes to bring their products to market in the Southwest region of Whole Foods Market. You can follow her on Twitter at @Epic_Appetite.

LAUREEN LENTZ is a law librarian and preservation activist who, along with Karen Gadbois and Sarah Elise Lewis, tracked lists upon lists of demolitions for the community on the Squandered Heritage blog—sometimes being the first to tell homeowners that their homes were on the chopping block.

BILL LOEHFELM grew up in Brooklyn and on Staten Island. In 1997, he moved to New Orleans, where he has taught high school and college, worked in an antique shop, and done absolutely everything there is to do in the bar and restaurant business (except cook). He received his MA from the University of New Orleans in 2005. He is the author of five novels. The most recent is *Doing the Devil's Work*, the new Maureen Coughlin adventure, from Sarah Crichton Books/FSG. Bill lives in New Orleans' Garden District with his wife, AC Lambeth, a writer and yoga instructor, and their two dogs.

WAYNE LEONARD joined Entergy, Louisiana's second-largest company and New Orleans' lone Fortune 500 firm, as chief operating officer in 1998 and served as CEO from 1999-2013.

JUSTIN LUNDGREN is a physiatrist, photographer and artist. He lives in Mid-City with his wife, Kiersta Kurtz-Burke, and their two children.

LUCKYDOG was born and raised in New Orleans and spent much of his professional career in leadership of international humanitarian assistance programs delivered in conflict areas. Luckydog was among the professional leadership of Doctors Without Borders in 1999 when the staff and volunteers of that organization were awarded the Nobel Peace Prize, and he has worked in over a dozen remote emergencies around the world. For the last several years, like so many New Orleanians, he has been immersed in building broad-based community-oriented cultural efforts in New Orleans and helping to rebuild his little corner of the city.

MATT MCBRIDE is a mechanical engineer whose Broadmoor house was flooded following Hurricane Katrina. He has served as a self-appointed watchdog over the work the U.S. Army Corps of Engineers since 2006. Scrutinizing the Corps' every move at fixthepumps.blogspot.com, he kept the public informed of what they were doing wrong, what they were doing right, and what they weren't doing at all.

ELIZABETH MCCRACKEN is the author of five books: *Here's Your Hat What's Your Hurry* (stories), the novels *The Giant's House and Niagara Falls All Over Again*, the memoir *An Exact Replica of a Figment of My Imagination*, and the forthcoming *Thunderstruck & Other Stories*. She has taught creative writing at Western Michigan University, the University of Oregon, the University of Houston, and the University of Iowa Writers' Workshop. She holds the James A. Michener Chair in Fiction at the University of Texas, Austin, and boy are her arms tired.

CREE MCCREE moved to her adopted hometown of New Orleans from New York City in 2001. The author of *Flea Market America*, she has written for a wide variety of publications, including *Spin, Details, High Times, No Depression* and *Oxford American*.

MOMINEM is the blog handle of the New Orleans-based creator of the *Tin Can Trailer Trash* blog (http://fematrailer.blogspot.com), where he offered regular musings on life and living in a FEMA trailer post-Katrina.

ASHLEY MORRIS was a New Orleans activist, computer science professor and prominent blogger whose legendary post-Katrina rant, "Fuck you, You Fucking Fucks," became the seminal post of the NOLA blogosphere and was immortalized by John Goodman in his performance as Creighton Bernette, a character *Treme* creator David Simon based on Morris.

MARK MOSELEY is an opinion writer for *The Lens* (thelensnola. org). He has also worked as *The Lens*' engagement specialist and coordinator for the Charter Schools Reporting Corps. In 2004 he stopped yelling at his TV and began a New Orleans blog called *Your Right Hand Thief*. After Katrina and the Federal Flood he helped create the Rising Tide conference, which grew into an annual social media event dedicated to the future of New Orleans. He lives in Broadmoor with his wife Jennifer, a Louisiana native, and their two daughters, Zoe and Violet.

JEANNE NATHAN: For forty years, Jeanne Nathan has worked in journalism, marketing, event and video production, and community organizing, including current work revitalizing the neighborhoods and communities in New Orleans. She has been behind some of the most successful cases of putting culture at the core of economic revival. She is a cofounder, with Robert Tannen, of the Contemporary Arts Center, and has spearheaded the formation of the Creative Alliance of New Orleans, a professional, membership organization aimed at increasing public and private investment in the creative sector. As adjunct faculty at Tulane School of Architecture, Jeanne has brought her students into the neighborhoods of the city to plan redevelopment projects.

SEAN NELSON is best known as the former lead singer of Seattle's Harvey Danger, a Seattle indie pop band whose curious fortune it was to have a song from their debut album turn into a radio and MTV hit during the sharp intake of breath that separated the twilight of the dubious "alternative" era and the period when the internet arose from the ashes of the rock and roll Rome that burned down while Limp Bizkit fiddled. He is Associate Editor Emeritus at *The Stranger*, co-owner of the independent label Barsuk Records, and the force behind the 2013 album *Make Good Choices*. You can follow him at @seantroversy.

JOSH NEUFELD is a Brooklyn-based cartoonist known for his nonfiction narratives of political and social upheaval, told through the voices of witnesses. Neufeld has been an Atlantic Center for the Arts Master Artist, a Knight-Wallace Fellow in journalism, and a Xeric Award winner. His works include *A.D: New Orleans After the Deluge*, about Hurricane Katrina (Pantheon Books).

NOLA FUGEES: From 2005-2010 the website *NOLAFugees.com* mixed investigative journalism, first-person reportage, political analysis, and vicious satire to develop an alternate chronicle of Reconstruction New Orleans as a city of profound uncertainty. Over five years, *NOLAFugees.com* published more than one hundred writers and collected the content from NOLAFugees.com in two nonfiction anthologies (*Year Zero*, 2006 and *Soul is Bulletproof*, 2008) and published the first collection of post-Katrina short fiction, *Life in the Wake* (2007).

JOSHUA NORMAN, a New Jersey native, earned a bachelor's degree from NYU in 2000, after which he joined the Peace Corps and spent two years in West Africa. He then earned a master's degree from Columbia University, and joined the staff of the *Sun Herald* of Biloxi, Miss., in June 2005. He is currently a senior editor for *CBSNews.com* in New York.

DAVID OLIVIER is a husband, father, programmer, writer, illustrator, photographer and musician. He has been blogging at *Slimbolala.blogspot.com* since 2005.

NIKKI PAGE is an artist, teacher and writer who lives in New Orleans.

DA PO'BOY lived in the New Orleans area and worked for a local TV news station before, during, and after Hurricane Katrina. POLIMOM misspent her youth in Algiers, and left a part of her heart there in New Orleans for always.

GREG PETERS, the late creator of the editorial comic strip *Suspect Device*, was an award-winning graphic designer, cartoonist, and writer for newspapers and publications including *Gambit Weekly*, *The Independent Weekly*, the *Times of Acadiana*, and the *Chicago Reader*. An avid blogger until his death in 2013, he created posters for the annual Rising Tide conference in New Orleans, and designed the cover for the Katrina anthology *A Howling in the Wires*, by Gallatin & Toulouse Press.

WADE RATHKE is a community and labor organizer who founded the Association of Community Organizations for Reform Now (ACORN) in 1970 and Service Employees International Union (SEIU) Local 100 in 1980. He was ACORN's chief organizer from its founding in 1970 until June 2, 2008, and continues to organize for their international arm. He is the publisher and editor-in-chief of *Social Policy*, a quarterly magazine for scholars and activists. The magazine's publishing arm has published three of his books. He and his partner, Beth Butler, live in New Orleans, Louisiana.

RICHARD READ has written about cars, videogames, travel, theatre, and pop culture for *Gawker*, *Fodors*, *High Gear Media*, and many points in-between. He's the editor of *Gaywheels*, a website devoted to LGBT car fans, and the coauthor of *The French Quarter Drinking Companion*, a field guide to some of New Orleans' best watering holes. Born in Mississippi, Richard has spent most of his life in New Orleans, which is, as luck would have it, the hometown of his biological mom. (It's a long story. Ask him about it when you have time.) He lives there with his partners, numerous hounds, many wonderful friends, and a moderately well-stocked bar. FRANCIE RICH paints portraits of people, dogs, cats and Barbies, usually with her trademarked stunning gold-leaf backgrounds. Her series of the 33 Chilean Miners (each individually done on 5x5-inch canvases) takes her breath away. She is currently working on portraits of daytime TV judges and the New Orleans attorneys that advertise on the shows. She teaches art history and lives on the Northshore with her husband, the artist John Hodge.

KALAMU YA SALAAM: New Orleans writer and educator Kalamu ya Salaam is senior staff with Students at the Center, a public high school writing program; moderator of *e-Drum*, a listserv for Black writers. Kalamu blogs at <kalamu.com/neogriot>. He can be reached at kalamu@mac.com.

HARRY SHEARER: For the past two decades Harry Shearer has enjoyed enormous success and planted the fruits of his talents in the heads of millions worldwide thanks to his voice work for *THE SIMPSONS*, where he plays a stable of characters: most notably Mr. Burns, Smithers, and the insufferable neighbour Ned Flanders. He directed and narrated the documentary feature *The Big Uneasy*, which revealed the reasons why New Orleans flooded during Hurricane Katrina. The film received stellar reviews for Shearer and his team of experts and whistleblowers. He has been blogging for *Huffington Post* since May 2005, and his satirical sandbox *LE SHOW* is heard weekly on radio stations around the world.

JON SMITH: Raised in and around New Orleans, Jon Smith enjoyed his region's deeply traditional culture as a birthright. After college, Jon did what anyone with anyone who studied Urban and Regional Planning in college would do: He got into the fine wine business. For the next 16 years he travelled the nation while representing several major wineries, broke bread with many chefs along the way, and ultimately settled back in New Orleans where his love of food, wine, and the culture of the Crescent City led him to open his own wine store, Cork & Bottle. During that time, in between pulling corks and running a cash register, Jon taught wine education courses and wrote a lot about wine. Since 2013, he has served as the Executive Director of the French Market Corporation, the oldest continually operating public market in the United States.

SWAMPISH THOUGHTS is a longtime New Orleanian by marriage, residence and inclination.

MICHAEL TISSERAND, the author of *Sugarcane Academy: How a New Orleans Teacher and His Storm-Struck Students Created a School to Remember* (Harvest), is currently working on a biography of New Orleans-born comic strip artist George Herriman.

EVE TROEH is the News Director at WWNO, where she oversees the station's expanding coverage of New Orleans and southeast Louisiana news stories, and develops New Orleans Public Radio's capability to report news of national significance for NPR. Follow her on Twitter at @evetroeh.

ROB WALKER, author of *Letters from New Orleans*, writes about design, technology, business, and other subjects. He's a regular contributor to *Design Observer*, writes *The Workologist* column for *The New York Times Sunday Business* section, and contributes to *Yahoo Tech*, *Fast Company*, and others. He is on the faculty of the School of Visual Arts' Products of Design MFA program and is involved with various side projects, such as Significant Objects (with Joshua Glenn), The Hypothetical Development Organization (with Ellen Susan and GK Darby), and Unconsumption.

JACK WARE, a technology consultant, was a prolific blogger during the years following Katrina. In 2010, he quietly helped direct the early trajectory of the ongoing claims process that followed the Deepwater Horizon explosion in the Gulf of Mexico. In 2014, inspired by the entrepreneurial spirit that has reinvigorated New Orleans, Ware created Valence Tech Solutions, an IT company that offers diverse technology solutions to enterprise clients. He plays saxophone with the Browncoat Brass Band and harumph! while remodeling the storm-damaged house he purchased in March of 2006. He lives with his wife and son.

DAR WOLNIK has worked as a community organizer on consumer and environmental campaigns since the 1980s, and for the last 15 years has focused on expanding the number and reach of farmers markets across the U.S. She splits her time between the French Quarter and her grandparents' home near Abita Springs and writes about all of it.